Trapped in the Gap

TRAPPED IN THE GAP

Doing Good in Indigenous Australia

Emma Kowal

berghahn
NEW YORK · OXFORD
www.berghahnbooks.com

Published in 2015 by
Berghahn Books
www.berghahnbooks.com

Library of Congress Cataloging-in-Publication Data
Kowal, Emma.
  Trapped in the gap : doing good in indigenous Australia / Emma Kowal.
    pages cm
  Includes bibliographical references and index.
  ISBN 978-1-78238-599-8 (hardback) -- ISBN 978-1-78238-604-9 (paperback) -- ISBN
978-1-78238-600-1 (ebook)
  1. Aboriginal Australians--Social conditions--21st century. 2. Aboriginal Australians-
-Services for. 3. Aboriginal Australians--Ethnic identity. 4. Whites--Australia--
Attitudes. 5. Race awareness--Australia. 6. Australia--Race relations. I. Title.
  DU124.S63K68 2015
  362.84'9915--dc23
                                                                    2014033556

British Library Cataloguing in Publication Data
A catalogue record for this book is available from the British Library

Printed on acid-free paper.

ISBN: 978-1-78238-599-8 hardback
ISBN: 978-1-78238-604-9 paperback
ISBN: 978-1-78238-600-1 ebook

To Yin, Maya and Eden, Sara, Ramona and Mandy.

CONTENTS

ILLUSTRATIONS

PREFACE

'You're an anthropologist and you study... White people?' I regularly receive a puzzled look from people when I tell them what I do. Anthropologists are supposed to study Indigenous tribes in remote locations, aren't they? Or at least something exciting, like drug addicts or slum dwellers. When I explain further that I study White anti-racist people in Australia who work in Indigenous health, the confusion often dissipates. 'I see, so you look at their motivations for working with Indigenous people', they say, assuming that my goal is to question the motivations of White people and show that really they are racist. 'No, I don't look at their motivations exactly. I am more interested in what it means to identify as an anti-racist, and what this tells us about the whole project of helping Indigenous people.' By this stage of the conversation, people either know exactly what I am talking about, or are more confused than ever.

Finding this object of study was the starting point of this book. It also marked the end point of ten-year journey that began at university in Melbourne in the early 1990s and ended in Darwin, four thousand kilometres and a world away. I was born and raised in Melbourne, the cosmopolitan Australian city, as the grandchild of four Jewish Holocaust survivors who fled rural Poland after the war. They worked in factories and sent their children to public schools where they excelled, went to university, and made the transition to the middle classes. I was brought up in an inner Melbourne suburb full of old White ladies and private schools. As I was a smart girl, good at maths and science, medicine was the obvious option, though I tempered it with a concurrent arts degree in history and anthropology. From the time I started at Melbourne University in the early 1990s, I was an activist, fighting against the introduction of university fees and for a free East Timor and women's rights. It seemed obvious to me that since I was so lucky, blessed with education and material security, I should devote my spare time and energy to helping those less fortunate – the oppressed of this world – whose suffering my privilege depended on.

I first became interested in Aboriginal justice issues in 1996 when I was in the national capital of Canberra to protest against budget cuts to the education sector by the conservative federal government led by John Howard. I was vaguely aware that the budget of the Aboriginal and Torres Strait Islander Commission (the government arm for Indigenous service delivery led by elected Indigenous leaders and later shut down by the Howard government) was also being cut. The day after the main protest at Parliament House was an Indigenous Day of Protest. A huge number and range of Indigenous groups participated from around the country. I was deeply affected by their stories. I decided then that the struggle for justice for Indigenous people was the primary struggle of this country. This became a kind of mantra, directing my energies away from other causes and into Indigenous activism.

I became involved in a newly formed Indigenous solidarity group on campus. Our work centred on educating non-Indigenous people about the history of colonisation and of Aboriginal resistance, issues in the contemporary Aboriginal community, and racism and the workings of Whiteness in our society. We collaborated with the local Koori community, and particularly with Kooris studying at Melbourne University. Near the end of my medical degree, I arranged to spend three months based at the Aboriginal community-controlled health centre at Utopia, a remote community in Central Australia. I loved the desert and the people there. I felt for the first time that I had found a medical job I could imagine myself doing – a doctor in a remote Aboriginal community. As soon as I finished my medical degree, at the age of twenty-five, I bought a second-hand four-wheel drive and drove four thousand kilometres to Darwin to begin my internship at the Royal Darwin Hospital (RDH), the only public hospital in Darwin and the referral centre for all of the Northern Territory and neighbouring parts of Queensland and Western Australia.

I arrived in Darwin between Christmas and New Year's Eve. Humidity was at its annual peak, and for three days I felt I was in a fog, unable to think of anything but the oppressive heat. I soon began work at RDH, where at least 60 per cent of the patients were Aboriginal, most of those from remote communities. The air-conditioned hospital was too cold for most of the Aboriginal patients, and the concreted area outside the main doors was always buzzing with life, with young kids running around and family groups sitting and talking in various Aboriginal languages, eating chips from the cafeteria and passing around cigarettes, with tubes and bags of bodily fluids protruding from hospital gowns.

During my last years of medical study I was drawn to prevention and public health, as it seemed the most effective way to improve the health of everyone, and a way to stem the massive flow of public money spent on overpriced drugs and diagnostic tests. Once someone sought medical attention it showed society had failed to improve the social conditions that made that person sick, and would make them sick again. It was clear to me that public health was where investments should be made.

It was not long after starting work in the hospital that I became interested in the Indigenous health research institute close by, the Darwin Institute of Indigenous Health. They held weekly meetings that many hospital staff attended, and I eagerly listened to tales of community health promotion projects where researchers supported local people to identify and resolve their own health priorities. Their presentations were littered with happy snaps of Indigenous people cheerfully participating in the research, kids playing up for the camera, island beaches, lily-strewn billabongs and damper roasting on the fire. In my personal journey of methodically applying myself to what I thought to be the most important cause in the most effective way, the Darwin Institute seemed the next logical step. Having trained as a doctor, Indigenous health was the most important area to work in; within Indigenous health, public health was the most effective way to improve health; and to ensure that public health methods worked as well as they could, we needed good quality public health research. I began infiltrating the institute, introducing myself to people after lunchtime meetings, having coffee with researchers after ward rounds, even learning a local Indigenous language in anticipation of remote community work. After a year of exhausting hospital work, I had lined up my first job at the institute as a public health researcher.

Finally, it was me that was flying on a tiny plane to a remote community, shyly meeting the council chairman and thanking him for letting me visit, explaining our project to Aboriginal Health Workers at the health centre with the aid of a brightly coloured flipchart, and tentatively trying out the Aboriginal language phrases I had learnt. White people who come to be known in an Aboriginal community through residence or frequent visits are 'adopted' into an Aboriginal family. Soon I too was adopted into the community I visited most as the sister of a single woman I was working with. I was instantly slotted into a kinship network that spanned the entire region, and I dutifully began to use the correct kin terms for the people I had already got to know – they turned out to be my mother-in-law, my brother's son, and my maternal grandmother.

After two years of intermittent remote community work, combined with long stretches in front of a computer in town, translating the work into quantifiable outcomes and lists of remaining challenges (accompanied by photographs like those I had once envied at the weekly seminars), I felt I was developing a sense of what Indigenous public health research was about. There were plenty of fabulous non-Indigenous people

**Figure 0.1 The author at Utopia with Patsy Ross, 2002.
Photograph: Yin Paradies. Used with permission.**

working at the institute – skilled, friendly, and committed to Indigenous self-determination – and there were a few people who seemed to be primarily concerned with furthering their own careers. The Indigenous staff at the institute, while in general less formally educated than most of the non-Indigenous staff, were mostly diligent and great to work with, although a few seemed to work short hours and to be more interested in self-promotion than getting the job done. While many staff tried to be innovative in their work, they sometimes complained that their bosses or their funders would not let them work in a way the community really wanted them to.

In other words, the institute was not that different from any other bureaucracy. But the rhetoric of the institute promised so much more. The buzzwords were all there: *Indigenous control of research, working with communities, capacity building, doing things differently*. There were all the structures that made the institute a space where there was an attempt to invert dominant power relations, through mechanisms like the Indigenous ethics committee with veto rights over projects that failed to meet Indigenous ethical principles, and the requirement by some funders to have Indigenous co-investigators, Indigenous reference groups, and the incorporation of Indigenous methodologies into research designs. I knew the legacy of exploitative, disempowering research practices, and I saw that the only solution to Indigenous health was for researchers to truly commit to Indigenous control (Humphery 2000; 2001; Henry et al. 2002a; Thomas 2004). For two years, I tried to work that way, and was impressed by the skill and commitment of many of my colleagues.

Having reached the pinnacle of my own instrumentalism, the place where the rhetoric and level of resources meant there was the most potential to find the 'real' solutions to Indigenous health, I found myself disillusioned. My callow enthusiasm was disappointed, for instance, at the power plays that went on between staff that overshadowed the coopera-tion that was needed; at the way that some projects which were widely promoted by the institute and government as 'the answer' seemed full of dysfunction on the inside; and at the ease with which staff would criticise other projects as disempowering or even racist, but would not offer any useful assistance. Above all, I came to question the arguments circulat-ing within the institute explaining why research had not worked in the past and why Indigenous control would fix the problem. The tendency to demonise White researchers in particular seemed, once I had got to know many of them and of course become one myself, an inadequate way to explain the situation.

I became increasingly aware that the moral politics of race and identity played a prominent role in public and private exchanges at the institute. In a seminar, for example, a question from an audience member about the method of payment of Indigenous community research staff could imply that the White researcher was not paying their Indigenous staff suf-ficiently and was therefore exploitative or racist. A detailed explanation and justification would always follow such a question to deflect the impli-cation, whether or not the implication was intended. Where projects were presented to the public, White researchers would take great pains to present an 'Indigenous face', editing themselves out of videos, preparing presentations for Indigenous colleagues to deliver but remaining silent themselves, and perhaps exaggerating the role of community members in the project. Conflicts between Indigenous staff could include questioning of the person's stated tribal affiliation or their very indigeneity. Whites were reluctant to question anything an Indigenous person said, even if it was clearly wrong. As I cynically wrote in my journal in the first months of my research: 'In the political world of Indigenous health we don't have arguments, we have positions. And the position of the "authen-tic Aboriginal voice" [see Chapter 5] trumps even the most eloquent argument, and has no need for it'.

Over time, I came to realise that much effort expended in the name of improving Indigenous health was directed at creating and maintaining racialised identities. In an *Indigenous* health institute, those who walk through the front doors every day are not just *people*, they are Indigenous people or non-Indigenous people. The institute is an always already racialised space. When the racial identities circulating in people's minds are examined more closely, they immediately multiply: the Indigenous people could be '[remote] community people', or 'urban people'; the non-Indigenous people could be 'White people' or both non-White and non-Indigenous; the Whites could be 'rednecks' or anti-racist (people who are both non-White and non-Indigenous are somewhat immune from being considered 'racist'); those not yet known to the viewer could best be classified as 'possibly-Indigenous' until their Indigenous status has subtly been ascertained. Much work went into maintaining one's racial identity. For non-Indigenous people, this meant maintaining a specific racial identity as a 'good' White person and not an ignorant, exploitative, 'racist' White person: part of the solution and not part of the problem.

I began to form an answer to that fundamental question I sometimes asked myself in times of frustration, a question that haunts many White anti-racists described in this book: 'What the hell are we White people actually doing here?' In the course of the research that led to this book, this question developed further: 'When a group of relatively intelligent, well-meaning people, supported by the state, attempt to enact a mode of difference that is non-oppressive, does this make any difference?' *Trapped in the Gap* is an attempt at an answer.

This book would not have been possible without generous material and intellectual support. The research was supported by an Australian National Health and Medical Research Council (NHMRC) Training Scholarship for Public Health Research and a VicHealth Ph.D. scholarship. Other funding was provided by the Australian Institute of Aboriginal and Torres Strait Islander Studies Conference Support Subsidy, the Northern Territory Department of Health & Community Services Studies Assistance Award, and student bursaries from the Society for Cultural Anthropology and the Cultural Research Network. Doug Lloyd of Northern Territory General Practice Education provided office space at a critical time and Ashley Greenwood provided invaluable assistance in the final stages.

A large number of colleagues and friends have generously engaged with my work in correspondence and in person over the years. Thanks to Cath Alderton, Jon Altman, Ian Anderson, Warwick Anderson, John Avery, Philip Batty, Nicholas Biddle, John Boulton, Maggie Brady, Victoria Burbank, John Cash, Richard Chenhall, Michael Christie, Gillian Cowlishaw, Cameo Dalley, Bill Day, Ruth DeSouza, Jennifer Devlin, Angela Durey, Peter Dwyer, Deane Fergie, Cressida Fforde, Martin Forsey,

Elizabeth Ganter, Graham Gee, Mick Gooda, Kelly Greenop, Ashley Greenwood, Pauline Guerin, Ghassan Hage, Chris Haynes, Chris Healy, Melinda Hinkson, Michael Jindra, Kirrily Jordan, Odette Kelada, Clare Land, Marcia Langton, Tess Lea, Mark Lock, Michael Lowe, Charlotte McCabe, Martha Macintyre, David Martin, Richard Martin, Francesca Merlan, Paul Memmott, Monica Minnegal, Terry Moore, Mark Moran, John Morton, Dirk Moses, Tim Neale, Yin Paradies, Glenn Pearson, Katya Pechenkina, Nic Peterson, Tim Pilbrow, Richard Potok, Beth Povinelli, Bruce Rigsby, Nicolas Rothwell, Tim Rowse, Will Sanders, Lisa Stefanoff, Patrick Sullivan, Peter Sutton, David Trigger, Michael Tynan, Eve Vincent, Charlie Ward, Elizabeth Watt and Jackie Yowell. Thanks especially to Jon Altman for suggesting the title of this book. Thanks to participants in the 'Race, Culture, Indigeneity and the Politics of Disadvantage' short course since 2003 for helping me to clarify my ideas.

Above all, I am grateful to all of those at the 'Institute' who participated in the research, and the then Director and senior researchers who supported this project. My research participants, who were both colleagues and friends, thought together with me about the complexities and dilemmas of Indigenous affairs. Thank you for sharing your intellectual journey and helping me with mine.

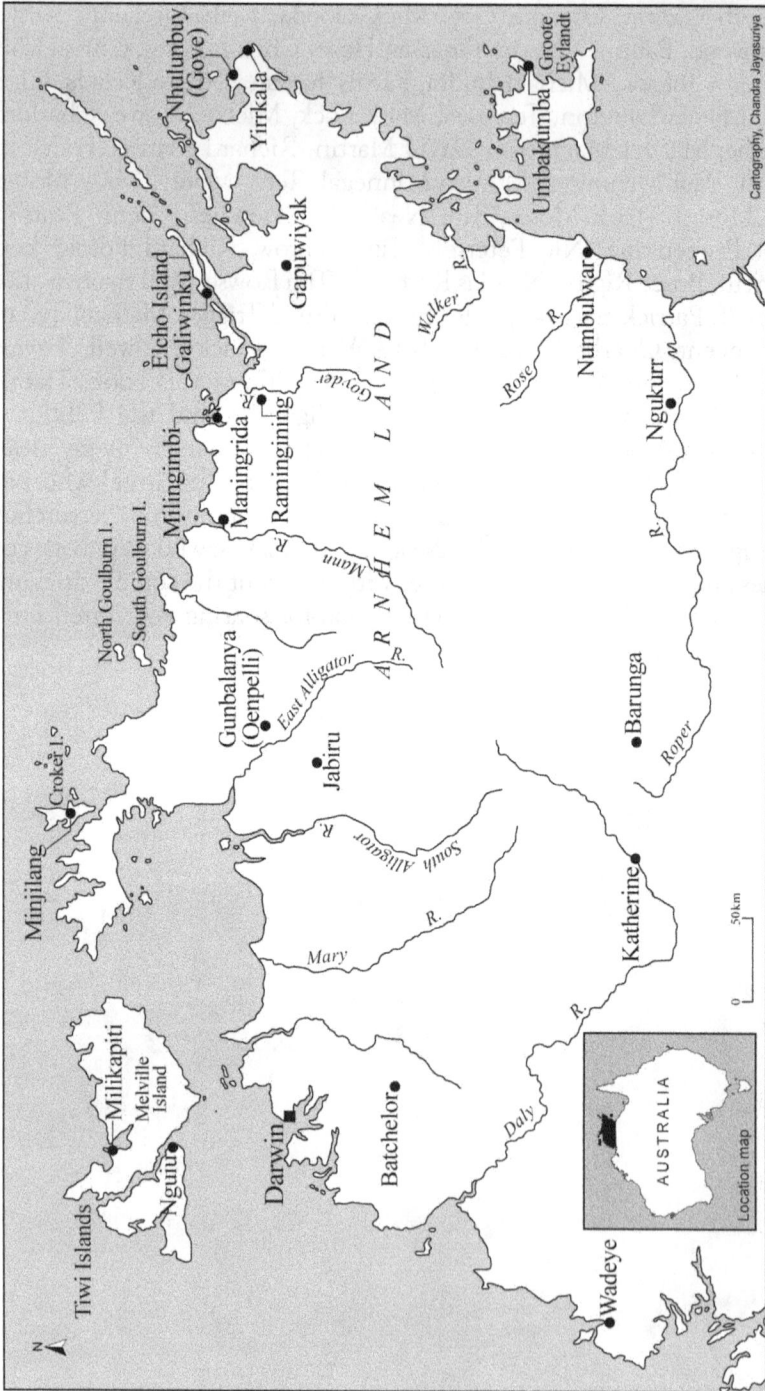

The top end of the Northern Territory showing Darwin and larger remote communities

INTRODUCTION

~~~~~~~~~~~~~~~~~~

Picture this: the remote coast of northern Australia, early in the twenty-first century. Endless unspoiled beaches framed by Casuarina pines. Soaring escarpments cradling spectacular twenty-thousand-year-old rock art galleries, roaring waterfalls and Edenic pools. Lush rainforests interspersed with tropical savannahs, teeming with birds, possums, wallabies and goannas. Food sources are everywhere: rivers brim with barramundi, oysters cling to rocks in the shallows, and nests of turtle eggs lie just beneath the sandy surface of the beach. But it is the world of the mangroves, those strange salt-loving trees that form dense forests along the shore, where the real bounty is found: plentiful crabs, shellfish and fish, and edible snakes and worms waiting for those who can decipher the subtle patterns of holes in the mud that reveal what lies beneath.

This is what white Australia knows as Arnhem Land:[1] ninety thousand square kilometres of Aboriginal land in the north-eastern corner of Australia's Northern Territory. From here it is six hundred kilometres to Darwin, the closest city and the territory's capital. Slightly closer than Darwin are the coasts of Papua New Guinea and Indonesian West Papua across the shallow Arafura Sea. This vast wilderness is cared for by Aboriginal Traditional Owners whose cosmology has a place for every living creature, physical feature and weather pattern within their dense kinship network. The European colonisation of Australia in 1788 made no immediate impression here. It took over eighty years before Darwin was founded in 1869, and it remained a small town of a few thousand people for another eighty years. Missionaries first moved into Arnhem Land when an Aboriginal Reserve was officially declared in 1931. They built five mission settlements that were handed over to local control in the 1970s, a move that reflected the politics of the dawning 'self-determination' era. It was not until the opening of a Bauxite mine in 1970 that 'development' made any impression at all, and the one mining town (Gove) is still the only place in Arnhem Land where there is a hospital, motel, restaurants or a high school.

Far from Darwin or Gove, our protagonist stands knee-deep in mangrove mud. The fetid smell of the mud is overpowering, and it distracts her from the intense humidity, the sting of sunburn and the itch of dozens of sandfly bites. She holds tight to a mangrove branch to retrieve her legs from their muddy enclosure with a sucking sound, then stumbles as she climbs over the branch and plunges again into the mud. The Aboriginal women and children she is with turn to wait for her, their own progress through the maze of mangroves seemingly effortless.

Anna is a White woman approaching forty.[2] She grew up in Sydney, the famous international city built around a stunning harbour. She recognises that her upbringing was privileged: a fifth-generation Australian of English and Irish heritage, professional parents, a stable nuclear family in a nice house, a good education at a private school and then university. But her progressive parents instilled in her a sense of responsibility to use her skills and knowledge to help those less fortunate than herself. As she moved into adolescence in the early 1980s, she began to realise that the vast majority of the world lived in poverty. Books that explored the race question in the United States, books like Black Like Me and Roots, influenced her growing critique of Western society. By the age of fifteen, she had decided that she wanted to work for the World Health Organization in developing countries.

At university in the late 1980s she was interested in health, so she did a science degree, majoring in health education and psychology. One day, a guest lecturer came to talk about her work with an Indigenous community, showing slides of the remote community where she worked and speaking passionately about the potential of self-determination to improve the poor state of Indigenous health. Anna was captivated. Suddenly, her desire to work for the WHO in far-flung places paled into insignificance when compared to the plight of Indigenous people in her own country. Embracing her new direction, she took all the Indigenous studies courses she could, hungry for knowledge about the history of Australian settler-colonisation and its devastating effect on Indigenous people. Indigenous people, she learned, lived twenty years less than non-Indigenous people. They suffered from nearly every health problem at much higher rates, from heart disease to suicide, and from kidney failure to drowning, as well as some diseases that are now hardly seen in the White population, like rheumatic fever and syphilis. The history of dispossession, oppression and racism had eroded the ability of Indigenous people to meet these health challenges. By the 1990s, the devastating and inter-generational effects of removing mixed-race Aboriginal children from their families – known as the 'stolen generations' – began to be widely known and loomed large in Anna's mind (Human Rights and Equal Opportunity Commission 1997). The cultural base of Indigenous society had been devastated, and with it, the spirit of its people. What was needed, she learned, was to empower Indigenous people to rebuild their culture and take back control of their communities.

Soon after finishing her degree, a position in Indigenous health promotion was advertised in Central Australia, and she jumped at the chance to work there. Over the next decade she had worked in a dozen different communities, developing culturally appropriate health education programmes and supporting Aboriginal Health Workers to deliver them. She eventually convinced her employer that health promotion is best delivered away from the health clinic, a place local Aboriginal people associate with sickness and generally avoid. She secured permission and funding for hunting trips where she takes a carload of Aboriginal people outside the community to nearby hunting grounds. Once the hunting or gathering is done, the group finds a shady spot on the beach and makes a fire for cooking the food and boiling water for tea. As the party sips strong sweet tea and feasts on grilled fish, crab and mussels, Anna produces a 'flip chart' from her bag. These large laminated books feature images of Aboriginal people engaged in health-promoting activities: buying canned fruit and vegetables and refusing sodas and crisps at the local store; hunting, fishing and walking to prevent obesity; or treating children for scabies sores and hanging clean sheets and mattresses in the sun (Figure 0.2).

The image of Indigenous men, women and children gathered on a beach to discuss the merits of various canned vegetables with a White woman who has travelled from afar to be there is pleasing to many White Australians. For decades, the poor health of Australia's Indigenous population – currently known as Aboriginal and Torres Strait Islander people[3] – has been of concern to many progressive white Australians. In the early 1970s, activists began to protest against the poor health status of Aboriginal people and call for government action to improve Indigenous mortality and living conditions (Tatz 1972). Aboriginal activists in partnership with activist doctors set up free health services staffed with volunteers in cities and towns around the country from the mid-1970s (Anderson 1988). It was not until the mid-1980s that Aboriginal

Figure 0.2 Helping you to make healthy food choices for good health and nutrition.
Source: The Aboriginal and Torres Strait Islander Guide to Healthy Eating Educator's Resource, Northern Territory Government, 2005.

health became a specific issue of concern to the federal government which directed the newly formed Australian Institute of Health (later renamed the Australian Institute of Health and Welfare) to collect data on Aboriginal health problems (Castles 1986). The first Aboriginal health strategy was released in 1989, followed by the first Aboriginal health textbooks (National Aboriginal Health Strategy Working Party 1989; Saggers and Gray 1991; Reid and Trompf 1991).

By the mid-1990s, the poor state of Aboriginal health was well known among White Australians. Central to the discourse of Aboriginal ill health that increasingly populated media sources was the most shameful health statistic of them all: Indigenous Australians have a life expectancy of twenty years less than other Australians. The immediate causes of this unequal burden of disease are chronic diseases such as heart disease, high blood pressure and kidney failure, respiratory disease and cancer related to smoking, and alcohol-related violence. The underlying causes, however, are recognised by progressive Australians to be colonisation, dispossession and the ongoing institutional racism that Indigenous people face in their everyday lives. The fact that this gap was far wider than comparable gaps between Indigenous and non-Indigenous life expectancy in Canada (seven years), New Zealand (five years) and the United States (three years) continues to be a source of national shame.[4] For many White Australians concerned about Indigenous health, these years of life not lived represent an organic barometer of continued colonial oppression.

The history of concern for Aboriginal health is closely tied to the politics of the self-determination era. In Australia, 'self-determination' has been the dominant trope for expressing the aspirations of Aboriginal and Torres Strait Islanders since the late 1960s. Self-determination was a reaction to the assimilation era (roughly 1950–70), when Indigenous collective life was judged to have been so damaged as to be irreparable, with the only humane course of action being the absorption of Indigenous people into 'mainstream' society. By the late 1960s, intellectuals such as C.D. Rowley and H.C. Coombs were arguing that Indigenous cultural life remained vital and should be encouraged (Rowley 1972b; Coombs and Smith 1994). Rather than Indigenous people assimilating to Western values, which Coombs thought indistinguishable from extermination (Rowse 2000), the proponents of self-determination argued that Australian legal and administrative structures should accommodate Indigenous forms of social life. In making this argument, these intellectuals took the lead from contemporaneous Indigenous leaders such as Joe McGuinness and Kath Walker (later Oodgeroo Noonuccal). Indigenous leaders effectively used the 'politics of embarrassment' over the plight of Indigenous people to leverage fledgling political commitment from governments and a strong affective response from White supporters in organisations such as the Federal Council for the Advancement of Aboriginal and Torres Strait Islanders (FCAATSI).[5] 'Cultural appropriateness' became a key mantra of activists and politicians alike, and the 'Aboriginal Corporation' was created to interact with government and service providers (Rowse 2005). From the early 1970s, Aboriginal health services, legal services, and housing cooperatives were set up as community-run organisations. The legal and administrative bases of the 'Aboriginal domain' (Rowse 1992) were expanded from the 1970s to 1990s by the Northern Territory land rights legislation (1976), the establishment of regional land councils and local government councils in remote communities, and later the national representative body, the Aboriginal and Torres Strait Islander Commission (ATSIC, established in 1990 and dismantled in 2004).

Since the late 1960s there has been an enormous increase in the number and diversity of people that identify as Indigenous. The definition of indigeneity shifted from various state and federal government definitions based on 'caste' to a pan-Indigenous approach advocated by

Indigenous activists. Since the early 1980s, the tripartite 'working definition' of indigeneity adopted by government agencies has been self-iden-
tification, descent (of unspecified amount) and community acceptance.
As a result of these shifts, Indigenous people are highly diverse both
within and between Indigenous communities, language groups and
regions. Although less urbanized than the general population, 74 per
cent of Aboriginal and Torres Strait Islander people live in urban and
regional areas, and 26 per cent live in remote areas. Only 12 per cent of
Aboriginal and Torres Strait Islander people speak an Indigenous language at home, with the remainder speaking English at home (Australian
Bureau of Statistics 2010). Over half of all Aboriginal and Torres Strait
Islanders have non-Indigenous partners, a figure that rises above 80 per
cent in urban areas (Khoo, Birrell and Heard 2009). These patterns, similar to Indigenous demography in North America and New Zealand, contribute to a highly diverse Indigenous population in terms of appearance,
ancestry, knowledge of traditional cultural practices and socioeconomic
position.

By the twenty-first century, Indigenous health and welfare formed a
small but significant part of state bureaucracy. In 2010–11, $4.6 billion[6]
was spent on Indigenous health, which represented 3.7 per cent of total
health spending. Per person, for every dollar spent on non-Indigenous
health, $1.47 was spent on Indigenous health (Australian Institute of
Health and Welfare 2013).[7] Although Indigenous advocates argue that
spending remains inadequate given the scale of Indigenous ill health
(Mooney, Wiseman and Jan 1998), spending on Indigenous health and
Indigenous programmes in general is nonetheless significant.

With funding comes a workforce to address the plight of Indigenous
communities. From the 1970s on, a generation of White people like
Anna, armed with progressive politics and professional degrees, left their
metropolitan homes to travel overseas to the global South or the 'fourth
world' of their own backyard: remote Indigenous Australia. As they see it,
the goal of White professionals is to facilitate community-led action on
the health problems that most concern Indigenous communities.[8] This
book explores the set of beliefs shared among White anti-racists about
Indigenous ill health and disadvantage as an object to be studied. Within
this knowledge system, 'community consultation' and 'self-determination'
are vital terms. These concepts and associated practices have been elabo-
rated in response to Indigenous critiques of Western development and
research, critiques that are paralleled in the international development
context (Escobar 1995; Smith 2012). They are what distinguish the work
of White anti-racists like Anna from the work of earlier generations of
White helpers, including the missionaries – the savers of souls – and the

assimilationists, who sought to absorb Aboriginal people into the White population. As I explore in this book, these two historical roles, now seen as arrogant and imprudent, form the psychological backdrop to the practice and experience of White anti-racism in contemporary Australia. Their counterparts in the global context – missionaries and colonial governments – perform the same function for international development workers.

Innumerable books, articles and reports offer advice as to how White anti-racists should listen to Indigenous voices, prioritise Indigenous needs, and draw on Indigenous decision-making processes. Anna has read many of these, and has tried to incorporate their messages into her work. But despite her concerted efforts, or perhaps because of them, she cannot shake off the feeling that her work may just be another neocolonial project to make Indigenous people conform to Western lifeworlds. As her reading of Indigenous and development critiques has made clear, nearly every health promotion message she advocates conflicts with the social practices of the Aboriginal people she works with. To maintain a healthy diet, they must refrain from sharing unhealthy food when their kin offer it to them (Dussart 2009). To reduce overcrowding and vandalism, they must turn away relatives, especially those affected by alcohol or drugs, who may arrive at the house at any time of the day or night (Peterson 1993; Schwab 1995). To stop smoking or drinking, they must isolate themselves from the social practices of sharing tobacco or alcohol that are deeply embedded in community life (Brady 1993; Johnston 2008). To ensure their children attend school regularly, they must override the autonomy granted to children in Aboriginal society (Hamilton 1981). While the processes of community consultation and self-determination offer hope that these contradictions can be avoided or overcome, Anna fears this is false hope.

Anna sits and drinks her tea under the shade of the Casuarina pines. To the observer, it would look no different from any other health promotion trip she has made. There is general chatter around the fire, most of it unintelligible to Anna. Others nearby attend to children or peer out to sea, perhaps spotting a crocodile or turtle in the distance. But today the sense of unease that has been building for months or maybe years reaches a tipping point. The flipchart in her backpack seems to weigh a ton, and she dreads the moment she will remove it and begin delivering the script.

Disturbing questions percolate in her mind as she contemplates the health promotion task at hand. How can the project to improve Aboriginal health be separated from projects that are widely judged as colonial and neocolonial? Is it even possible for White people and organisations to help disadvantaged others? Or is the desire to help others indistinguishable from the desire to dominate them? 'What is the point?' she tells me later. 'Who are we to say what's right and what's wrong, and what's healthy and what isn't?'

Anna is deeply worried that the Aboriginal people she works with will reap no benefit from her efforts. She remembers that when she started working in Aboriginal communities, she longed for the time when she would develop deep relationships with people and truly understand their culture. Then, she hoped, her health promotion efforts would be effective.

But the longer she works in communities, the more she feels the messages she is delivering are irrelevant. She fears that all her efforts at incorporating local values and words from the local language are superficial, merely Western imperialism in sheep's clothing. Even worse, she suspects that the relationships she has developed mean that community members participate in her activities not because they are truly interested, but because of their ties with her.

Far from enabling her to work in a culturally appropriate way, her knowledge of the community where she works has further clouded questions of motivation and benefit. 'We bring money and resources into the community, and say "we've got this big bucket of money, it's for really good things and we could do this and we could do that"', she explains. 'The community feel obligated to take it on board. Obligated because of their connection with us, you know? I've been working there for a long time and they feel the pressure to say yes, so they're not disappointing us.'

Although she has tried for years to work in a way that is congruent with what she perceives as Indigenous cultural values, Anna feels her very presence in the community brings a Western influence that 'contaminates' the field. 'I think it's really hard when there's non-Indigenous people involved because you don't get a true representation of the Indigenous perspective', she tells me. Her comment suggests that Indigenous people are prevented from expressing, and perhaps even feeling, their true views when a White person is present. The picture Anna sketches here is one where White people attempt to mould Aboriginal desires, and Aboriginal people passively participate out of kindness, coercion or perhaps boredom.

Some would consider Anna's account to be a product of 'burnout', or her underlying racism towards Indigenous people, or perhaps evidence of inadequate engagement with Indigenous communities. This book argues that experiences like Anna's are not (just) a personal crisis or a flawed character, or even a symptom of policy failure, but a microcosm of the global politics of inequality and its alleviation.

Trapped in the Gap

This book presents a study of White anti-racists. Located at the inter-section of anthropology, whiteness studies, and postcolonial studies, it challenges current understandings of racial inequality and its alleviation. It explores the gap between the promises of liberal multiculturalism and the experiences of Whites who seek to help Australia's Indigenous minor-ity, generating new insights into the politics of difference in post-settler states. It also contributes to a growing literature on global inequalities in material and social goods, exploring the ways that White professionals mobilise concepts of race, culture and indigeneity in the name of improv-ing the health of Indigenous communities.

The book is set in the contemporary city of Darwin, a key site for reckoning with the ongoing crisis in Indigenous health and well-being. Darwin's diverse population of 100,030 is made up of long-term Darwinians – multiracial families that embody a local history of Indigenous, South-East Asian and European contact – a large contin-gent of Indigenous visitors from remote communities, and the newcom-ers: White bureaucrats, military personnel and miners, as well as the liberal 'do-gooders' that are the focus of this book. Since the dawn of the Aboriginal 'self-determination' era in the late 1960s, many White Australians have personally taken on the challenge of improving the health and well-being of the nation's most disadvantaged group. For many of those who hope to right the wrongs of colonisation, and restore the good health denied to Indigenous people by dispossession and discrimination, Darwin is the destination of choice.

While the city itself is home to ten thousand Indigenous people, it is the engine room for efforts to help the forty-five thousand Indigenous people living in small communities scattered over a territory that is larger than most countries. Through carefully considered and culturally appro-priate health programmes, White anti-racists hope to 'close the gap' between Indigenous and non-Indigenous health and social outcomes, normalising Indigenous life expectancy.

But the path to better health for Indigenous Australians has not been straightforward. Despite improved health services and better access to education and housing, Indigenous health has not greatly improved (Wilson, Condon and Barnes 2007). School attendance is poor, and 'lifestyle' diseases such as diabetes and heart disease are at endemic levels.

For the White people who have tried to help Indigenous Australians, their inability to close the gap is disturbing. Their belief in the project of

Indigenous health improvement is slowly but inexorably eroded by multiple misgivings. They experience two equal and opposing fears. First, they understand that improving Indigenous health requires systemic change, and they question their ability to overcome the institutional racism of post-settler society. While 'the gap' remains as an organic barometer of continued colonial oppression, they fear they are doing too little. At the same time, they fear they are doing too much. Encounters with radically different Indigenous ways of life leave White anti-racists concerned that their efforts to improve the health and social status of Indigenous people might be furthering the neocolonial expansion of biopolitical norms. If the 'gap' is due, at least in part, to the ways of life requisite to cultural survival, it follows that erasing the gap erodes Indigenous cultural distinctiveness. Despite the postcolonial mantra of community control, White anti-racists worry that their labours will be judged as indistinguishable from those of racist bureaucrats and missionaries of the past.

This ambivalence is common among those White people in the 'contact zone' (Pratt 1992), the place where anti-racism meets radical difference (see Chapter 3). Within these spaces, both White anti-racists and Indigenous subjects are 'trapped in the gap'. This polysemic phrase condenses the arguments of this book in three senses. First is the 'gap' between the promises of liberal multicultural policy and the reality of both government inefficiency and the radical difference of many Indigenous lifeworlds (Povinelli 2002b). Then there is the statistical gap between Indigenous and non-Indigenous outcomes that holds the promise of a future where full citizenship rights can be enjoyed (at such time when the gap is finally closed). As I will discuss, White anti-racists fear this statistical gap may also be where the distinctiveness of Indigenous people resides, whether this distinctiveness derives from cultural difference or colonial violence. The final gap, drawing on the psychic register, is that between self and other, and between one's self-representation and one's 'true' self. This untold story of the fears and doubts that plague White anti-racists 'trapped in the gap' epitomises the underlying dilemmas of the liberal multicultural project and international development efforts.[9]

The Culture of White Anti-racism

This book approaches White anti-racists as a transnational cultural group. As both 'White' and 'anti-racist' are highly contested and often provocative terms, my use of them requires explanation. In Chapter 3 I sketch the demography of this group and its internal divisions. Here I will focus on my theoretical and conceptual frame. My use of the term 'White' in this ethnography draws on whiteness studies.[10] It does not intimate that all my research participants had white skin, or even that they all identified as White (though both of these conditions apply to most of them). Rather, it implies that they willingly and unwillingly, knowingly and unknowingly participate in the racialised societal structure that positions them as 'White' and accordingly grants them the privileges associated with the dominant Australian culture. According to this schema, a non-White person (including an Indigenous person) with sufficient Western education, income, class privilege, and other forms of status can enact whiteness through dress, talk or behaviour, and receive its associated privileges.

The term 'anti-racist' is often used normatively to describe a person or action that is 'objectively' anti-racist. To use the label in this way immediately invites questions as to whether the object in question is 'really' anti-racist or 'actually' racism in disguise.[11] In contrast to this usage, I take an anthropological perspective and consider anti-racism to be a culture, discourse and identity. I am not interested in judging whether people are 'really' racist or not. Rather, I seek to understand what it means to be a person who identifies as anti-racist. The normative use of anti-racism, in particular the constant suspicion and self-questioning that accompanies it, are aspects of the subjectivity to be studied, rather than discourses to be reproduced.

While most in the group under study would not object to the label 'White anti-racist', they would more readily self-identify as 'non-Indigenous'. I choose not to use the latter term as it conceals rather than reveals important aspects of White anti-racist identity. The term 'non-Indigenous' is obviously defined in opposition to Indigenous Australians. But contained within it is a second dichotomy between conservatives and progressives.[12] Few Australians would actively define themselves as 'non-Indigenous', that is, lacking in indigeneity, or use this term in conversation. The majority of Australians would be more likely to call themselves simply 'Australian', and/or identify with their ethnic minority, and may object to being labelled 'non-Indigenous'. To claim the label of 'non-Indigenous' is an act of distinguishing oneself from other Australians who are not preoccupied with the plight of Indigenous people. It is partly for the purposes of illuminating this double dichotomy that I describe this group as 'White anti-racist' rather than 'non-Indigenous'. The use of this term also highlights the transnational aspects of this identity, and begins to explain why the views of a White Australian Indigenous rights activist are surprisingly similar to a Danish development worker in Tanzania (Eriksson Baaz 2005).

For so many engaged in the task of helping non-White populations, from the neighbourhood centre to the refugee camp, anxiety and confusion are common feelings. Those who identify as 'White anti-racists' experience a mixture of ambivalence and desire, suffering and humiliation, friendship and love. Their attempts to assist, help, encourage and facilitate racialised subjects profoundly influence progressive movements around the world, including anti-racism, Indigenous rights, development and multiculturalism. Yet because White anti-racists are not usually considered to be cultural group, they have generally escaped anthropological attention.

While scholars such as John Hartigan Jr., David Roediger and Matt Wray have extended our historical and anthropological knowledge of the White working classes, few scholars have considered either middle-class Whites or White anti-racists (Roediger 1991; Hartigan 1999, 2005; Wray 2006). The work that does exist is rarely based on empirical research on White anti-racists and consequently is ethnographically thin (Moon and Flores 2000; Bonnett 2000a, 2006; O'Brien 2003, 2009; Ahmed 2004).[13] Within the field of whiteness studies, for example, this group are often depicted as naive perpetuators of imperialism or as racists in disguise (see Chapter 6).

Furthermore, the whole concept of White anti-racism is questioned. It is argued that the structure of racial hierarchy means that actions intended by Whites to be anti-racist merely act to reinforce White privilege (see, for example, Jensen 2006). While such conceptions are useful for making whiteness visible and problematising it, they provide no traction in understanding White anti-racists or their concomitant bureaucracies and social movements. Rather than taking White anti-racism as a moral position to be defended, this book considers White anti-racists as a cultural group to be analysed emically.

This perspective allows for new insights into White anti-racism. *Trapped in the Gap* presents, as an anthropological problem, aspects of behaviour that have previously remained at the level of anecdote, such as the tendency of White anti-racists to erase White agency and amplify non-White agency, and their willingness to withstand and even seek out suffering that ranges from physical hardship to humiliation (see Chapter 6; also Kulick 2006).

Drawing on Erving Goffman (1959), we can think of White anti-racism as something that is 'performed'. Anti-racism is thus produced through a complex combination of conscious and unconscious gestures and words, intentional and inadvertent slips in the routine, and the various practices that allow groups to monitor and police performances of a shared identity. The performance of White anti-racist identities is most discernible in relatively public spaces, like in conferences, seminars and publications (see chapters 3, 4 and 5). But in the analysis of anti-racist performances, the 'backstage' is just as important as the front stage. Backstage is where the audience is not allowed and the members of the team can freely interact without the pressure of staying in character. The backstage has supportive functions such as teaching new members of the team how to perform and checking for offensive aspects of the performance (ibid.: 112).[14]

My own position as a 'native ethnographer' (a White anti-racist studying other White anti-racists; and see Narayan 1993) allowed direct access to the 'backstage' where performances of White anti-racism were rehearsed and deliberated. Physically, the backstage includes the corridors of the institute, the tearoom, closed meetings of researchers, and social gatherings on the large back verandas of Darwin homes. In the front stage (in public seminars, conferences, and in publications), the belief system and subjectivities of White anti-racists are carefully cultivated and preserved. It is backstage 'where suppressed facts make an appearance' (Goffman 1959: 12) and where White anti-racists ask the disquieting questions like those that Anna posed.

The Global Gap

Anna is not alone in questioning her ability to help, and even her right to inhabit the field of development. This state of unsettling self-reflection was a common feature among White anti-racists in the ethnography described in this book. It may, in fact, be a feature common to White anti-racists worldwide.

This latter claim is supported by studies of White development workers. One example is Barbara Heron's *Desire for Development* (2007).[15] Heron is an ex-development worker with experience in Africa who conducted interview research on fellow development workers. She argues in her book that her research subjects were not sufficiently aware of their privileged position and their role in the oppressive global politics that are the real cause of 'underdevelopment'. However, all of those she interviewed were troubled by their position of power to some extent. Most were concerned, for example, by the idea that they might be 'changing the culture' of development recipients and reinforcing structures of racial privilege.

Carol was perhaps the most reflective and self-critical of all the development workers Heron interviewed. Carol developed a love for Africa after travelling extensively through the continent and feeling a sense of freedom there that she relished. She returned to work as a teacher in a government school in 'South Africa'.[16] At the time she was interviewed by Heron, she had left development work and was in graduate school. She revealed a high level of ambivalence about her ability to help as a development worker. We see this, for example, in her discussion of how she struggled to justify her presence in the development scene:

> What I told myself was, 'Well the [South African] government, which happens to be made up of all black [South Africans], apart from one who happens to be a White [South African], are building a lot of schools and they can't staff the schools with [South Africans] so they are asking for foreign teachers. So I'm not going as some missionary who believes she knows what's right, I am going because I've been requested.' And that was my way of justifying it. And then I sort of justified it by saying, 'Well if I can produce two teachers and put myself and one other expat out of a job, then I could justify being there'. And then I *further* justified it by saying, 'And besides, I'm not going there to teach, I'm going there to learn. And if I can bring *back* sensitivity and so forth to my own culture and change as a person, then that's for the best. So I'm not going to leave any marks on [South Africa], I'm going to have [South Africa] leave marks on me... So these were the reasons I told myself it was okay for me to go. But it's not okay because it is such an unbalanced relationship. (Heron 2007: 48)

As this quotation illustrates, Carol was highly aware of the privilege she received by virtue of being White. She attempted to counter the effects of this privilege by minimising her agency (an effect discussed in chapters 2 and 6). Her multiple justifications of her presence in [South Africa] diminished her agency in deciding to go ('I've been requested'), in stating that her presence would only be temporary (she aimed to put herself 'out of a job'), and in declaring that she would not 'do' anything herself, but would instead be acted on 'by' [South Africa]. Elsewhere in the book, she describes her efforts 'not to impose herself' by remaining silent as much as she could in staff meetings at her school. Her ultimate goal was 'to live a life that is as harmless as possible' (Heron 2007: 103, 135).

Both Carol and Anna shared a fear of dominating others, and harboured suspicions that their 'unbalanced relationship' with the recipients of development would make this domination inevitable. Both women actively tried to counter their privilege and found the experience wanting. They were left with disturbing and unanswered questions about their ability to help.

In Heron's book as a whole, as in other similar works, the questioning anti-racist is presented as the exception.[17] Heron and others argue that, for most development workers, anti-racism is a veneer that conceals a system of buttressing White anti-racist narcissism. Whites don't really love the marginalised; they love being the saviour of the marginalised. Paulette Goudge (2003) explores this argument through the concept of White privilege. White development workers are privileged in countless ways – they are in positions of power, they are paid more, they can come and go as they choose, and they are given special treatment. For her, White privilege is a constant reminder of the global oppression of the South by the North, and the privileged White body of the development worker can only reinforce this system of oppression, even in the act of alleviating it. She argues that White anti-racists deliberately ignore their privilege and the inequitable geopolitical relations it represents because of their narcissistic need to save and be loved by the oppressed. Goudge and Heron approve only of those few anti-racists who, like Carol, recognise the need to manage their inherent harmfulness.

But what about spaces where the questioning anti-racist is the rule, rather than the exception? What if the institutions that employ White anti-racists encourage them to recognise their privilege and act to counter it? What difference does it make? The White people involved in this study of anti-racists in Darwin more closely resembled Carol than the other, less sophisticated development workers that Goudge and Heron criticise. Perhaps due to their positioning as White settlers in the post-settler state, most found their racial privilege difficult to ignore and were often troubled by it. They worked at an Indigenous health research institute that encouraged and in some instances required them to work collaboratively with Indigenous people, and to both structure and modify their projects in response to Indigenous concerns.

Heron and Goudge would consider these anti-racists and this institution as success stories. But for me, they are the starting point. From my perspective, the troubled anti-racist is not the answer to global inequality, but the beginning of a new line of inquiry. Why does normative White anti-racism as espoused by scholars entail endless self-questioning to the point where the possibility of anti-racism itself is in doubt? Is it true that being privileged contaminates the act of helping, or development, irrevocably? And if so, what does this say about the possibility of help across racial and other lines of privilege? Are there any viable alternatives for White anti-racists who wish to help others without oppressing them?

By taking the White anti-racist as its object of study, this book offers some answers to these questions. I begin in Chapter 1 by considering how 'good' can be studied. Turning the anthropological gaze on people who are both privileged and trying to 'do good' raises suspicion of various kinds among participants and audiences. Rather than viewing these suspicions as a barrier to research, I draw them out to discuss the political and practical challenges of studying benevolence and the methodogical tools I used to address them. Chapter 2 outlines the main argument of the book, which is that the efforts to improve Indigenous health and social outcomes since the late 1960s have relied on a particular mode of Indigenous difference I call 'remediable difference'. Remediable difference works to manage the tension between two competing processes internal to Indigenous affairs: attaining statistical equality (explored as 'remedialism') and maintaining essential Indigenous difference (explored as 'Orientalism'). I recount how remediable difference was commonly unravelled by contact between White anti-racists and radically different Indigenous people, threatening the perceived moral integrity of both.

Subsequent chapters of the book explore different aspects of the overarching argument and White anti-racist culture. Chapter 3 zeroes in on the suburbs of Darwin, where White anti-racists at the institute live, to examine the 'contact zone'. An unremarkable suburban supermarket is the stage where radically different Indigenous 'long grassers' interact with White anti-racist residents. Other parts are played by Whites who openly object to the drunken disorder of long grassers, and activists who minimise long grassers' impact and defend their 'right to sleep' in public places.

Chapter 4 focuses on the 'performance' of White anti-racist identities through an examination of 'Welcome to Country' ceremonies. These are ceremonies conducted at the beginning of an event where an Indigenous 'Traditional Owner' for a specific locality welcomes those present, usually in a short speech. A corresponding ritual is an 'Acknowledgement of Country', whereby a non-Indigenous person acknowledges the Traditional Owners. I analyse this rich post-settler colonial ritual as an 'anti-racist speech act' to illustrate its multiple and ambiguous meanings.

The 'mutual recognition' of White anti-racists and Indigenous people is the subject of Chapter 5. I show how the process of 'conditional recognition' described by scholars, whereby minorities are recognised by the state, is a mutual process. Alongside the recognition of Indigenous people, White anti-racists at the institute seek recognition as anti-racist. Indigenous people are invited to take up two conflicting modes of recognition (that correspond with Orientalism and remedialism): the 'authentic Indigenous voice' that attests to essential Indigenous difference, and the 'self-improving' Indigenous person who offers a path to statistical equality. White anti-racists seek recognition by recognising Indigenous people in dense performances that oscillate between these conflicting modes.

Chapter 6 explores the novel concept of 'white stigma'. Although thinking of whiteness and privilege as stigmatised is counter-intuitive, it is a useful heuristic in spaces like the institute, where there is a deliberate attempt to invert colonial power relations. The management of white stigma explains some key behaviours of White anti-racists, such as a reluctance to claim any agency in Indigenous improvement and a tendency to tolerate suffering. I show how stigmatised whiteness is central to the normative discourse of whiteness studies and critiques of international development, fields where the management of white stigma is likely to be as important as it is at the institute.

The conclusion considers the consequences of the book's arguments for the current Australian political context and for the broader project of multicultural recognition. I finish with a reflection on the potential for alternative identity forms. Much of the book has interrogated White anti-racist identities and found internal contradictions that make them virtually unliveable for many. I relate these arguments to scholarship critiquing 'minority' identities – a category that includes indigeneity.

A range of scholars, including Indigenous Australian academics, have questioned whether identities rooted in past and present oppressions can only reinforce their own marginalisation. They argue that truly emancipatory identities must be grounded in a vision of an alternative future, rather than sourcing identity from the wounds of the past and the antagonisms of the present. This work suggests the fundamental problem with indigeneity, as it is recognised by progressive political forms, is that equitable Indigenous futures are bound to oppressive pasts.

I examine the various 'post-racial' options proposed that might transcend the 'wounded attachments' of minority identity, and find that forms of hybridity emerge as the most promising alternative.[18] Some scholars are refusing the mould of indigeneity, fashioning their own identities that may lie between existing categories. Such experiments in self-formation provide examples that White anti-racists may look to in conducting their own identity experiments when the space of recognition becomes too claustrophobic. The aim could be to form non-oppositional, non-stigmatised, non-settler identities – not to let White people 'off the hook' or to ignore white privilege, but to move towards a society that does not work against the flourishing of its citizens. Giving up current modes of recognition of indigeneity and White anti-racism would come at enormous political cost – a cost borne disproportionately by Indigenous people – but it may also offer new possibilities. Given the exhaustion of current modes of recognition, these possibilities are worth exploring.

Notes

1. In this passage I refer to an area that is technically north-east Arnhem Land but generally referred to as 'Arnhem Land'.
2. All names and identifying details of people have been changed to protect the privacy of research participants.

3. The acceptable term for Indigenous Australians periodically changes and is subject to contestation. Using the terms that will be developed in this book, one could say it is a key site for White anti-racist performances: knowing the right term and why the previous term is racist is an important skill for displaying one's anti-racism. Currently, the term 'first peoples' appears to be emerging in influential sites and may eventually replace 'Aboriginal and Torres Strait Islander'.

4. Note however that a revision in the method of calculating life expectancy means that the 'gap' is now much lower (12 years for men, 9.5 for women) and is comparable to the gap for Canada and less than some calculations, thus reducing the rhetorical power of the life expectancy statistic (Australian Bureau of Statistics 2009).

5. For an account of FCAATSI, including the intra-organisational racial politics that led to its demise, see Taffe 2005. For the 'politics of embarrassment', see Dyck 1985.

6. All figures are in Australian dollars.

7. To provide a sense of the increasing rate of spending, in 2006–7 just under $3 billion was spent on Indigenous health, which represented 3.1 per cent of total health spending, and a ratio of 1.25:1 compared to spending on non-Indigenous people (Australian Institute of Health and Welfare 2009).

8. For an early formulation of this approach, see Spark, Donovan and Howat 1991.

9. The research for this book consisted of fourteen months of participant-observation among health researchers at an Indigenous research institute in the Northern Territory, interviews with eighteen White health researchers from around Australia, and extensive document analysis of Indigenous health articles, policy documents, ethical guidelines and websites.

10. Foundational works include McIntosh 1990; Frankenberg 1993; and Dyer 1997.

11. As I discuss in Chapter 6, much scholarship in whiteness studies takes this perspective, as well as popular discourses.

12. These terms are necessarily generalising, as I explore in Chapter 4. I mean them here to refer to Australians who are concerned about Indigenous disadvantage and who think governments must take more action to assist (progressives) and those who do not see it as a crucial issue or who see the major fault lying with the Indigenous people themselves (conservatives). See Chapter 3 for more detailed description of 'progressives' and 'anti-racists'.

13. Hughey's recent work (2012) on anti-racists is based on a major empirical project and is discussed in Chapter 6.

14. Note that the 'backstage' is still a 'stage', and there are other aspects of any subjectivity that are hidden at all times or not consciously known. My combined use of subjectivity and performativity comes close to Haraway's use of the concept of 'figurations' (Haraway 1997: 11).

15. See also Kaufmann 1997; Crewe and Harrison 1998; Allahyari 2000; Goudge 2003; Eriksson Baaz 2005; Arvidson 2008; and Mosse 2011.

16. Heron substituted South Africa for the real country to protect the identity of the interviewee.

17. Through a circular logic used in whiteness studies (see Chapter 6), even where White anti-racists appear to be critical of systems of power they are often portrayed as simply reinforcing their own privilege. Thus Heron can describe how most of the development workers she interviewed were highly critical of the development enter-

prise, yet she focuses on how some viewed their own work as exceptions to this rule. She argues that therefore 'our critiques of [development] have the effect of enshrining us in virtue' (Heron 2007: 103).

18. On 'wounded attachments', see Brown 1995. For other theoretical approaches, see the conclusion.

Chapter 1

STUDYING 'GOOD'

It was anthropologist Laura Nader's famous call in 1972 for anthropologists to 'study up' that inspired a generation of anthropological scholarship of the 'West'. She challenged anthropologists to shift our gaze to the 'study of the colonizers rather than the colonized, the culture of power rather than the culture of the powerless, the culture of affluence rather than the culture of poverty' (Nader 1972: 289).[1]

Since that call, a growing body of anthropological work has emerged examining all kinds of Western institutions, cultures and cultural processes, as well as elite groups within societies around the world. While much work has examined the workings of oppressive forms of power, a small subset of that work has examined elite groups that have benevolence as their explicit mission. Some examples are the humanitarian organisation 'Doctors Without Borders' (Médecins Sans Frontières; see Redfield 2013), participatory development projects in India (Mosse 2001), AIDS activism in the Ivory Coast (Nguyen 2005), and self-determination in remote Indigenous communities (Cowlishaw 1999). Studying activists of various kinds raises specific methodological and ethical problems. All anthropologists who study 'up' or 'across' must contend with the unease of their research subjects who may not see themselves as the natural objects of anthropological attention. To take as an anthropological object something that most people see as inherently good is to invite a particular kind of suspicion.

The first question in people's minds, if not on their lips, will concern the motives of the researcher: why do you want to study people that are 'doing good'? If your reason for analysing them is not to offer good publicity, the assumption will be that you want to criticise them. Specifically, your motives will be interpreted in one of two ways. The anthropologist who analyses a benevolent project which is based on encouraging community participation might be interpreted as a right-wing conservative who thinks that participation is a waste of time and whose analysis will seek to show that participation is irrelevant, unimportant or unworkable, regardless of how well it is done. Alternatively, she might be taken to be a progressive who believes passionately in participation and whose analysis will argue it is not being done adequately. As either option spells trouble, such objects of anthropological attention are likely to be wary.[2]

In describing his ethnography of a development project in India, David Mosse details the political obstacles he overcame to see his work in print. While most of his development colleagues and research participants agreed wholeheartedly with his analysis of how a successful aid project was constructed, a number of those in managerial positions at the aid agency objected strongly to his work. They felt he was unfairly critical of their development project and would harm their reputation. They made their concerns widely known to the book's publisher, his head of department, the ethics committee of his university and the chair of his professional organisation (Mosse 2005a: ix–x).

The sensitivities that produced this reaction also existed in my field site, a space where benevolence held sway. Without exception, those non-Indigenous people who participated in my research were working in Indigenous health because they wanted to help Indigenous people. Despite the widespread suspicion of one's own and others' motivations as befitting a 'mercenary' (discussed in Chapter 6), none of those I worked with could seriously be categorised that way.

My desire to study this group generated a range of responses from actual and potential research participants. First and foremost, there was great interest in my work. I benefited from the intense interest in the ethics of Indigenous research and the efforts to 'decolonize' it (Smith 2012). There was enough overlap between my project and the desire for White anti-racists to be 'critically reflexive' for there to be substantial support for my project. Fieldwork often consisted of a 'para-ethnographic' space, where participants and I discussed together the contradictions and ambiguities of working in Indigenous affairs (Holmes and Marcus 2005).

However, this interest and support was laced with ambivalence. Making White anti-racists visible as a 'cultural group' by studying them makes many people in this group uncomfortable as they experience the range of fears mentioned above. Would I portray them as racist? Would I show them up as too concerned with their own reputations (motivated by a desire to conceal their racism, or by narcissism), or as blasé and ignorant of the racial context they worked in? As I discuss in Chapter 6, White anti-racists would prefer to disappear from the scene than be placed on centre stage.

These concerns also related to the institute as a whole, expressed through concern about how I would portray the institute and its staff. I was largely able to counter this as I had previously worked in the institute, and most people knew that depicting it and its staff as 'racist' was not my goal. Nevertheless, after public discussions of my work some in the audience would inevitably believe I was unfairly arguing that White researchers are racist. Others had the opposite concern. Some who saw White people as furthering the colonial project thought I was being too easy on White people if I was not actively criticising them. In view of the centuries of racist acts by White people towards Indigenous people, some thought my moral stance should be to uncover the ongoing racism of White researchers. Given my failure to do this, my research has been accused of being 'White therapy', implying that I merely make White people feel better about their racism, or better able to deny it.[3]

A factor in these reactions to my work was my insider status as an employee of the institute and, related to this, my membership of the specific group under study. I identified (and still do) as a White Australian and as an anti-racist, and sought to work with other White anti-racists as a 'native ethnographer' to more effectively address Indigenous disadvantage. My identification with the group under study led to its own set of moral problems, distinct from yet overlapping with the quandaries of studying benevolence.[4] My intermittent use of 'we' and 'them' to refer to White anti-racists in this book makes visible my vacillation between 'objective' observer and group participant, between subject and object.

Another form of response to my research was to protect Indigenous people from potential harm from my work. An academic from my university department asked me plainly whether I supported the 'Indigenous Research Reform Agenda', an approach to research characterised by emancipatory politics that privileges Indigenous voices (Rigney 1999). When I responded by trying to explain that my approach to anthropology meant that nothing was immune from critical analysis, he replied that if he thought that my work would 'in any way harm the [Indigenous] community', he would intervene to stop it.[5] Another White academic was openly hostile to my project because 'analysis/representation of non-Indigenous health researchers and of Indigenous co-researchers has the potential to offend and harm both groups'.

At times, I found that this academic had a point. When discussing sensitive issues such as race and the portrayal of indigeneity and whiteness, there seemed to be endless potential for misinterpretation. For example, any discussion of negative *representations* of Indigenous people and culture were interpreted by some as a negative portrayal of Indigenous people. When I shared a chapter I had written with a research participant that explored the ways that 'culture' is used in constructions of Indigenous ill health, she objected to my discussion of how Indigenous culture was constructed in some Indigenous health literature as 'damaged' by colonisation (Kowal 2006a). Using the word 'damaged' was offensive, she said. I pointed out that the sentence did not say that Indigenous culture 'was' damaged, but that some people wrote and talked about it 'as if' it were damaged – but this made little impact.[6] The need for some progressive non-Indigenous people to remain recognisably 'anti-racist', what I explore in this book as the 'performance' of anti-racist subjectivities (see chapters 3 to 5), means that any association of a negative attribute with Indigenous people is highly problematic, even where the intent is to understand the discourses that anti-racists share and reproduce.

The preoccupation of White anti-racists with their self-presentation affected the content of this book. Senior people in my field site and some participants were highly concerned that participants may be identifiable if I described individuals in any detail. This was a difficult issue to navigate, given that the hallmark of anthropological scholarship is precisely detailed descriptions of individuals and events. Partly as a result, the essays that make up this book draw on a wide range of sources in addition to field notes and interview transcripts from my research at the institute.[7] While the argument has been developed through participant-observation with a research team of eighteen people and long interviews with eighteen others who worked at the institute, I illustrate my arguments with a mix of material from policy, media and academic sources in addition to my direct research data. In addition, two chapters apply the main arguments of the book to contexts beyond the institute: 'long grassers' in Darwin, and Welcome to Country ceremonies.

Overall, the White anti-racists I have had contact with expressed more concern about possible epistemological violence to Indigenous people resulting from my work, rather than possible damage to White reputations. This is ironic from my perspective. After all, my project was inspired in part by prominent Indigenous activist Gary Foley who took a keen interest in the Indigenous solidarity student activist group I helped to found in 1997 at the University of Melbourne. As Foley used to advise, 'don't worry about us [Indigenous people], you work on your own mob'. I came to recognise the naivety of my assumption that directing research efforts towards White people, rather than Indigenous people, would shelter me from accusations of harming Indigenous people. I see now my focus on White people partly reflects the desire of White anti-racists to minimise our seemingly inherent capacity to damage Indigenous people – a desire I interrogate in chapters 2 and 6. Another factor that influenced how this range of criticisms was deployed, and sometimes withheld, was the indigeneity of my supervisor. Having an Indigenous professor for a supervisor – certainly one of the most influential and respected Indigenous academics in Australia – was important for the political viability of my research. Notwithstanding his intellectual contributions, my perceived ability to have captured his coveted attention was crucial in the acceptance of my work and my presence in the field, and in Indigenous health forums generally.

Concerns that my project may actively harm Indigenous people were matched by concerns that the project may not benefit them – an act of harm by omission. Echoing criticisms of 'White therapy', one researcher thought it was 'indulgent' to try and understand the position of White researchers, asking bluntly, 'Who benefits from your research?'[8] My pleas that Indigenous people *might* indirectly benefit from the improved research practices that *might* result from my research were far from convincing from her perspective. Another found my case for the inherent value of anthropological understanding morally unacceptable: 'it's not good enough anymore, just to understand … because, meanwhile, Aboriginal communities are still having inexcusable rates of violence and chronic disease'.[9]

This is a hazard of working as a cultural anthropologist in an arena where discourses of 'urgent need' circulate freely. Here's a crude but effective exercise: type into a Google search the words 'Indigenous', 'health', 'Australia' and 'urgent need', and you get 1.8 million hits. The links on the first page tell us that the following are all urgently needed: housing, the alleviation of poverty and youth suicide, Indigenous health personnel, education on cultural safety, better planning and coordination of funding, better Aboriginal health promotion, and research that preserves cultural heritage. This sense of urgency and desperation is something I have shared at times, most acutely in my attempts to deliver quality medical care to Indigenous people in Darwin. In this environment of crisis, some see research of any kind as a waste of precious resources. As one audience member commented at an institute seminar on mental health research: 'Isn't it trite to give people a questionnaire when kids in Arnhem Land are hanging themselves every night? Shouldn't we be trying to find out how to fix the problem instead?'[10]

While this discourse on urgent need casts moral uncertainty over any research effort, it is particularly difficult to carve out a foothold for critical analysis that has 'understanding' as its aim. This is the converse of the problem that Charles Hale has discussed. Hale is an anthropologist of Latin America and a proponent of 'activist research', a type of anthropology that unashamedly admits dual loyalties to the intellectual endeavour and to the emancipation of the oppressed. This method produces 'emancipatory knowledge' (Hale 2006). While he complains of being ostracised by anthropological colleagues for practising activist research, my problem is the risk of being ostracised at my field site for *not* doing activist research. It may be that all subjects of anthropological research expect anthropologists to take up the subjects' moral positionings as their own, but when one is 'studying up' this expectation has particular weight, as Cris Shore has argued (Shore 2002; see also Conroy 2009).

A number of theorists have addressed the political consequences of critiquing emancipatory discourses. Stephen Muecke explains that literary criticism of Indigenous texts that transcend the automatic praise of Indigenous authors results in 'an intensification of the scrutiny of these social fields where power relations are exercised, rather than the endorsement of romances of liberation' (Muecke 2005: 119). This scrutiny can have uncertain political outcomes.

Anna Tsing's ethnography of environmentalism in Indonesia takes these moral and political dilemmas seriously. She sees the kinds of issues I discuss here as an opposition between scholarly theory and activist practice. She tracks how anthropologists' outright support for activist movements gave way to more finely grained critique in the 1990s. These analyses have made important contributions to activist discourses, for instance through questioning the concepts of 'community' and 'participation', but they have also 'dampened the spirit of advocacy, making those who wanted to change the world seem self-aggrandizing, if effective, or silly, if not' (Tsing 2005: 265). She argues that academic scholarship needs to re-engage with practitioners, learning to 'tell a story that both acknowledges imperial power and leaves room for possibility… to encourage critical purchase without cutting off the strings of hope' (ibid.: 267). Similarly, in this study of White anti-racist people, I do not aim to denigrate their quest to minimise human suffering, but to understand it better.

How are anthropologists to remain loyal to their intellectual agendas, while negotiating the politics of their field sites, respecting the viewpoints of their activist subjects and not 'cutting off the strings of hope'? In my work, a crucial tool for this task has been the mapping out of three different modes of analysis.

David Mosse discusses the first two modes in his analysis of research on development policy. He argues that the two dominant views of policy are 'instrumental' and 'critical'. The *instrumental* view sees development policy as shaping development in a more or less positivist way; the goal of commentary on development policy would thus be to improve development. In contrast, a *critical* view 'sees policy as a rationalising technical discourse concealing hidden purposes of bureaucratic power or dominance' (Mosse 2004: 641), a view typified by the early critiques of development two decades ago (Ferguson 1990; Escobar 1995). Within these formulations, development is a form of neocolonial domination to be resisted. As Mosse is not instrumental in his approach, the aid officials he studied interpreted his work as critical. These modes of analysis are mirrored in the reception of my work among some White anti-racists who thought I was out to show them up as ineffectual, or to criticise the whole enterprise of health improvement as fruitless or racist. Mosse argues that neither the instrumental nor critical perspective is useful for achieving his goal of 'opening up the implementation black box so as to address the relationship between policy and practice' (Mosse 2005a: 5).

For this task of understanding, a third mode of analysis is required, that of critique. To establish this third mode, it is helpful to insist on a distinction between *critique*, which seeks to understand an object of study through careful analysis of its construction, and *criticism*, which can include critique but which also seeks to pass moral judgment. As Foucault put it: 'A critique is not a matter of saying that things are not right as they are. It is a matter of pointing out on what kinds of assumptions, what kinds of familiar, unchallenged, unconsidered modes of thought the practices that we accept rest' (Foucault 1988: 155).

Bourdieu approached the same point from a different direction, writing that 'good intentions so often make bad sociology' (Bourdieu 1990: 5). He rejected sociology based on 'the logic of the trial' that seeks to accuse one's objects of study of wrongdoing (or alternatively, defend them from such accusations) (idem 1993: 42). He concurred with Foucault that social research must seek only to expose the hidden truths of a particular social field – what I characterise as 'critique'.

In practice, it is difficult to sustain the distinction between instrumental and critical approaches on one hand and critique on the other. Many people are incredulous that anyone can claim to be studying something without trying to judge it or change it for the better. Such sceptics are common within social fields where 'doing good' is the underlying principle of behaviour and belief.

In carving out a space for critique of benevolent forms, the concept of 'methodological agnosticism' is useful. This term was first proposed by religious studies scholar Ninian Smart to argue that scholars of religion should seek to neither confirm nor deny the existence of God, but instead to understand the variety and meanings of religious belief (Smart 1973). I adapt the term here to mean a deliberate non-belief about what White anti-racism, cultural appropriateness, or self-determination really do or should consist of. This incorporates agnosticism about reality – for example, agnosticism about what Indigenous programmes 'really' achieve and whether anti-racists are 'really' racist – and moral agnosticism – agnosticism about what Indigenous programmes and anti-racists should do or be. For the purposes of understanding White anti-racists' constructions of Indigenous health and illness and their effects on how problems and solutions are framed, the 'objective reality' of these things are taken to be unknown and unknowable. Where representations contradict each other, as they often do, it is not my role to privilege one source over another as the authoritative one. Rather, my task is to understand how certain representations come to be accepted as truth, and others come to be contested.

In place of the 'tough-minded suspension of disbelief' that Fernandez has called for, this is a 'suspension of belief' in emancipatory narratives common among the cultural group under study (Fernandez 1990: 159). Methodological agnosticism, or put differently, strategic non-belief, is both particularly necessary and particularly difficult in social fields that involve powerful moral positioning.[11] As I asked informants for their views about Indigenous disadvantage and, in return, was often asked about my own opinions, the temptation to 'perform' anti-racism and commit to a moral position was often strong.

Methodological agnosticism is not without its own moral hazards. While it may be analytically useful to insist that we cannot know reality, reality matters nonetheless. Indigenous people really get sick and die, and governments spend real money on the problem. How can the scholar remain agnostic about a reality that is as grave as it is for many Indigenous Australians?

Bruno Latour has usefully considered the political implications of critique. He was motivated among other things by the science wars over climate change, where some climate change sceptics use the idea that knowledge is a 'social construction' to argue against cutting greenhouse gas emissions (Latour 2004b). In regretting that a basic principle of critique he helped to create had gone so awry, he reiterated the distinction between social constructivism (as it is commonly understood) and constructivism (Latour and Woolgar 1979). To say something is socially constructed is taken to mean that it is not 'real', but merely an effect of either pressing social forces or the projection of individual desires. So to say that Indigenous culture is socially constructed, in this sense, might be taken as saying that it is really the effect of colonisation and oppression, or alternatively, that it is a projection of White people's romanticisation.

In contrast, constructivism rejects the idea that 'reality' and 'construction' are opposites: rather, reality is the result of sound constructions. To say that Indigenous culture is 'constructed' points to the numerous discourses that give it meaning, from anthropological concepts of culture to global discourses of Indigenous rights. A constructivist scholar is someone who 'adds reality ... and not subtract reality' (Latour 2004b: 232) by elucidating 'the collective process that ends up as solid constructs through the mobilization of heterogeneous crafts, ingredients and coordination' (Latour 2003: 31).

In my everyday life, I am very grateful that the representation of a red light for stop and the civil discourse of refraining from violence towards strangers are compelling to most people. I take the authority of these constructions for granted. But as an anthropologist, my job is to analyse compelling representations that occur in my field of interest. The outcome of such research is admittedly uncertain. As Hage puts it in his exposition of Bourdieu's epistemology and anti-racist sociology, good scholarship is 'inherently subversive', uncovering knowledge that has been hidden in order to sustain the dominant order (Hage 1995: 60). When the social field of interest is a place where benevolence is the 'dominant order', those invested in this field may understandably be apprehensive. However, uncovering the underlying assumptions of White anti-racist beliefs, as I do in the next chapter and throughout this book, is crucial in order for us to identify the limits and opportunities of dominant constructions, and imagine how we might think and act differently.

I have laid out here a toolkit to establish a space for critique in a climate of urgent need and dense moral and racial politics. This does not resolve the challenges of studying benevolence, but defines a methodological and ethical position from which to face them.

Notes

1. See also Stocking 1982: xi; Marcus 1998; and Marcus and Fischer's discussion (1986) of the 'repatriation of anthropology'.
2. George Marcus, in his foundational work on the anthropology of elites, has outlined the moral and methodological dangers of either sympathising with or disapproving of the elite subjects of anthropological research (Marcus 1983).
3. Hughey makes a similar critique of anti-racist activism as 'white confessionalism' (Hughey 2012).

4. These particular politics of knowledge production are also common to anthropologists of development (who are often development practitioners themselves).
5. Journal, 2 May 2005: 9.
6. Field Notes, 20 Oct. 2004: 2, 20.
7. Kaufmann (1997) describes a similar anxiety about anonymity in her 'partial ethnography' of development practitioners.
8. Field Notes, 10 Oct. 2004: 2, 5.
9. Transcript 8, 7.
10. Field Notes, 4 Apr. 2005: 3, 64. For discussions of the ethics of social research in the context of crisis, see Kroll-Smith and Couch 1990; Fassin 2011; and Redfield 2013.
11. Other relevant work making this point includes Burchell's view that the anthropologist should engage a 'non-identitarian posture' (Burchell 1993), engaging in critical analysis and leaving it to others to make axiological and ontological judgements. In their collection on the anthropology of policy, Shore and Wright argue that research on policy 'involves detaching and repositioning oneself sufficiently far enough from the norms and categories of thought that give security and meaning to the moral universe of one's society in order to interrogate the supposed natural or axiomatic "order of things"' (Shore and Wright 1997: 17).

Chapter 2

THE CULTURE OF WHITE ANTI-RACISM

The one thing that most people who work in Indigenous affairs can agree on is that Aboriginal people are, in general, different from non-Aboriginal people. They have a different history. They have a different culture. Some, especially in the north and the centre of the country, have a different language. They have different family structures, different expectations, different communication styles, and different social worlds.

But what kind of difference is this? The particular way that we think of Aboriginal difference has a major impact on how we try to address Indigenous disadvantage. Past ideas of difference, when mainstream Western science saw Aboriginal people as the bottom rung of the human species – barely human at all – have become a source of shame for many Australians (see Stocking 1968; Stepan 1982; McGregor 1997). Equally, many of us would disagree with the idea that Aboriginal people are no different from the rest of us. Dominant concepts of Aboriginal difference lie somewhere between absolute difference and absolute sameness.

My approach to this question draws from my analysis of non-Indigenous people who seek to address Indigenous disadvantage. For some decades, scholars of Indigenous Australia have recognised how Indigenous and White society are interdependent social worlds. More than that, each only makes sense in terms of the other (Merlan 2006). But the recognition that to understand indigeneity we must understand whiteness, and vice versa, is not reflected in what scholars study and write about. While a number of studies of Indigenous Australia mention in passing the White people within their purview, there has been very little dedicated study of the non-Indigenous half of the intercultural field. (This reflects, at least in part, the methodological and ethical challenges I discussed in the previous chapter.)

This study is one of the few exceptions.[1] My research on White, left-wing, middle-class professional people who work in Indigenous health offers an opportunity to understand the kind of 'different' that Aboriginal people are, as seen by the bureaucratic and programme machinery that is designed to help them. If we think of the full scope of Indigenous difference as 'everything that Indigenous people do', the way that Indigenous difference is thought of by the state and the broader society will always be an incomplete picture, a particular viewpoint with some aspects kept out of the frame. Indigenous difference is made intelligible to White anti-racists through the concept of 'remediable difference': a difference that can be improved. Remediable difference is a useful concept for explaining the culture of White anti-racism. This chapter outlines my account of remediable difference as a particular form of difference that acts to manage a tension inherent to progressive constructions of Indigenous disadvantage.

In the Preface I described my move from Melbourne to Darwin at the end of 2000. I aimed to combine my medical training with my political beliefs to help to redress the harm that Indigenous people have suffered under European colonisation. After a few years working in Indigenous public health and clinical medicine, I began to have doubts about the whole system. I could see how the health care and research bureaucracy were trying to change in order to hear Indigenous voices and give Indigenous people more power, through mechanisms like employing Indigenous people and supporting their professional development, having Indigenous reference groups for research projects, cultural awareness training and so on, but it rarely seemed to have the desired effect. Lots of other people that I worked with seemed frustrated with the system too. Publicly many people would say that the bureaucracies were not doing enough to change, or that non-Indigenous people were not sharing power effectively. Privately, people might say that they were disillusioned or cynical about the ability of White people to have a positive impact on Indigenous health at all.

Gradually, I began to see this as an anthropological problem. I began asking the question: what does it mean for a group of well-meaning, White, left-wing, middle-class people to leave their metropolitan homes to come to the north of Australia and try to empower a group of Indigenous people to take action to improve their own health outcomes? How do we understand this particular mix of people and beliefs? I thought about this in historical perspective, in the context of the post-1970s Indigenous rights movement that many of us are directly influenced by, and the longer history of White people trying to help Indigenous people. Soon enough, I was studying my own tribe.

In studying this tribe, I was trying to understand their subjectivity. In my usage, this term means something broader than what is generally understood by the more common term 'identity'.[2] An identity is a type of person or an aspect of being a person that people can identify with or be identified with, such as woman, White person, mountain climber, violinist, injecting drug user, and so on. Subjectivity is the sum of all the knowledge, beliefs, actions and technologies that make it possible to have a particular identity. To take an example, the subjectivity of a 'mountain climber' is the product of the concept of leisure, middle-class affluence, discourses of White masculinity and environmentalism, and the magazines, websites and films that form a mountain climbing subculture. All of these things produce the subjectivity of the mountain climber.

The subjectivity that I was interested in was that of 'White anti-racists'. This term needs explaining. As mentioned in the Introduction, I use it as shorthand for non-Indigenous, left-wing, middle-class professionals who work in Indigenous affairs. I use the word 'White' because most people in this group are visibly white, and because White refers to the dominant culture that all people in this group are part of and feel comfortable in, even if they do not have white skin themselves.[3] The second half of the term – 'anti-racist' – refers to someone who defines him or herself as that, or as 'not racist'. It is not an objective label but a self-identified one (although in the next chapter I examine the empirical evidence for the social groups I term 'progressives' and 'anti-racists'). I am not interested in judging whether particular people are 'actually' racist or not. Rather, I am interested in what it means for someone to think of him or herself as anti-racist, as many people interested in Indigenous affairs do (me included).

Just like the subjectivity of the mountain climber, the subjectivity of White anti-racists can be broken down into its constituent parts. I was working and living in an environment where there were lots of White anti-racist people working with Indigenous people, in health, education, the environment, law, music, and many other areas. Although we were a diverse group, we shared common beliefs and ideals. My task was to understand all the aspects that produced the subjectivity we all identified with (but usually could not name).

An important part of understanding White anti-racists was unpacking the knowledge system that underpins this subjectivity. We all have belief systems that help us to make sense of the world we live in. If you are a Christian, you might believe that good deeds will be rewarded with a place in heaven after death. If you are a neoliberal, you might believe that the free market is the best way to provide the needs of the populace. White anti-racists have a certain understanding of Indigenous disadvantage, its causes and its cures, which differ from say, the understanding of Andrew Bolt (radio broadcaster, television presenter and blogger) or Alan Jones (radio broadcaster), the two most prominent figures in the conservative public sphere. What do White anti-racists believe in? How is this knowledge about Indigenous people structured; what is left in, and what is left out?

The knowledge that White anti-racist people have about Indigenous disadvantage is the set of beliefs usually associated with the 'self-determination' era. It includes beliefs that Indigenous people are the first peoples of Australia; that their culture has been maintained for thousands of years, perhaps the 'oldest' culture in the world; that they have a special relationship to country and a complex social system; that their culture is in some ways superior to Western culture (for example, in the way they live 'in harmony' with the land); that their culture has been severely decimated by colonisation; that their current problems stem from dispossession, displacement, racism and intergenerational trauma; that the Australian people and Australian governments must accept responsibility for the injury inflicted on people and culture, and should invest more resources in Indigenous programmes. Self-determination is central to this knowledge: a belief that Indigenous people must be in control of efforts to improve their lives, but non-Indigenous people must be available to provide adequate support. This set of ideas represents the dominant belief system among progressive Australians from around the early 1970s.[4]

As a white Indigenous solidarity activist, public health researcher, and in various other White anti-racist roles I have inhabited, I have participated in producing and reproducing this set of beliefs. Now, as an anthropologist of anti-racist White people, I examine it as an object of study. Understanding this set of beliefs is a key way to understand the subjectivity of White anti-racists. (While this chapter focuses on beliefs, elsewhere in the book I discuss the actions of White anti-racists, such as 'performances' – chapters 3 and 5; 'speech acts' – Chapter 4; and behaviours to manage 'white stigma' – Chapter 6.)

In many ways, all knowledge about Indigenous people is a meditation on equality and difference. How different they are from us, and how equal they should be, are two questions that dominate or linger on the margins of every speech, tearoom chat, online forum and dinner party conversation about Indigenous issues. Beliefs about Indigenous disadvantage can be seen as attempts to solve the central dilemma of Indigenous affairs: the tension between equality and difference.

Right-wing commentators might resolve this tension by arguing that Indigenous people are inherently different from non-Indigenous people (whether this difference is seen as genetic or the result of welfare dependency) and will never be equal. White anti-racist beliefs resolve this tension differently, by arguing that Indigenous people are culturally different, and equality can be achieved if this difference is taken into account. This latter argument draws on a specific construction of Indigenous difference: 'remediable difference', defined as a difference that can be improved.[5]

This construction of Indigenous difference serves many White anti-racists well. For others, exposure to a more extreme form of difference that I call 'radical difference' destabilises remediable difference and makes it untenable.[6] This chapter will explain the concepts of remediable difference and radical difference and show that they account for the beliefs of White anti-racists and the broader project of Indigenous improvement in post-settler colonial Australia. Before we get to that part of the story, I first dwell on how equality and difference are understood by White anti-racists.

* * *

In recent years, 'closing the gap' has become the virtual slogan of Indigenous affairs. It seems straightforward that we would measure certain outcomes like life expectancy, employment, and home ownership, graph them, and do all we can to close the gap. But the imperative to do this draws on a historically and culturally specific set of beliefs and norms largely described through the concept of liberalism, the school of political thought born in seventeenth-century Europe that takes freedom and happiness as its goals. In liberal theorist John Grey's account, the central tenets of liberalism are individualism, equality, a universal sense of morality (of right and wrong), and a sense that our lives can be improved through good government.[7] Western democracies are all liberal in the sense that they broadly believe that individuals should all be supported to fulfil their life goals to the best of their ability.

In the context of Indigenous disadvantage, liberalism emphasises the rights of Indigenous people to standards of living equal to those of non-Indigenous people, and the responsibilities of the state to effect this improvement. Liberalism underlies the belief that the lives of Indigenous people, so badly affected by colonisation, can be improved through reasoned intervention. It entails a set of assumptions about what a 'good' life requires, such as functional housing, Western education, employment opportunities, and freedom from addiction and illness. The idea of 'inequality' is central to the expression of liberalism. We produce a myriad of statistics about those things we consider to constitute a good life, and we strive to equalise the outcomes for non-Indigenous and Indigenous people, to make the lines on the graph converge. If one image could sum up the work of equality within the belief system of White anti-racists, it would look something like this.

Rate per 1,000

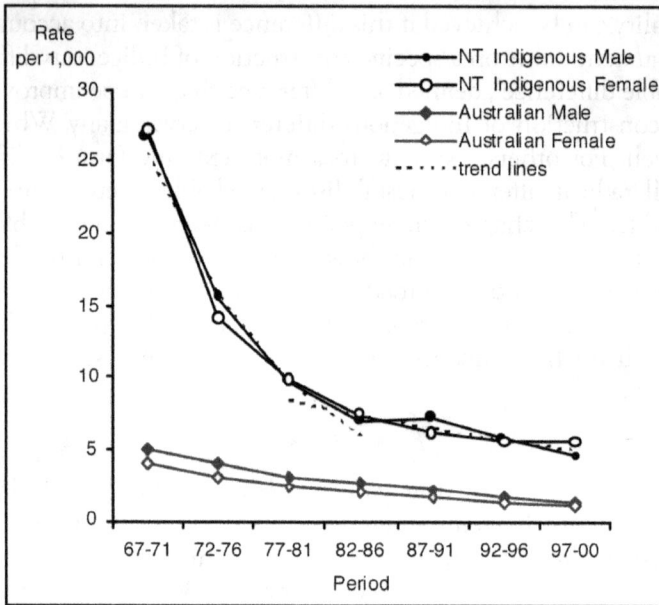

Figure 1.1 Mortality trends for Indigenous 0–4-year-olds, 1967–2000 in the Northern Territory.
Source: Condon et al. 2004. Used with kind permission of the authors.

Remedialism is a powerful force driving White anti-racist beliefs. But an adequate explanation requires something more. Equality explains why we want to help those less fortunate people in our society, but it does not explain why we identify a particular disadvantaged group such as 'Indigenous people', rather than, say, homeless people, the mentally ill, or the colour-blind, all groups that might also have gaps that we could measure and try to close. Neither does remedialism explain the belief that Indigenous people themselves need to be in charge of efforts to address inequality.

What distinguishes White anti-racist beliefs from other forms of liberalism is the importance of difference. The idea that Indigenous people are different – whether this difference is thought to be grounded in culture, social exclusion, or something else – is central to how Indigenous disadvantage is understood within the dominant society, and by White anti-racists in particular.

The idea of 'Orientalism' is a useful way to think about how difference works within White anti-racist beliefs. This term originally meant 'the study of the East' (though often referring to practically everything outside Europe), but in the last decades it has taken on a different meaning through the work of Palestinian theorist Edward Said and other postcolonial scholars. Said argued that the Western scholarly work on 'the Orient' actually functioned something like a reverse mirror. Rather than seeing the Orient with a genuine clarity, the Western scholar projected onto the Orient everything that Europe was not (backward, dirty, immoral), so that the West could be reassured of what they were (civilised, clean, virtuous). The Orient was 'essentialised', that is, reduced to a number of characteristics that supposedly contained the 'essence' of the Orient (Said 1978).

In the case of Indigenous people, past essentialist accounts have represented them, for example, as primitive and barbaric 'stone-age' people of low intelligence, an anachronistic remnant of European man's own past. This depiction functioned to reinforce notions of the European as the pinnacle of human progress and rationality. These images of the West that always accompany Orientalism (usually implicitly) have been called Occidentalism (Carrier 1995). Orientalism and Occidentalism are more than 'just' images and words. They are powerful discourses that have underpinned Western colonisation. The meanings they create and reflect facilitated the European occupation of Australia and the principle of *terra nullius*. Most Europeans assumed that such a 'primitive' people who did not make permanent settlements could not have a sense of ownership at all, let alone a complex system of land ownership. This kind of Orientalism is marginalised today and unequivocally labelled as racist in the public sphere, although it survives in many pockets of Australia (and is particularly evident in the Comments sections of certain media websites and blogs).

Another thread of 'essentialist' depictions of Indigenous people sees them in a more positive light. These are the images we so often see associated with 'feel-good' stories in the media: dark-skinned Indigenous people who enjoy a deep spiritual connection with the natural world. For clarity, I refer to this form of Orientalism as 'positive Orientalism' and the denigrating form as 'negative Orientalism'. Just as negative Orientalism has a (usually implicit) counterpart in positive depictions of the West, positive Orientalism has a double in negative depictions of the West. For example, the spiritual well-being of Indigenous people is invoked to suggest the spiritual poverty of Western lifestyles. In calling this 'positive', I do not mean to imply that I think positive Orientalism is a good thing. This simple inversion of negative Orientalism, valorising all things Indigenous and rebuking all things Western, is as inaccurate as its opposite.

Positive and negative Orientalism map onto two forms of Indigenous difference I call 'sanitised' and 'unsanitised'.[8] Sanitised difference is those differences generally perceived as 'good' by White anti-racists (along with many other Australians who are not invested in an anti-racist identity): kinship, hunting skills, language, art, living on breathtaking outstations, unspoiled beaches and billabongs teeming with wildlife. The 'unsanitised' differences of Indigenous social life are those aspects that most anti-racists view as 'bad' or, at the very least, problematic: massive overcrowding, vandalised houses, dirty or broken toilets causing constant illnesses, children not attending school, eating fried food and drinking coke from the take away for most meals, or gambling away welfare money while children go hungry – not to mention the darkest aspects of unsanitised social life in many communities: substance abuse, domestic violence and child abuse.[9]

These divisions between the delightful, the unfortunate, and the abhorrent may seem self-evident to liberal readers. Of course, detailed knowledge about the country and its flora and fauna integrated into a glorious cosmology is a 'good' thing; and of course, having children kept up by their relatives' noisy drunken fights night after night is a 'bad' thing. As mentioned in Chapter 1, engaging with the arguments presented here requires a suspension of belief. Let us assume a null anthropological hypothesis: that culture is what people do, full stop. Let us assume that any categories we impose on what people do (such as moral and immoral) achieve some end.[10] Often this 'end' is an extremely good idea, such as imposing law and order sufficient to make a community liveable. But the divisions that progressive logic read into Indigenous lifeworlds perform other functions, namely, expressing White anti-racist beliefs and maintaining the viability of White anti-racist subjectivities.

The distinction between sanitised and unsanitised difference reflects the moral sensibilities of White anti-racists.[11] As I will illustrate, sanitised difference corresponds to the territory of remediable difference, and unsanitised difference maps onto radical difference. White anti-racist beliefs about Indigenous disadvantage hinge on the assumption that 'closing the gap' acts to erase unsanitised difference and preserve sanitised difference. This division is central to remediable difference. We will see how the preservation of sanitised difference manages the tension between remedialism and Orientalism, promising that the imagined future of statistical equality will produce recognisably Indigenous subjects.

Although the term 'Orientalism' can be taken as an accusation of wrongdoing or even racism, I do not use it in this way. By drawing on this concept to explore the role of difference in White anti-racist beliefs, I do not mean to imply that White anti-racists are, in fact, racists. Rather, I mean to point to the drawbacks of designating one group as 'different' from another group, especially when these two groups are viewed as not just different from each other, but opposed to one another by definition – in this case, as Indigenous and non-Indigenous. Once we define two groups in this way, it is almost impossible not to essentialise these groups in relation to one another, whether these assumptions are in the form of 'Western, good – Indigenous, bad', or 'Indigenous, good – Western, bad'. Scholars such as Charles Taylor, Elizabeth Povinelli and Wendy Brown have, in different ways, questioned the limits of a politics based on protecting or repairing a culture defined in opposition to the dominant society (see, for example, Taylor 1994; Brown 1995; and Povinelli 2002b). Their varying approaches are collected under the banner of the 'politics of difference' or the 'politics of recognition' (for more on this, see Chapter 5). I will return to the limits of difference below.

* * *

I have argued that the beliefs of White anti-racists are underpinned by the idea that Indigenous people are distinctively different from White people (difference), and the idea that White people have both the ability and an obligation to improve the lives of Indigenous people (equality). A closer examination of these ideas reveals the potential for tension between them. If Indigenous people are completely different from non-Indigenous people, then how can we be sure all of them want to be equal to us, or that equality means the same thing to them as it does to us? Can inequality be a chosen expression of difference in some circumstances? If some aspects of Indigenous distinctiveness are related to inequality, then when we close the gap and make Indigenous people statistically equal to non-Indigenous people, could we be making them less Indigenous?[12]

Many non-Indigenous people who work in Indigenous affairs have grappled with these questions. Others find such questions are puzzling, preposterous, or even racist. I interpret the former questioning group as those White anti-racists for whom remediable difference is failing in the face of radical difference. For the latter unquestioning group, remediable difference is functioning perfectly well.

For the White anti-racists I studied who worked with Indigenous communities in the Northern Territory, these unsettling questions almost inevitably made their way into conversations between colleagues and friends, over coffees, during long bush drives, or over beers on back verandahs. The conversations these questions provoke eroded remediable difference and the broader belief system it supports.

Recall that I define 'remediable difference' as 'a difference that can be brought into the norm'. Remediable difference means that Indigenous people are different to 'us' – to non-Indigenous people – but not so different that they are beyond the reach of our interventions. To explain the failure of remediable difference, I will take a close look at one common White anti-racist belief about Indigenous health: what I call the 'information deficit model'.

The 'information deficit model' is the idea that Indigenous people are unhealthy because they lack correct health information. According to this model, if they were provided with good health information in a linguistically and culturally accessible manner, they would take their medicines, stop smoking, eat nutritious food, send their children to school, and perform any of the other personal and social tasks required to 'close the gap'.

This model of health behaviour has been criticised in the mainstream context (see, for example, Lupton 1995), but it survives quite well in the mainstream and particularly in Indigenous health. An important example in Indigenous health is the book *Djambatj Mala: Why Warriors Lie Down and Die*, published in 2000. The author is Richard Trudgen, a mechanic turned successful cross-cultural consultant for Aboriginal Resource and Development Services (ARDS), a Christian organisation based in Arnhem Land.

In one part of the book, Trudgen tells the story of David, a man who was told by doctors for thirteen years that his kidneys were failing because of diabetes, and that he should eat a diet low in sugar and salt and give up smoking. He had not acted on any of this advice, and he was soon to be forced to move from his community into Darwin to receive renal dialysis. But this changed when Trudgen acted as an interpreter during a twenty-minute consultation with a doctor. David had a 'very good knowledge of English' and had travelled widely as a national Indigenous leader. But his 'different world view' meant that he did not understand the Western concepts he had been hearing for years until Trudgen explained them to him using metaphors he understood, like comparing kidney function to an engine filter. Once Trudgen had properly explained to him why he should stop smoking and restrict his sugar and salt intake, he immediately did so, and his health dramatically improved (Trudgen 2000: 98–101).

This story had a strong impact on me when I first read it, soon after moving to Darwin, and others I have known had similar reactions. It made so much sense that Indigenous people would stop smoking and eat the right foods if they truly knew what the consequences were. I now understand the appeal of this story as 'remediable difference': a difference that will respond to reasoned intervention. In this case, David's apparent inability to follow dietary advice that would greatly benefit him was remedied by Trudgen's linguistic intervention. After some years working in the field I began to doubt the logic of this story, and I will talk about the unravelling of White anti-racist beliefs below. But for now, this story should be read as an example of this belief system.

At this point, some readers may be wondering why I am making such a big deal of this information deficit model. Surely it is reasonable to say that Indigenous people from remote communities lack Western health information, given their isolation from mass communication, poor literacy, and culturally distinct health beliefs. And surely it is reasonable to think this is a major reason why they smoke more, drink harmfully more, and are more likely to be obese (Australian Bureau of Statistics 2006).

For the purposes of destabilising this view, I draw on a study into health promotion in remote Northern Territory communities. It should be remembered that it is very likely that Indigenous people lack some health knowledge, and that health information is both important and useful. My goal is not to vilify the field of health promotion, but to illustrate how and why remediable difference is so appealing to White anti-racists.

So, is Indigenous ill health due to a lack of knowledge about their health problems? One answer to this is provided in research on smoking. A study of six remote Northern Territory communities asked residents in 1999 whether they believed that smoking causes lung cancer and/or heart disease: 85 per cent believed that lung cancer is linked to tobacco use, and 82 per cent that heart disease is linked to it. In contrast, data collected at around the same time from the general Australian population indicated that only 60 per cent believed smoking causes lung cancer and only 32 per cent believed it causes heart disease. But this higher level of knowledge was not reflected in lower rates of smoking: 68 per cent of Indigenous people in these NT communities smoked, in contrast to 24 per cent of all Australians at that time; and knowing the dangers of smoking did not mean people were more likely to give it up (Trotter 1997; Australian Bureau of Statistics 2001, 2003; Ivers et al. 2006).

There are a multitude of reasons why Indigenous people might smoke at higher levels than non-Indigenous people, some of which were cited in the article that reported on this study, but a lack of health information does not appear to be one of them. According to this study and others, Indigenous people in these remote communities are *more* informed than other Australians about the dangers of smoking. Yet they are nearly three times more likely to smoke.

I rehearse this example to make the point that the idea that Indigenous people know better than the general population that smoking is bad for you, but smoke anyway, makes many White anti-racist people feel uncomfortable. This knowledge contradicts the 'information deficit model' and it goes against remediable difference. But why do White anti-racist beliefs, including the information deficit model, appeal to us so much that their contradiction causes unease?

This is because the information deficit model means that White anti-racists do not have to change Indigenous people. All we need to do is provide information in an appropriately modified fashion, and Indigenous people will change themselves. This is remediable difference – Indigenous people are different, but they will respond to health interventions in the same way that anyone would, providing their cultural difference is taken into account. There are two distinct aspects of this appeal. The information deficit model (among other aspects of White anti-racist beliefs) implies that, first, we are not actually changing Indigenous people when we try to make them healthier, and second, they do not need to be changed. The distinction I am making between these two statements needs explaining. As we will see, these statements act to preserve the moral status of White anti-racists and Indigenous people, respectively.

* * *

The information deficit model is one example of a larger category of causes of Indigenous disadvantage. This larger category is 'structure', a concept that social theorists oppose to 'agency'.[13] Structure describes the way that our choices are shaped. Where and how we were brought up, our level of education, our gender, race and ethnicity, our sexuality, our first language, and many other factors all have a strong effect on whether we choose to finish school, to have children and at what age, to use condoms, to smoke, to exercise, or to get up in the morning at all. Agency describes what we do with the hand that life has dealt us. We all know a family where the siblings have had similar life chances – similar structural determinants – but things end up very differently for them. Within disadvantaged families, some children succeed in education and employment and eschew drugs despite the odds against them; within privileged families, some descend into substance abuse and unemployment despite the opportunities available. Every life choice that every person makes is some mix of structural and agential forces. Structural factors greatly influence what choices are available, but there is always an element, a moment of choice, that remains. This basic formula applies to Indigenous people no less than other Australians.

When a White anti-racist feels uncomfortable about the idea that Indigenous people might smoke despite knowing better than other Australians that it is bad for you, they are uncomfortable that Indigenous agency might play a role in ill health. White anti-racist beliefs about Indigenous people assume instead that Indigenous disadvantage is wholly due to structural factors. I (with co-author Yin Paradies) have called this phenomenon 'overstructuration'. Overstructuration is the tendency to downplay agential explanations and highlight structural explanations for any given situation.[14]

My research at the Institute involved running a workshop for health professionals that aimed to teach critical analysis and introduce anthropological, sociological and psychological theories that help to understand Indigenous disadvantage and the culture of Indigenous affairs. One section of the workshop vividly illustrates overstructuration.[15] Participants were divided into four groups, and each group was asked to consider one of four health problems that afflict Indigenous communities: diabetes and coronary heart disease; end-stage renal disease; poor housing and environmental health; and poor obstetric and infant outcomes.[16] Each group was asked to think of all the reasons that Indigenous Australians suffer these problems at higher rates than non-Indigenous Australians. Participants were specifically asked to include 'non-politically correct' (non-PC) reasons. 'Political correctness' was not formally defined. Participants were left to decide what they thought was politically correct and incorrect within their groups.

After generating many different reasons, the groups were asked to come together and arrange their reasons into categories of their choosing (reproduced in stylised form in Figure 1.2).

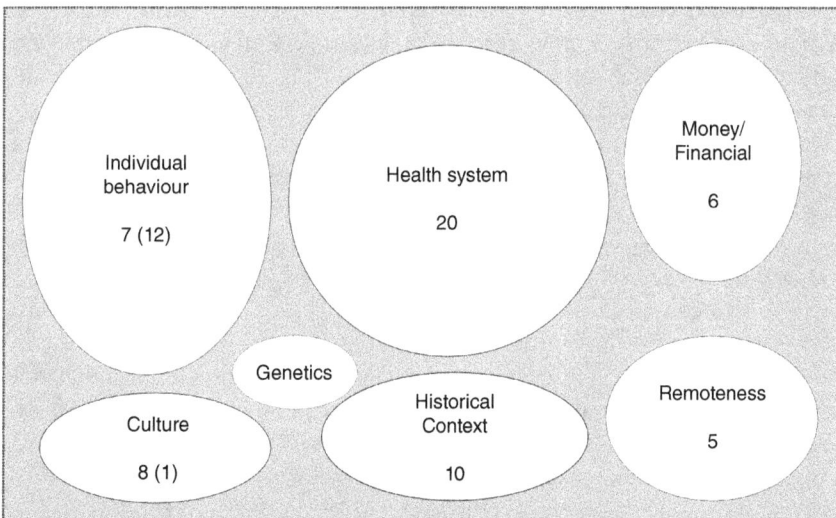

Figure 1.2 Schematic representation of explanations for ill health created by workshop participants (numbers of non-politically correct reasons are shown in brackets).

Source: Kowal and Paradies 2005. Used with permission.

Table 1.1 Reasons given for excess Indigenous ill health by category

Category	Number ('non-PC' subset)	Examples
Individual Behaviour	19 (12)	Having kids too young*, bad diet*, people just throw their rubbish everywhere*, want to share in a non-healthful behaviour identity (such as 'drinking culture')
Culture	9 (1)	Community dysfunction, different beliefs about health behaviour
Health System	20 (0)	Culturally inappropriate interventions, cycle of disadvantage, lack of interpreters, institutional racism
Historical Context	10 (0)	Past and present discrimination, forced changes in ways of living
Money/Financial	6 (0)	Poverty, welfare dependency
Remoteness	5 (0)	Expensive to provide care, problems with maintenance of health hardware
Genetics	1 (1)	Genetics

Source: Kowal and Paradies 2005. Used with permission.

Examples of reasons in each category are given in Table 1.1. Reasons that were identified as 'non-PC' are marked with an asterisk.

The results of this exercise illustrate the overstructuration inherent to White anti-racist beliefs. There was a clear tendency towards structural attributions for Indigenous ill health, including reasons grouped under the 'health system', 'historical context', 'money/financial', and 'remoteness' categories. Complementary to this, there was discomfort with explanations that stressed agency, demonstrated by the fact that nearly all the reasons identified as 'politically incorrect' were within the individual/behavioural category. That is, participants were more likely to blame the system, and were reluctant to nominate Indigenous people's choices or actions as a cause of their ill health.[17]

Let us consider how this idea of 'political correctness' functioned.[18] We did not define it, yet everyone knew what it was, and what it was not: all four groups came up with similar examples of political incorrectness. 'Political correctness' was acting as a placeholder for White anti-racist beliefs, the liberal values that are dominant within Indigenous health discourse: 'politically incorrect' reasons were those that contradicted these beliefs.[19] This exercise showed that White anti-racist beliefs are disturbed by Indigenous agency.

This disturbance is also illustrated by the reasons within the 'individual/behavioural' category that participants did *not* consider to be politically incorrect. Terms like 'wanting to share in a non-healthful behaviour identity' (that is, wanting to be a 'smoker', 'drinker' or 'petrol sniffer') were necessary in order to speak of Indigenous agency in an acceptable way. This laborious phrase indicates the lengths to which White anti-racists must go in order to feel comfortable with the fact that Indigenous people may make morally unsound decisions, such as frequently drinking to excess.

It must be kept in mind that overstructuration is an anti-racist discourse. It is a response to 'victim-blaming', a term given to expressions of Indigenous agency that place the blame for Indigenous ill health entirely on the actions of Indigenous people. One victim-blamer disliked by many at the institute was the then federal health minister (currently prime minister) Tony Abbott, who commented in an interview that 'Aborigines would be healthier if they chose to eat better and exercise more' (Anonymous 2005). The article that takes this quote as a headline was prominently displayed on the doors of some institute offices as a protest at the racist ignorance of the federal government. At face value, the headline is banal health promotion orthodoxy – no one can deny nutrition and physical activity are key determinants of health. If the statement was made in relation to non-Indigenous people it would never justify the status of a headline. But in the context of Indigenous affairs, where overstructuration is central to anti-racist beliefs, any expression of Indigenous agency without substantial qualification is suspect.

I am not quibbling with the anti-racist intent or the anti-racist effect of overstructuration. The prefix 'over' in overstructuration does not imply that it is wrong to emphasise structure and downplay agency, but that it has origins and consequences that exceed the intent of the White anti-racists. 'Over' refers to the asymmetry of an argument that cannot comfortably accommodate Indigenous agency. This leads us to question what function this asymmetry performs within White anti-racist beliefs.

Overstructuration contributes to 'remediable difference' by locating 'the problem' externally to Indigenous people. Indigenous ill health becomes an unfortunate effect of circumstances ameliorable through external action. The Indigenous person burdened by these extenuating circumstances is understood as hypothetically healthy, *if only* the state had successfully educated them, helped them to find work, and provided them with suitable housing. The behaviours that affect health – smoking, eating and exercising – are constructed as a direct function of external factors. Indigenous agency is presumed to be a mirror image of White anti-racist agency, desiring the same things: a clean house populated with cooperative family members who attend school and work and provide a steady income. This Indigenous agency is imagined to be like a jack-in-the-box, constrained only by structural forces, always ready to spring forth and climb the social ladder when those obstacles are finally removed. Remediable difference does not allow for any other form of Indigenous agency.

This discussion is not designed to flip things the other way: to convince you that Indigenous people do not want a better life, that Indigenous disadvantage is entirely the fault of Indigenous people and that no government programmes can ever help. Rather, I want to highlight, to make visible, the assumptions that White anti-racist beliefs are based on. The full spectrum of Indigenous social life cannot be admitted – only the part of it that is congruent with remediable difference.

White anti-racists will look for any structural reason available to explain Indigenous disadvantage. And clearly, there are plenty to choose from, not just lack of health information but lack of services and jobs, poor quality education, lack of affordable fresh food, institutional racism, transgenerational trauma, and dispossession. When we intervene in Indigenous lives, we like to think of ourselves as tinkering with the structural factors that determine health. If White anti-racist beliefs admitted that Indigenous agency had some impact on Indigenous disadvantage, then White anti-racists would have to act on Indigenous people directly to address it. This idea makes us uncomfortable. As one colleague said to me, 'We don't do social engineering; we just make structural changes to make healthy choices easier'. 'Social engineering' implies trying to change Indigenous people, and this grates against White anti-racist beliefs.

* * *

An emphasis on structural factors is crucial to White anti-racist beliefs because it assures us that we are not changing Indigenous people when we try to address their disadvantage. Why do we shrink from the idea of changing Indigenous people? Above all, it is because we do not want to hurt Indigenous people. We do not want to hurt Indigenous people like White people have done in the past, and like those White people we regard as 'racist' continue to do today.

This suggests a second set of aversions internal to White anti-racist beliefs. I argued above that White anti-racists do not like the idea that Indigenous agency may contribute to Indigenous ill health. Neither do we care much for White agency. White anti-racist beliefs are built around the idea that White agency is dangerous. We are suspicious that if White people do anything to Indigenous people, they will hurt them. One colleague said, 'It's like the more we do the more damage we do'. Another said, 'I'm not wanting to drive the process at all, I want to give the process away'. As I will return to in Chapter 6, within this belief system White agency behaves like a stigma, contaminating everything it comes into contact with.

As a result of this aversion, White anti-racists become good at minimising what they do. One colleague discussing a project with Aboriginal health workers said, 'I was merely just facilitating what they had been doing for a long time'. She used not only the passive verb 'facilitate', but two qualifiers – 'merely' and 'just' – in order to diminish her agency in the project. White agency is also literally concealed when we edit ourselves out of project DVDs or duck out of the way of a photographer so that a purely 'Aboriginal' image is produced.

White anti-racists do not like the idea that we might be changing Indigenous people, because we worry that any act we perform on Indigenous people will hurt them. I also argued that White anti-racists don't like the idea that Indigenous people might need changing. Why did I draw that distinction?

Here we need to revisit the discussion of Indigenous agency. Remediable difference only allows a limited view of Indigenous agency whereby Indigenous people are assumed to value most highly the same things as most White anti-racists, and will spring into action to obtain them the moment that structural barriers are removed. This vision of Indigenous agency is convenient for anti-racists who do not need to *do* anything to Indigenous people. Their domain of action can be limited to structures, making health information clearer and ensuring Indigenous people are able to access what they need to be healthy.[20] The end product is a morally pure Indigenous agency and a harmless, near invisible White agency.

But what if remediable difference was illusive? What if Indigenous people were, instead, radically different from non-Indigenous people? If Indigenous people were radically different to non-Indigenous people, then they may not stop their kids from missing school or drinking coke for breakfast, or stop their relatives from trashing the house, or stop smoking, even if they know these are bad and they seem to have the means to stop them. If Indigenous people have radically different priorities to White people, then maybe when White people try to make them more healthy, they are also fundamentally changing them, perhaps even making them less Indigenous. At the moment when a White anti-racist begins to entertain this set of musings, remediable difference begins to unravel.

Here it is important to note that I am not saying that Indigenous people *are* radically different from White people. Some might be radically different in certain ways but very similar in other ways; others may 'appear' to closely resemble the average White person but in fact may be very different. To be sure, the full spectrum of personalities and social circumstances are represented within the Indigenous population, if at different proportions to the general population. The point is that White anti-racist people worry a lot that Indigenous people *might* be radically different, and that their efforts might have the effect of diminishing this cultural difference and making Indigenous people less different to White people.

We return here to the fear that White people have of hurting Indigenous people. The main component of this fear of hurting is the fear of being assimilationist. Ever since the 'Bringing Them Home' report was released in 1997 and brought the issue of the 'Stolen Generations' to national attention, the figure of the assimilationist has loomed large in the fears of the White anti-racist (Human Rights and Equal Opportunity Commission 1997). When colleagues at the institute described what they try not to do, or criticised other researchers, they commonly used the word 'imposing'. As one phrased it, 'we shouldn't impose a Western idea of length of life on people'.[21] Or as a researcher explained her plan for an exercise programme in a remote community: 'I want to reintroduce exercise by saying it is an Aboriginal concept; it is not just imposing a Western view' (McDonald 2003: 23). She feared imposing a Western view, of exercise in this case. She feared it because it casts her in the role of modern-day assimilationist or modern-day missionary, a subject I take up in Chapter 6.

If Indigenous people really have radically different priorities, then the project of improving their health, of making the lines on the graph converge, becomes a burden imposed upon them. As one colleague mused about a project he was involved in, 'The thing that bothers me is if it hasn't been taken up well and the community don't own it, well do they really want it?' There is a dual threat contained here: the fear that Indigenous people are not the innocent moral victims of structural causes but are actively determining their own radically different fates, and the fear that White anti-racist efforts to help them are merely the most recent colonial imposition. The moral status of White anti-racists and disadvantaged Indigenous people are intimately related.

White anti-racist beliefs serve as a defence against this twin loss of viable subjectivities. Remediable difference staves off this scenario and preserves a space for ethical White action, a space where White anti-racists can try to help Indigenous people without harming them. But once the possibility of radical difference has reared its ugly head, for many White anti-racists there is no return to certainty. When this belief system unravels, White anti-racists are left living with the uncertainty of a sullied subject position. They can no longer ensure that they are not damaging Indigenous people when they try to help them, and the possibility of an ethical White anti-racist subjectivity is severely threatened.

The disconcertment that remains once White anti-racist beliefs are unravelled can be understood through two dilemmas: the dilemma of 'history continuity' and the dilemma of 'social improvement'. The first dilemma refers to the inconvenient truth that history is continuous. It is the fact that the health department of the Northern Territory government of 2015 is the continuation of the health department of the 1930s that participated in stealing children. It is the fact that many Aboriginal communities were missions and are still called missions by the locals, and that White anti-racists fill many roles that were for many decades filled by missionaries. And ultimately, it is the fact that the authority of Australian governments is continuous with the authority of those who invaded the land. White anti-racists try to create historical *discontinuity* to show they are different from their predecessors, but the fact that we have to do that reveals that we are worried we might not be any different from the forebears we consider to be racist, or at best, misguided. My point is not to argue that we are or are not different from our predecessors (we are undoubtedly the same in some ways, and different in others), but that to worry about this is integral to White anti-racist subjectivities.

The dilemma of social improvement is the fear that improving Indigenous health will inevitably make Indigenous people resemble White people. As discussed above, this has much to do with the concept of radical difference. If you believe, or even suspect, that some Indigenous people have a radically different idea of what it means to be healthy, it may follow that our ideas of good health are imposed on people. As one colleague put it, 'who are we to say what's right and what's wrong and what's healthy and what isn't?'[22] Once White anti-racists begin to suspect that dominant definitions of being healthy are not necessarily universal, they worry that making Indigenous people 'healthy' may be a form of assimilation.

There is a statistical way of looking at this. I have argued that statistical inequality – 'closing the gap' – is the focus of remedialism. But Indigeneity is not the only gap. There are others. There is the income gap, the education gap, the class gap, and the gap between privileged and deprived neighbourhoods (Turrell et al. 2006).[23] Whichever graph you care to look at, those who have the best health and are always represented on the top line of the graph are White, middle-class, educated people. It is a mix of structural and agential factors that is responsible for their good health – everything from exposing young children to books, having only a few people per house, buying and cooking nutritious food, not smoking, experiencing less stress, and regularly accessing high-quality health care (Australian Bureau of Statistics 2003). To the extent that the statistics we measure construct what we mean by 'healthy', 'healthy' is equivalent to having a good income, a professional job, a high level of education, and living in a privileged area. These are characteristics racialised as White.[24]

As the 'gap' narrows, the more closely the ways of life of the lower line resemble that of the upper line. The question that irks the White anti-racist is whether a culturally distinct way of life gives you a different line on the graph. If so, when we eliminate the gap, do we eliminate this distinctiveness? Lea expresses the dilemma this way, 'Can the good health that arises out of the historical symbiosis of capitalism, colonialism and neo-liberal democracy in the modern era be generalised across colonised spaces without imposing its own structuring (Indigenous-culture-destroying) social and historical inheritance?' (Lea 2002: 12).

As a prominent Indigenous researcher put it in an institute seminar, 'we [Indigenous people] might one day have the same health statistics as everyone else but not at the cost of being indistinguishable from non-Aboriginal Australia'.[25] Historically, 'indistinguishability' – incorporation into the White majority – has been the destiny of minority groups that are socioeconomically successful (Ignatiev 1995; Brodkin 1998; Zhou 2004). But unlike other ethnic minorities, Indigenous Australians are defined in opposition to White settlers. Being indistinguishable is thus tantamount to social death, and remedialism becomes cultural genocide.

Dominant White anti-racist beliefs avoid this quandary by associating the gap exclusively with unsanitised difference. Indigenous ill health is attributed to oppression. Therefore, when oppression is lifted, Indigenous people will shed their unsanitised difference (the substance use, the gambling, the truancy, the violence) and become healthy subjects. As unsanitised difference is divorced from sanitised difference (cosmology, hunting, art, kinship), the 'good' aspects of Indigenous culture can be quarantined from this transition from unhealthy to healthy.[26] Once the transition is made, these elements will remain to ensure that these newly healthy subjects are recognisably Indigenous. While this form of reasoning is highly effective in Indigenous health discourse, it ceases to protect White anti-racists from the dilemma of social improvement once the distinction between sanitised and unsanitised difference has been undermined. White anti-racists begin to suspect that Indigenous difference cannot be effectively divided into good difference and bad difference. The moral certainty of remediable difference is replaced with the impossible choice of either radical difference or sameness.

* * *

The process I have described of White anti-racist beliefs unravelling in the face of radical difference is common, but by no means universal. For some White anti-racists, remediable difference serves them well, preserving their own morality as 'facilitators' of improvement, and the morality of Indigenous people as deserving and self-determining recipients. For this group of White anti-racists, their experiences may reinforce their beliefs that Indigenous-led programmes are more likely to succeed; that Indigenous agency will seek to 'close the gap' when given the opportunity; and that programme failure is always attributable to inadequate funding or inadequate Indigenous control. Those White anti-racists who are exposed to radically different Indigenous ways of life, or who experience serial programme failure, may be more likely to experience the challenge to their belief system posed by the dilemmas I have outlined.

Neither the persistence of White anti-racist beliefs and remediable difference, nor their collapse, is wholly good or bad. Any belief system offers opportunities and presents limits. Remediable difference provides an assurance that Indigenous people do want to change to be more like White, middle-class people and will retain essential differences when they do, and that White anti-racists who effect these changes are not like assimilationists or missionaries of the past. The limits of this belief system are that there is no guarantee these assurances are true, and that it necessitates a partial view of Indigenous life, partitioning sanitised and unsanitised difference and filtering out those aspects of experience that threaten to contradict the division.

Similarly, as I will return to in the Conclusion, the breakdown of White anti-racist beliefs offers an opportunity for rethinking Indigenous affairs, but also extreme limitations. There is no good solution to the tension between equality and difference. The tension is managed by each paradigm of Indigenous affairs until the weaknesses of that belief system leads to its undoing – typically, thirty years after its emergence. Protection, assimilation, self-determination, and whatever era is emerging now are all attempts to manage this tension, each with their strengths and weaknesses.

Where this unravelling of White anti-racist beliefs does occur, it is dealt with in a variety of ways. Some who experience it leave Indigenous affairs for good. I suspect this explains much of the phenomenon known as 'burnout'.[27] Others cling tightly to their belief system, warding off the threat that the dilemmas of historical continuity and social improvement pose to remediable difference. If some person or situation suggests that we are just like the missionaries or assimilationists of the past, they will argue that we are different because, unlike them, we really respect Indigenous culture, or that nowadays Indigenous people are leading projects them-selves. If some person or situation suggests that improving Indigenous health might erode the cultural distinctiveness of Indigenous people, they will reject this strongly and perhaps stress that Indigenous people want the same things that we want, if only they were given the opportunity to get them. This strategy works well for many people who manage to keep these dilemmas at bay.

Another response is what I call 'the fantasy of White withdrawal'. This is when a White anti-racist muses about a future time when we can with-draw our damaging influence altogether and leave Indigenous people to their own devices. This view, which was not very common, could reflect a belief that efforts to 'close the gap' were assimilation and should stop, or alternatively that Indigenous people had superior ways of improving their health and social circumstances that would only manifest when the contaminating influence of White people was removed.

Finally, there is the strategy of acceptance. These White anti-racists were aware of the ethical quandaries inherent to their subject position, but they keep on working anyway. They do this not by rehabilitating the sullied subjectivity of White anti-racism, but by abandoning it altogether. As one colleague put it: 'I don't have any great illusions about, you know, what I might achieve working in Aboriginal health compared to some-body else. But, you know, I would prefer to be doing that; I would prefer to have this sort of complexity'.[28] Others expressed this sentiment in terms of friendship: 'You realise you're not going to make a lot of difference. I came to a place [an understanding] where I was happy to… journey with people, and see the common humanity, the normal aspects of friendship'.[29] Rather than defend the right to think of themselves as 'anti-racist' – as countering the legacy of colonialism through their work with Indigenous people – these whites retreated from anti-racism. They supplanted the centrality of doing good with other factors on which to base their work in Indigenous affairs, such as their personal preference for interesting and challenging work, and the pleasure of working cross-culturally.

* * *

While remediable difference is powerful and useful, it often fails to match up with the experiences of White anti-racists, and may ultimately be a dead end. As discussed above, and as I will return to in the Conclusion, a strand of political theory argues that a situation where a privileged group tries to help a disadvantaged group is bound to fail, because, paradoxi-cally, the very act of identifying an oppressed group (such as 'Indigenous people') condemns them to remain oppressed, even when they are identified solely for the purposes of helping them.

This argument would predict that the only way out of this circular situation is to forge new identities for White and Indigenous people that are not oppositional.[30] However, the political implications of giving up 'White' and 'Indigenous' subjectivities are fraught. It is difficult to know whether placing pleasure or 'normal friendship' at the centre of Australian race relations would be a radical act that transcends oppressive identities, or a conservative 'colour-blind' step that conceals and intensifies racial inequality. Such a move may imply giving up the gains made through the politics of difference, such as native title, Aboriginal funding programmes and the entire Indigenous bureaucracy, which apart from anything else is the major employer of Indigenous Australians.

As I will return to in the Conclusion, it is not a matter of standing by or abandoning dominant modes of subjectivity in contemporary Australia – we are stuck with them for the foreseeable future, and many agree that they have provided some measure of social justice. The point is to understand the limits and opportunities of our current modes of subjectivity and recognition, and to think through the limits and opportunities of the alternatives.

Notes

1. The other scholar to do this systematically is Tess Lea (2008).
2. My use of 'subjectivity' draws on Foucault's notion of subjection, Bourdieu's notion of habitus and Elias's historical analysis of the Western subject (Bourdieu 1977; Elias 1978; Foucault 1983). For a collection of anthropological work on subjectivity that draws on a range of different genealogies of the concept, see Biehl, Good and Kleinman 2011.
3. This definition of 'White' draws on the field of 'whiteness studies'.
4. Literature from the early 1970s on Indigenous disadvantage sets a tone that was followed very closely for the next thirty years – see, for example, Tatz 1972. Things have changed over the last five to ten years, as I discuss in the Conclusion.
5. My thinking about improvement has been influenced by Tania Murray Li (2007).
6. My understanding of radical difference draws on literature on alterity; see, for example, Taussig 1993 and Povinelli 2001, 2002b. Van Alphen usefully identifies three broad philosophical approaches to alterity. Much post-Hegelian philosophy takes a *hermeneutical* approach that sees alterity as a device that gives meaning to the self, either through a struggle to assimilate the other into the self or through the act of excluding the other. The *epistemological* approach focuses on how knowledge about both the self and the other is produced, an approach typified by Foucault. The *psychological* approach draws on Freudian theory to argue that the 'other' is actually a part of the self that is repressed and thus becomes both strange and feared. Importantly, in all of these modes of inquiry, alterity does not exist in isolation but is the result of a relationship. Although alterity is so often, perhaps routinely, transformed by the

viewer into an essence intrinsic to the person viewed as different, it is important to remember that *alterity is a relation*. What functions as alterity for one person may, in turn, see them as alterior (van Alphen 1991).

7. John Gray describes the core principles of liberalism in this way: '[I]t is *individualist*, in that it asserts the primacy of the person against any collectivity; *egalitarian*, in that it confers on all human beings the same moral status; *universalist*, affirming the moral unity of the species; and *meliorist*, in that it asserts the open-ended improvability, by the use of critical reason, of human life' (Gray 1995: 86, my emphasis).

8. The term was inspired partly by Briggs's use of 'sanitary citizenship' in a somewhat difference context (Briggs and Mantini-Briggs 2003).

9. Child sexual abuse in Indigenous communities has frequently been splashed across national headlines, particularly from the mid-2000s (Australian Broadcasting Corporation 2006). My inclusion of these extreme behaviours in the ledger of unsanitised difference is not intended to imply that these phenomena do not occur in White disadvantaged communities (or in White privileged communities for that matter), or that these things are tolerated in the communities that suffer them.

10. This idea has a long genealogy in the social sciences; see, for example, Benedict 1934.

11. This division is also a feature of anthropological discourse. 'Unsanitised' cultural aspects, such as gambling, swearing, fighting and alcohol use generate a greater range of explanations and academic controversy than 'sanitised' cultural aspects. For example, Macdonald's discussion of alcohol use among the Wiradjuri argues that fighting 'should not simply be attributed to too much alcohol (for often it is absent altogether), to violence characteristic of those of low socio-economic status (as in a culture of poverty thesis), or to the ravages of colonisation'. Her argument is that fighting is 'an integral part of the social system and essential to its working', a functional and instrumental aspect of Aboriginal culture. So, drinking might be straightforward deviance in the context of substance abuse; or a reflection of class oppression; or the effects of colonial oppression; or (her argument) a rational and culturally based dispute-resolution process. This is a far broader range of explanations than those offered for kinship practices elsewhere in that collection (Macdonald 1988: 187, 191).

12. I am far from the first to raise these questions. Tim Rowse, for example, posed them in the context of the Community Development Employment Program (CDEP). CDEP is similar to a 'work for the dole' programme, where participants work four hours a day for pay similar to unemployment benefits. Community organisations coordinate CDEP programmes, and the goal is to create jobs. Rowse asks whether the demonstrated inability of CDEP to create mainstream employment is a defeat for the goals of equality or a victory for the goals of difference, as Indigenous people choose the flexible and unorthodox work practices accommodated by CDEP (Rowse 2002; see also Rowse 2012). Note that CDEP programmes were radically scaled back as part of the Northern Territory Emergency Intervention (discussed in the Conclusion).

13. For classic accounts, see Bourdieu 1977 and Giddens 1990. For a useful reformulation, see Hays 1994.

14. The following few paragraphs are adapted from Kowal and Paradies 2005.

15. Workshop participants gave written consent for de-identified minutes of the workshop to be used for research purposes. The workshop is now called 'Race, Culture, Indigeneity and the Politics of Disadvantage'. The twelve workshops I have run subsequently have all shown very similar results to those reported here.

16. These problems are well known to practitioners in Indigenous health (Trewin and Madden 2003).
17. This tension between focusing on 'upstream/distal' structural causes or 'downstream/proximal' behavioural causes of disease is the subject of much debate in public health, sometimes staged as a contest between social epidemiology and biomedicine – see Lupton 1995.
18. There is a growing scholarship on 'political correctness' that highlights the multivalence of the concept; see, for example, Friedman 1999 and Fairclough 2003. I argue here that in this case 'political correctness' corresponded to White anti-racist beliefs.
19. White anti-racists may not always agree with the belief system dominant within Indigenous affairs (particularly after they have been exposed to radical difference, as I will explore in the next chapter), but they know they are supposed to agree with it. One workshop participant exhibited mock-contestation when considering whether a reason for Indigenous ill health needed a star to indicate it was 'politically incorrect': 'Janice discusses the reason "poor knowledge of hygiene" her group has come up with: "Is this politically incorrect? I don't know. I know it's supposed to be!" She chuckles and marks it with a star' (Field Notes, 6 Apr. 2005).
20. This limitation of White anti-racist action to structural domains is implausible for two quite different reasons. First, improving health necessarily involves changes in individual behaviour, whether or not this is the direct 'aim' of an intervention. Second, changing structures is incredibly difficult and generally outside health professionals' sphere of influence, whether one is talking about the redistribution of resources through progressive taxation or the provision of affordable housing.
21. Field Notes, 5 Nov. 2004.
22. Transcript 9, 13.
23. People with blue-collar jobs, the less educated, the poor and those in poor neighbourhoods are more likely to smoke, be obese, add salt to their food, and suffer poorer health (Turrell et al. 2006). Note that these gaps in income, education and place of residence also apply *within* the Indigenous population – for example, there are large differences in the health status of Indigenous people from remote versus non-remote areas (Australian Bureau of Statistics 2004b). The gaps are substantial; for instance, Indigenous males in New South Wales are more urbanised, richer, and better educated than Indigenous males in the Northern Territory, and have a median age of death which is nearly ten years higher (Australian Bureau of Statistics 2004a).
24. It is difficult to identify the 'White' population in Australia, as 'White' is not an ethnic identifier in statistical collections, as it is in the United States. For a long time we have only identified the country of birth, with a question on 'ancestry' included in the 2001 census. Nevertheless, the culture of the educated middle-class is predominantly a White one in Australia, as in most other English-speaking countries. The success of migrants from south-east and south Asia and their descendants in recent decades does not necessarily threaten the racialisation of privilege as white – see Wu 2002; Zhou 2004.
25. Field Notes, 3 Jun. 2005.
26. In some Indigenous health discourse, sanitised culture is not only depicted as unaffected by the substantial societal change required for remote Indigenous people to share the same statistics as other Australians, but is considered to be the therapy that will improve health – see Sutton 2001; Brady 2004; Kowal 2006a.
27. 'Burnout' refers to professionals becoming frustrated with their work environment and leaving. It is a serious problem in Indigenous health, compounding critical

personnel shortages and lack of continuity of care. For recent discussions of the problem see Hayes and Bonner 2010; and Roche et al. 2013.

28. Transcript 6, 17.
29. Field Notes, 6 Apr. 2005.
30. For a review of work on dichotomous identities in Indigenous affairs, see C. Dalley and R. Martin (forthcoming 2015) *Dichotomous Identities?: Aboriginal and Non-Aboriginal People in Australia*, a special issue of *The Australian Journal of Anthropology*.

Chapter 3

Tiwi 'Long Grassers'

⤛•⤜

This chapter explores the 'contact zone' where varieties of Indigenous and non-Indigenous people encounter and recognise each other. It offers a detailed description of Darwin, the tropical capital that the White anti-racists of interest in this book call 'home'. The narrative begins elsewhere, in the remote community of Gunbalanya on 'Open Day', an annual event when the public are briefly granted easy access. The chapter then moves to Tiwi, a suburb of Darwin, where displaced members of the Maningrida community, known locally as 'long grassers', live in the open and drink heavily. Long grassers are Indigenous people who come from remote communities but live (temporarily or permanently) in informal camps around Darwin, drinking alcohol to excess and trying to avoid the authorities who seek to enforce laws against camping and minimise their effects on other Darwin residents.[1] Long grassers represent the most extreme form of radical difference cohabiting urban space.

My use of the 'contact zone' in this chapter draws on Mary Louise Pratt's well-known term for spaces where the colonised and the coloniser meet. It is a concept that 'foreground[s] the interactive, improvisational dimensions of colonial encounters so easily ignored by diffusionist accounts of conquest and domination … emphasiz[ing] how subjects are constituted in and by their relations with each other'. The contact zone is thus a space that must be understood 'in terms of co-presence, interaction, interlocking understandings and practices, often within radically asymmetrical relations of power' (Pratt 1992: 7).

Darwin, the isolated capital of Australia's Northern Territory, is an exemplary post-settler colonial contact zone. Many different subcultures of White, Indigenous, and other people make up its 100,030 residents. I present a series of stories that epitomise the contact zones of urban Darwin: the fused doors of a block of public toilets; filing cards of ATM PIN numbers written in Chinese; a sorcery report; and a shared pouch of tobacco. Within these narratives, multiple subgroups of non-Indigenous residents respond to the problem of radical difference that long grassers pose. I explore these contrasting responses to elucidate the particular group of 'White anti-racists' I am interested in.

Long grassers in the suburb of Tiwi are a multivalent symbol. The varied reactions to the disorder their bodies create mark out the different subjective territories of White and Indigenous identity. In what follows, five different perspectives on Tiwi long grassers are presented: activists fighting for long-grasser rights; White anti-racists who live in Tiwi; White Tiwi residents who do not seek recognition as anti-racists and would be identified by many as 'racist', 'conservative' or 'rednecks';[2] the local council who must respond to the 'long-grasser problem'; and Indigenous researchers who are not long grassers themselves but have close relatives living in the long grass.

Although not included in the national census, long grassers form the background of many development decisions, election promises, tourism campaigns, dinner-party conversations, tea-room stories, and letters to the local paper. They are defended by activists who minimise their impact and excuse any offensiveness with talk of kinship obligations and lack of appropriate accommodation or substance misuse treatment services.[3] They are criticised by outraged White residents who emphasise their environmental and social impact on the urban landscape and population. They are euphemistically discussed by bureaucrats and other polite citizens who seek to erect aesthetic fences around public facilities. For White anti-racists who live in Darwin, long grassers present a challenge to their performances of anti-racism and to the beliefs they hold about Indigenous disadvantage and its remediation.

A distinction between 'activist' discourses and White anti-racist residents of Tiwi is important in this account. White anti-racists who live in contact zones can be distinguished from those who remain within the large metropoles of southern Australia. On the whole, 'southern' White anti-racists can avoid the challenges of the contact zone, and their commitments to White anti-racist beliefs remain unshaken.[4] As a result, activist discourses reflect 'unadulterated' anti-racist norms as outlined in the previous chapter. For many anti-racists living in the contact zone, the beliefs they bring to the north are challenged by their personal and professional experiences in contact zones. Instead of certainty, they experience confusion and incommensurability.

Most of the White anti-racist subjects of this book began their careers in Indigenous health as 'southern' White anti-racists, and moved to Darwin precisely because of their anti-racist beliefs.[5] Organisations with their roots in the early 1990s, such as 'Reconciliation Australia' and 'Australians for Native Title and Reconciliation',[6] provide White Australians who aspire to anti-racism with the tools they need: a knowledge of the history of racial injustice, complex explanations for contemporary Indigenous disadvantage, ideas for how the government can improve the situation of Indigenous communities, and action that they themselves can take, such as donating money, volunteering, signing e-petitions and attending rallies.

When these aspirations and beliefs meet the reality of life in a contact zone like Darwin, interesting things happen. Few of the young left-wing professionals I studied, who, like me, moved to the north to work with Indigenous people, have found their views unaltered – and nor have I. We do not become right-wing – far from it – but we talk about things in a different way.[7]

Living and working in contact zones profoundly disturbs the received knowledge system of White anti-racists. Through their knowledge of the complex material and affective ties that bind long grassers, alcohol and local shop owners to each other, the standpoint of the White anti-racist residents of Tiwi belies both the racist discourse of their outraged neighbours and the sanitising anti-racist discourse of metropolitan activists.

Anti-racist Australia

Before zeroing in on Tiwi (via Gunbalanya and Maningrida), it is high time I described in greater detail the subgroup of Australians I call 'anti-racist'. As I have mentioned at various points, the dominant political culture of Australia can be characterised as 'progressive', but only a minority of Australians are 'anti-racist' as I understand the term.

In gaining an empirical foothold on these categories, a reasonable place to begin is the 2012 report of the Australian Reconciliation Barometer. Inspired by the South African Reconciliation Barometer, this biannual survey conducted since 2008 asks a representative sample of over one thousand Australians for their views on Indigenous issues.[8] The results reflect a populace largely hospitable to Indigenous issues. For example, 87 per cent of those polled in 2012 believed the relationship between Indigenous people and other Australians was 'fairly' or 'very' important to them. Groups that were more likely to see this relationship as important to them were women, those over sixty years of age, and those who had frequent or occasional contact with Indigenous people. Seventy-one per cent believed that Indigenous culture is important to Australia's identity as a nation and that Indigenous history should be a compulsory part of the history curriculum in schools. Over 80 per cent thought it is important to know about Indigenous history and culture, and that discrimination is a cause of Indigenous disadvantage. Sixty-four per cent agreed that previous race-based policies continue to affect some Indigenous people today and 72 per cent believed that some Indigenous people need help to overcome disadvantage and that the government should act to help them. Two-thirds believed that (then Prime Minister) Kevin Rudd's 2008 Apology to the Stolen Generations (see Chapter 4) was important for the relationship between Indigenous people and other Australians. The question of intercultural marriage has long been a key indicator of racial attitudes. In this survey, 58 per cent reported that they would feel fine if a child of theirs married an Indigenous person, with another 28 per cent feeling neutral.

When we shift to talking about action, the numbers shrink somewhat: 41 per cent of those surveyed reported frequent (10 per cent) or occasional (31 per cent) contact with Indigenous people, although 65 per cent would like to have frequent (16 per cent) or occasional (49 per cent) contact. Only 36 per cent agreed that they 'would like to do something to help disadvantaged Indigenous people', with another 48 per cent neither disagreeing nor agreeing.

What emerges from this picture is a broad consensus that Indigenous issues are important, that Indigenous people suffer from the legacy of past racism and ongoing discrimination, and that Indigenous history and culture should be taught in schools. Upwards of two-thirds of those surveyed agreed with such sentiments. This is what I refer to as the progressive norms of Australian society shared by most Australians. Only a minority – around 15–20 per cent depending on the question – are explicitly antagonistic towards Indigenous issues. These are people who are concerned about a family member marrying an Indigenous person (14 per cent), who disagree that Indigenous people hold a special place as the first Australians (14 per cent), who are not proud of Indigenous culture (14 per cent) or who think that Indigenous people have greater access to opportunities than other Australians (13 per cent). This socially conservative minority is the heartland of commentators such as Andrew Bolt and Alan Jones.

On the other side of the political spectrum, anti-racists are a subset of progressives. As a group they are similar in size to what I refer to as conservatives, at around 15–20 per cent of the surveyed population. They go further than recognising the importance of Indigenous issues: they strongly support them and take action. Action is the key attribute of 'doing good', as opposed to just thinking it.[9] To be sure, anti-racists support Indigenous issues in thought as well, but more strongly than other progressives. On the Reconciliation Barometer, they are the ones who 'strongly' agree that Australia is better off because it has many different cultures (19 per cent), that they would be happy if a family member married an Indigenous person (19 per cent), that they are proud of Indigenous culture (16 per cent), and that the government should put measures in place to help Indigenous people in specific ways (14 per cent). Anti-racists are those who reported taking some form of action to support Indigenous people in the preceding twelve months such as donating time or money to Indigenous causes (16 per cent), educating themselves about Indigenous history, culture and people (25 per cent) or building personal relationships with Indigenous people (18 per cent). Another way to distinguish anti-racists from other progressives might be their willingness to embrace a 'non-Indigenous' identity (as discussed in the Introduction). Progressives would not object to being interpreted by others as 'non-Indigenous', but anti-racists would actively and spontaneously identify that way in social situations.

The Reconciliation Barometer is an ideal means to delineate those anti-racists who are passionate about Indigenous issues, but there are many breeds of anti-racist. For our purposes, a useful distinction might be between those who are primarily concerned with Indigenous issues and those that worry more about the treatment of refugees or Islamophobia. Whether a person becomes one or the other variety of anti-racist may be a matter of personal history, or preference, or superior NGO marketing by 'Australians for Native Title and Reconciliation' as compared to 'A Just Australia' (an NGO that supports refugees).

Even within the group that concern themselves with Indigenous issues (and some may shift between Indigenous, refugee and other anti-racist causes over time), there are subgroups with distinct disciplinary and professional cultures. Had my fieldwork been conducted with Indigenous rights activists, land-rights lawyers, academic anthropologists, artists, teachers, or environmental scientists, the particular contradictions that trouble anti-racists would have been different. Lawyers in Aboriginal legal services might feel ambivalent when they seek shorter sentences for violent offenders on the basis that cultural factors arguably played a part in the offence. Environmental scientists may worry they are imposing conservation principles on Indigenous people.[10] I believe that the main arguments of this book would apply to these other kinds of White anti-racists, if refracted through a specific professional and disciplinary lens. Exactly how well they apply, as well as the shifts in White anti-racist identity over time (see the Conclusion), are empirical questions that future research may address.

Approaching the Contact Zone

Darwin, the capital of Australia's Northern Territory, is the home of the Darwin Institute of Indigenous Health and the White anti-racists who work there. It is one of Australia's frontier towns. The relatively high Indigenous population of the town is central to its political and economic fabric.[11] However, the Darwin community is made up of diverse cultures and subcultures of which 'Indigenous' and 'non-Indigenous' are only the broadest and bluntest classifications.

Tiwi is one of many Darwin suburbs that are named after Aboriginal tribes of the Northern Territory.[12] Darwin was first settled by Europeans in 1869, and over its first century it became a centre for pearling, cattle farming, mining, and defence industries. In the twentieth century, the industry that came to dominate all others was government administration, and by the 1960s the transient but growing population of public servants and construction workers urgently required more accommodation. The 'northern suburbs' of Darwin, as they are called, that form an arch from Jingili to Karama (see Figure 2.1), were rapidly developed and filled with basic three-bedroom government houses on large blocks, which were later converted to private housing stock.[13]

The geography of each of Darwin's northern suburbs varies on a theme: main roads form the borders of the suburb, two winding, intersecting avenues shape the arterial infrastructure, and smaller circuits branch off them, ending with cul-de-sacs. Most of the dwellings are single level, three-bedroom houses on 900 m^2 blocks, interspersed with 'elevated' two-storey houses and the occasional block of flats. Walking paths link the winding roads, and every house is within one hundred metres of a small park with shady trees and colourful play equipment in varying states of repair. Minimal, slow traffic was the aim, and planners are generous with speed bumps. At the centre of each suburb is a large park comprising a sports ground, community facilities (usually a childcare centre and primary school or, in the case of Tiwi, a childcare centre and old age home) and a small shopping complex designed like a concrete bunker with wire mesh shutters that descend over the windows as night falls. In some suburbs, the shopping complex (referred to by locals as 'the shops') might include a fish and chip shop, hairdresser, or restaurant. As the Tiwi shops

Figure 2.1 Map of Darwin, including northern suburbs.

are very close to the Casuarina shopping centre – the only mall in Darwin – Tiwi has only a supermarket and the Darwin premises of a health promotion NGO, Diabetes Australia.

Like most of Darwin, the northern suburbs are ethnically and socially mixed. In a deliberate attempt at social diversity, the 'Part-Coloured Housing Program' in the 1950s saw blocks retained as public housing scattered through areas of private dwellings.[14] With few exceptions, most

White, middle-class people in the northern suburbs live in close proximity to non-White familes – poor as well as middle-class.

Statistics and their gaps are central themes of this book. Although the Tiwi long grassers are all too prominent in the social life of Tiwi (to the consternation of many residents, as we will see), they are absent from the statistical record of the suburb. The definite count of the Australian population is conducted once every five years. The 2011 Census recorded the population of Darwin as 78,684, of whom 8.4 per cent were Indigenous.[15] Tiwi has one of highest proportions of Indigenous people of any suburb, recorded as 14 per cent.

The Indigenous people counted in Tiwi on census night in 2011 comprised at least three social groupings that vary in terms of socioeconomic status, culture and ancestry. One group is made up of families that have been in Darwin for generations (some of whom would belong to the group who are the 'Traditional Owners' of Darwin, the Larrakia) as well as those who have moved from other large cities for employment opportunities. Those in this group would be a mix of renters and homeowners. Most of them would have some non-Indigenous ancestors from a range of backgrounds: largely Anglo-Australian, but also Filipino, Chinese, Japanese and Greek. Many of these families would include members of the 'Stolen Generations', when children of mixed ancestry were removed from their families and institutionalised (Cummings 1990; Austin 1993; Pilkington and Garimara 1996; Human Rights and Equal Opportunity Commission 1997). Members of these families occupy varying class positions, from well-educated professionals to the chronically unemployed, many of them marrying non-Indigenous people. Standard English or Aboriginal English would often be their first language, peppered with words from Indigenous languages they identify with.

The second group of Aboriginal Tiwi residents counted in the statistics are more recent arrivals to Darwin from remote communities. They are likely to live in public housing and few, if any, would own their homes. Most would have been born at the Royal Darwin Hospital or one of the four other regional hospitals in the Northern Territory, but all would identify with one or more remote communities where they or their parents grew up. This group would be further down the social gradient: less educated and less likely to be employed, but more likely to have welfare as their only income, to have chronic heart or kidney disease, and to be incarcerated. They would be more likely to speak an Indigenous language at home and less likely to have non-Indigenous partners or relatives. The cultural capital these people possess sometimes gains them employment as hospital interpreters, clerks in the government welfare office, or Indigenous support workers in primary schools. These households may serve as a town base for visitors from the remote communities they have connections to (see Figure 2.1). These homes can get grossly overcrowded when a big football game is on, or an important elder is sick in town.[16]

A third group of Indigenous residents of Darwin counted on census night would be visiting temporarily from remote communities and staying at an Aboriginal hostel. These hostels are run by a government-funded Aboriginal agency and provide an air-conditioned room and three meals for $23 a night. The hostel in Tiwi, called Daisy Yarmirr Aboriginal Hostel (or 'Daisy Y' for short), is named after a famous Aboriginal Health Worker. Its seventy-five beds are mostly taken up with remote Indigenous people who are visiting the nearby hospital for appointments or escorting sick relatives.

The Indigenous residents of Tiwi that are the focus of this chapter are yet another distinct group. Unlike the other groups I have sketched here, they are not counted on census night and their very right to 'reside' in suburban spaces is highly contingent and contested by various authorities.[17] Neither homeowners nor Traditional Owners, Tiwi long grassers present a challenge to some non-Indigenous Australians who seek to recognise the deserving victims of colonialism.

Open Day

My interest in the Tiwi long-grass community was piqued after I had lived in Tiwi for a couple of years. The story begins with a song that was performed at the remote community of Gunbalanya, three and a half hours from Darwin down the Arnhem highway. To get there, you drive through the northern section of the World Heritage-listed Kakadu National Park, past floodplains and savannahs, to where the road dips down through the East Alligator River. It was the annual community Open Day and I made the trip with a friend who also worked in Indigenous health. We relished the day ahead; it was an opportunity to relax with friends, listen to bands, buy a piece of art, all while supporting an Aboriginal community. In the late dry season the community was accessible by a road that crossed a river. We drove through the river and saw the serrated prehistoric backs of crocodiles swish through the water. Cahill's Crossing, usually closed to those without a permit to visit Aboriginal Lands, was open to all. The final twenty-five miles from the crossing to the community was breathtaking. The road of corrugated red earth wound along the escarpment and under the stark blue sky. We admired the craggy cliffs with small groves of paper bark trees at their base and imagined the spectacular rock paintings hidden inside. Behind the community lay the billabong, noisy with a thousand birds and under the graceful watch of Injulak Hill.

As we drove into the community we passed some dilapidated houses alongside new houses painted with bright colours. The yards of the houses, both old and new, were strewn with rubbish. No residents could be seen here: they were all watching the football down at the community oval. In contrast to the houses, the civic part of the community that hosted the Open Day activities was buzzing with life, and the school, the oval, the club, the youth centre and the arts centre were all spotless and shining. Local musicians from Darwin and surrounding remote communities played all day to around two hundred visitors, mostly White people from Darwin and tourists from other parts of Australia. In the community arts centre, woven baskets, screen-printed T-shirts and small bark paintings were purchased.

Apart from the rubbish-strewn yards, the only other visible sign of social disorder on this special day was a large blackboard behind the bar at the community hotel. On it, dozens of names written in white chalk were prominently displayed: 'JOSIE NABURLAMAN – LUNCH ONLY. TIMMY MORRIS – NO LUNCH'. It documented the drinking restrictions placed by the Aboriginal community council on people who had committed violence or other forms of disorder while drunk. Some were restricted from drinking during the evening opening hours of 5.30 – 8.30 P.M. and could only drink during the 'lunch' hours from 10.30 A.M. – 12.30 P.M. Others could not be served at all. These restrictions are just one example of the complex politics of Aboriginal drinking in remote communities. Licensed clubs (colloquially called 'wet canteens') are commonly held responsible for much alcohol-related violence and sexual assault. But supporters argue that providing alcohol in a controlled environment is better than the exploitative black-market trade in alcohol that flourishes in 'dry' communities (Gray et al. 2005).[18] The club in this community tried to manage the effects of alcohol though restricted opening hours, bouncers (who that day all appeared to be White) who stand at the door and make sure no banned or underage people enter, and harm minimisation messages. 'Drink Less for Your Family', advised the banner prominently displayed over the bar. As the sun went down, all the visitors sat on the lawns, slowly drinking beer and watching the band. Some old Aboriginal women sat towards the back of the lawns on benches, but most of the Aboriginal locals crowded under the shelter of the bar, watching the visitors.

Later, I went to the youth club where more bands played until midnight. By then, most of the day's visitors had returned back to Darwin. Only a core of White people in their twenties and thirties who were prepared to camp out on the oval remained. I knew nearly all of them from my social circle in Darwin. They were artists, musicians, film-makers, teachers, community development workers, and a few doctors, lawyers and environmental scientists. We congregated around the sound technician, a friend of ours, towards the front of the basketball court that served as an outdoor concert hall. The stage in front of us was the tray of a long truck. The side bleachers were bursting with chattering and laughing children and young people. Adults, babies and toddlers filled the court behind us. Those whom the bouncer had judged to be drunk were barred from entering the youth centre, and stood watching the band from behind the wire fence at the back of the court.

Soon after I arrived, the next band came on. They were the Letterstick Band and had travelled here from another Aboriginal community, Maningrida. Maningrida was just two hundred kilometres away, but on the rough dirt roads it takes eight hours to drive there, and the road is impassable in the wet months from December to April. As with most Aboriginal community bands, there were at least a dozen people on stage, including four guitarists, four singers, a didgeridoo player, and unusually an African man playing a djembe. School-age children flooded the dance floor, screaming and jumping. Young girls in tight-fitting clothes gyrated their hips to the music, arms held high, and then ran back to the bleachers between songs. Older teenage girls in oversized basketball shirts over long skirts formed small dancing circles, swaying from side to side, some holding their babies on their hips.

My friends and I were too shy to dance at first, perhaps because we did not want to 'take over' and intrude on the local space. We sat on the court behind the dancers, watching. After a few songs, some people worked up the courage to dance, and soon others in the group joined in. The good feeling amongst our group of friends was palpable as we danced in the cool, dry-season evening to a fusion of reggae, rock, traditional singing, and sometimes a hint of country or gospel.

The Letterstick Band sang in their local language of Gidjingarli. Like most of the audience who do not speak Gidjingarli, I could only appreciate the music. I later found out that the lyrics were about their traditional country, their clan identity, hunting and the history of their people, but also lost love and the harms of petrol sniffing.[19] Then I heard a catchy song with the distinctive chorus 'Tiwi Warriors, Tiwi Warriors'. My cultural radar, honed by ten years of engagement with all things Indigenous, sensed an incongruity. Why is a Maningrida band singing about the Tiwi Islands, a very different community over five hundred kilometres away? It is a cultural faux pas of the highest order to speak for or about another 'mob'.[20] Although I was curious, I did not expect to find an explanation for this. Being a White anti-racist who knows a little about Indigenous culture is so often an experience of knowing only how much we do not know.

As it happens, I was lucky enough to solve this particular mystery not long afterwards. A friend living at Maningrida (as his wife taught at the school) told me that the 'Tiwi Warriors' in the song are not from the Tiwi Islands north of Darwin at all – although the Tiwi people are indeed famous for being fierce warriors.[21] The song is about the far-less-famous locality of Tiwi in the northern suburbs of Darwin, where I was living at the time. The 'warriors' the song referred to were not Tiwi Islanders but people from the Maningrida songwriter's extended family who live in Darwin as 'long grassers' and congregate at the Tiwi shops. The lyrics translate as such:[22]

> I was camping outside in the bush
> When I saw that person there, he made me cry
> He was sleeping on the ground, I called out An-mujumburr
>
> Tiwi Warriors, Tiwi Warriors
> Tiwi Warriors, Tiwi Warriors, yeah.
>
> Night time, we made a fire
> Everyone sitting around, the wine's no good
> It made us sick
>
> Tiwi Warriors, Tiwi Warriors
> Tiwi Warriors, Tiwi Warriors, yeah.
>
> In the morning, I woke up and saw someone
> It was An-mujumburr, the wine's no good
> He was sitting drinking wine, I came and sat with him.

As an anthropologist of White anti-racism, I do not offer an anthropological analysis of the Aboriginal lifeworlds captured in these lyrics. Rather, I approach the song as an artefact of the contact zone. First and foremost, it will be encountered by the White anti-racist as modern Aboriginal music from the Maningrida community marketed by a savvy local record label, Skinnyfish Music.[23] If the White listener is puzzled by the title of the song, as I was, their curiosity will not easily be sated as the album provides no English translations. For the White anti-racist reader who is privy to the translation above, I propose that the message of the song is ambivalent. The lyrics seem to portray drinking in a negative light ('the wine's no good/It made us sick'). However, the conviviality of camping together in a family group is also discernable. Did An-mujumburr make the songwriter 'cry' out of sadness at his plight or out of the joy of reunion?[24] This indeterminacy is typical of encounters with difference in the contact zone of Darwin.

Below, I explore various perspectives on long grassers expressed by Tiwi residents and by more distant commentators. For White activists, Tiwi long grassers are symbols of resistance to colonial domination. For council authorities and many Tiwi residents, they are a source of anger and frustration. White anti-racists who live in Tiwi offer a third perspective that tends to minimise the social disruption of long grassers without denying it. The dense racial politics and the indeterminacy of the long-grasser problem at the Tiwi shops make this a paradigmatic contact zone. Through this extended example, I demonstrate how the knowledge system held by White anti-racist activists is challenged by the proximity of radically different ways of living.

The 'Long-Grasser Problem' at the Tiwi Shops

It is likely that long grassers have formed part of the Darwin landscape since the establishment of the settlement.[25] For decades the largest group making up unofficial camps on the fringes of town would have been Larrakia people directly displaced by White settlement. Over the last three or four decades, people from communities across the Northern Territory and beyond have found their way into long-grasser camps. There are many such camps around Darwin. Most are specific to one language group or a number of neighbouring language groups, while in some, people from disparate communities intermingle. The area around the Tiwi shops has been dominated for a long time by people from Maningrida in western Arnhem Land, who make camps at various places along the coastal reserve and meet at Tiwi shops to access food and alcohol. Figure 2.2 is an example of an established camp.[26] Tiwi is one of the hotspots for long grassers in the northern suburbs, judging from the volume of letters to the local paper from outraged residents.[27] Seeing groups of people bedding down for the night on the concrete under the shop awnings is a common experience for other Tiwi residents.

Long grassers have been politically active for many years, fighting alongside their allies (Indigenous and non-Indigenous activists) against the council and government for recognition of land rights to their camps and the provision of specific services. They have had some successes, and have a representative organisation that produces its own newsletter (Day 1994).[28] Long grassers attract a range of responses from both Darwin residents and the wider Australian community. Advocates attempt to counter images of long grassers as deviant, and emphasise the 'cultural'

Figure 2.2 A long-grasser camp on the outskirts of Darwin. Left to right:
Stanley Fry (inside van), unknown woman, Pauline Stewart (mostly obscured),
Lena Fry, Bonita Dempsey, Lewis Stewart, Len Stewart.
Photograph: Bill Day. Used with kind permission.

attributes of their behaviours. They stress the continuities between colonial dispossession of Indigenous peoples and the bureaucratic attacks on
long-grasser camps. Their narratives illustrate some of the features of
anti-racist discourse discussed in the previous chapter.

One example of such a narrative is from prominent Indigenous academic Marcia Langton, who draws on anthropologist Basil Sansom's
groundbreaking work *The Camp at Wallaby Cross* (1980) to explain the
long-grasser 'lifestyle':

> [Long grassers are a] community of people with a distinct culture, not
> of alcoholic homeless urban poor, but rather a fluctuating and rule gov-
> erned community of permanent resident hosts and cashed up guests who by
> sharing their money with their hosts come under their camp's protection.
> Camp life requires detailed insider knowledge of the social rules and laws.
> [Sansom] describes how alcohol often functions as a system of savings and
> amongst the camp residents because it is easy to calculate credit (by the
> can), whereas it is difficult to use foodstuffs as a currency with consistent
> units. (Langton, Morris, and Palmer 1998)

What might appear to the casual observer to be 'alcoholic homeless urban poor' is revealed by the anthropologist-advocate to be a 'rule governed community'. 'Deviant' behaviour is reframed as 'a distinct culture', demanding the same level of respect for long-grasser communities that is shown by many to 'traditional' Indigenous culture. As explained in the previous chapter, here too Indigenous difference is divided into two portions: the 'unsanitised' (such as drinking, gambling, not attending school, and violence) and the 'sanitised' (ceremony, art and hunting). The narrative of the quote above attempts to shift the reader's categorisation of long-grasser behaviour from the unsanitised to the sanitised. This discursive strategy is part of the repertoire of anti-racist beliefs and is ultimately threatened by the proximity of radical difference in the contact zone.

In another part of the article, Langton and colleagues emphasise the structural cause of the long-grasser problem, namely the public housing shortage in Darwin, and set this in a historical context of colonial displacement and frontier violence: 'What is happening to the "homeless" of Darwin is what happened to the Aboriginal nations in the nineteenth century, without the unfettered murder. Instead, the laws and regulations pertaining to "illegal camping" and "trespass" are used by the Northern Territory police to achieve the same result' (Langton, Morris, and Palmer 1998).[29]

Other advocates stress the racism inherent in the harassment of Indigenous homeless people forced to live outdoors, while the White population, who displaced the local Traditional Owners (the Larrakia people) in the first place, profits from tourists attracted to the art and culture of the very people they oppress. The final, incontrovertible fact used to argue for long-grasser rights is their Aboriginality: '[H]omeless Aborigines feel that despite their apparent lack of rights insinuated by the derogatory "long grass" and "itinerant" labels, they have more claim to be Darwin residents than most of those attempting to expel them' (Day 2005a). The violation of collective rights and the presence of cultural laws among 'homeless Aborigines' are recurrent themes in activist discourse.

A subgroup of the non-Indigenous population of Tiwi provides an alternative perspective on long grassers diametrically opposed to activist views. The protagonists here are the outraged White residents who experience long grassers as a severe disturbance. Their narratives of distress tend to draw on personal experiences of proximate social disruption. They portray themselves as the 'real' victims, powerless against the forces of political correctness that scare the authorities into inaction. Their outrage spills into the letters page of the local paper, the Northern Territory News (known locally as the 'NT News'):

Every, and I mean every, night for the past month I have had this mob set up camp near my residence with the accompanying consequences of fights, foul language, using my fence as a toilet and leaving a mountain of rubbish behind. Everybody that matters knows about it – the local member, Darwin City Council, the police and night patrol, but does anybody do anything about it?… I have had visitors from south[ern Australia] staying with me for a fortnight. One evening, after a pleasant night out at the theatre, we decided to sit on the veranda and have a cup of coffee before retiring. Fat chance. The sound of branches being snapped off trees to hit each other over the head with, yelling and screaming and language that would make the drover's dog wince[30] put paid to that idea. (Kerr 2005)

Leaving aside the drunken fights, foul language and distress caused to nearby residents, the major concern is the lack of toilet facilities. Campers [at the Tiwi shops] use the nearest tree or shrub to do their ablutions. No action has been taken by any authority to rectify the problem and the health risks grow daily. Only this morning, I witnessed thirty-odd people doing what comes naturally first thing in the morning. It is offensive and an ever-present health danger. (John 2005)

Here, the 'rule governed community' of the activist narrative becomes unwanted drunken chaos and uncontrolled bodily substances intruding into the public and private spaces claimed by law-abiding residents. Neither the colonial historical context nor the personal histories of long grassers appear in these narratives, just as the activist narratives above were devoid of the violence and human waste that are material realities of long-grasser life. As I will discuss, White anti-racists, who share urban space with both outraged residents and long grassers, present a third perspective that neither denies the unsanitised difference that long grassers present nor omits their socio-historical context.

Yet another voice in the debate is that of government. The Darwin City Council has a political imperative to respond to the long-grasser issue in a way that will satisfy these outraged letter-writers whilst avoiding accusations of racism.[31] Long-grasser politics surfaced in 2005 in Tiwi when the council allocated $200,000 to upgrade the Tiwi shops. In line with council protocol, meetings were called to facilitate public consultation on the upgrade. The minutes of the meeting reveal that the upgrade was seen by many as an opportunity to deal with the 'problem' of long grassers. Two stakeholders with a keen interest in the outcome were those in charge of the only two establishments in the small shopping complex: Tiwi Supermarket and the Darwin office of the national non-government organisation (NGO) Diabetes Australia. Tiwi Supermarket is a small business that sells basic grocery items, clothes and alcohol. The food is generally nutritionally poor, as it is in most Darwin suburban shops.

Few fresh fruits or vegetables are sold, while canned foods, soft drinks, confectionary, cigarettes and alcohol are over-represented. All items are vastly overpriced compared to the three large chain supermarkets at the nearby Casuarina Square shopping centre. White residents of the suburb generally only use the Tiwi shops to buy the NT News and the odd grocery item. The owner of the supermarket was present at the consultation meeting, but the minutes indicate that he said very little. As I will explore below, his silence may be explained by the complex and unorthodox relationships between long grassers and his family-owned business.

The other key stakeholder at the meeting was the regional director of Diabetes Australia. Diabetes Australia is a resource centre where Darwin's diabetics can access diabetes education, subsidised health equipment and support groups. According to an informant who used to work there, the service is used mostly by White people, although the organisation has tried to remedy this with the employment of an Aboriginal Health Worker. In contrast to the supermarket owner, the regional director of Diabetes Australia had a great deal to say about the potential of the upgrade to address the 'long-grasser problem'.

The consultation meeting, held in February 2005, was also attended by representatives of the Darwin City Council, the landscape architect firm designing the upgrade, and the Northern Territory government's Department of Infrastructure Planning and Environment, as well as four members of the public. It is not clear whether any of those attending the meeting identified as Indigenous, although the minutes suggest that this is unlikely.[32]

Much discussion at the meeting centred on how to make the shops unattractive to long grassers. Long grassers themselves were absent both from the meeting and from the minutes. Although they are everywhere implied, they are referred to indirectly only once as the 'homeless issue'. Elsewhere their effects (e.g. 'noise and gatherings') are named without connection to their human source. The mode of discussion of long grassers at the meeting is a distinct approach to indigeneity that could be located somewhere in the gulf between overt racism and anti-racism. Participants were very careful about what they said, seemingly aware that the project of deterring long grassers from the shops was a potentially racist project, if explicitly stated. And yet the shared agenda of those present was to minimise the presence of long grassers in their lives.

The meeting began by discussing the need to have bright lights with recessed fittings, and to paint the awnings white 'to assist in reflecting greater light'. A member of the public requested that 'segregated' seating for elderly local residents be provided 'away from noise and gatherings'. The proposal to build a fence around the shops was also the subject of much discussion. A member of the public present 'suggested [the] style of fencing to be robust', while the Diabetes Australia representative believed 'fencing could add an aesthetic quality'.

The representative from Diabetes Australia was particularly vocal, stating that she has 'realistic concerns that stem from three of her clients refusing to visit Diabetes Australia due to anti-social behaviour issues'. She expressed concern that the plan for a sloped surface from the inner edge of the footpath towards the building, an anti-long grasser engineering feature designed to prevent people from leaning against shop fronts, could actually be comfortable.

Later in the meeting, the 'homeless issue' was discussed directly. The Diabetes Australia representative expressed 'concern that $200,000 [allocated to the upgrade] may be wasted if other measures are not taken to stop anti-social behaviour'. The Tiwi Supermarket owner shared his scepticism, adding that 'the new concrete paving may not be able to wear the intense use (up to one hundred and twenty people congregating at one time) over the long term'. All were in agreement that 'proposed extra lighting will help this issue', as bright lighting will discourage people from sleeping under the shop awnings. In response, the council employee offered to conduct a 'Crime Prevention through Environmental Design' audit on the shops, and suggested 'the installation of a shelter and tap elsewhere in [a] nearby park would be useful to deal with the problem, especially if the itinerants are consulted about its location' (Clouston Associates 2005).

The tone of the meeting was a far cry from the activist narratives above, but it also departed from the outraged letter-writers. The drunken fights, foul language and excrement of the NT News letters are reduced in these minutes to much more palatable terms – 'the homeless issue', 'other issues', and 'anti-social behaviour'. The solutions suggested are robust: aesthetic fencing (presumably locked at night), sloped surfaces that will hopefully be uncomfortable, strong lighting reflecting off bright white surfaces, 'segregated' seating for the (mostly White) residents of the nearby old people's home, and a shelter and tap 'elsewhere' coaxing long grassers away from more desirable public spaces. There is even a technical term for this careful, deliberate shaping of long grasser-repellent surroundings: 'Crime Prevention through Environmental Design'. The desired outcome of these measures was to manage radical difference through its deletion, transforming the contact zone into a space of benign multiculturalism.

This euphemistic discussion of how to make life harder for Tiwi long grassers would not be condoned by all residents. Those in the social group of most interest to me have devoted their professional lives to helping Indigenous people. It is unlikely they would be sufficiently disturbed by long-grasser behaviour to attend such a consultation meeting. Sitting on a bench in the courtyard of the Darwin Institute of Indigenous Health with one of the subjects of this study, who is also a neighbour, I discussed the proposals made in the meeting. She was quick to defend long grassers:

> There isn't such a bad problem there at Tiwi shops, there's not much vandalism or anything. You know, I walk the dogs with my kids every day for years now along the Casuarina reserve, that's practically my backyard, and there's only been one time I've called the police – one time there was a man there and he was letting it all hang out [exposing his genitals] and calling out to us, I was there with my kids, so I went back and called the police. That was the only time. The people there, you see them every day, there's some that are connected with people staying at Daisy Y [Aboriginal hostel] but there's permanent camps there, lots of Maningrida people camping there, and every day you wave, or say hello. I've never had any trouble.[33]

Somewhat incongruously, straight after telling me that she has 'never had any trouble', she goes on to relate two other incidents of 'trouble' – one when a woman burst out onto the path from the mangroves, crying and saying she has been assaulted, and another when a man lay drunk, barely conscious across the path ('normally people would go and lie in the bush, but he was right across the path'). But these incidents are experienced as exceptions to the rule of successful coexistence. This narrative differs from the activist narratives above. She does not appeal to evocations of a distinct long-grasser culture, housing shortages or histories of dispossession to make her arguments. Like the outraged letter-writers, her narrative is based on experience of radical difference, although her mode of experience and style of expression is profoundly dissimilar.

A similar perspective on long grassers was offered by a colleague who worked at Diabetes Australia. I asked her whether White people are really too afraid to access their diabetes education and discounted health equipment because of long grassers at the Tiwi shops, as the Diabetes Australia representative at the meeting had claimed. She replied:

> A few people are too scared to come, but only a few of them. It's not a problem most of the time. Last year a woman smashed the glass though and she had blood running all down her onto the ground. The main problem is the area around the back is used as a toilet so it smells really bad. They want to put up a fence like a pool fence around the shops, but it's like keeping people out that way.[34]

She minimises the possible harm, in contrast with the Regional Director at the meeting who warns that the $200,000 upgrade will be 'wasted'

without urgent action. Similar to my colleague encountering long grassers on her family walks, this woman juxtaposes reassuring statements
(long grassers are 'not a problem most of the time') with a dramatic
image of scattered shards of glass and a woman standing in a pool of her
own blood. White anti-racists in the contact zone periodically witness
the unsanitised difference of long-grasser life in Darwin (as well as radical difference, both unsanitised and sanitised, in the Indigenous remote
communities where they work). Although they tend to play down the
effects of drunken disturbances – in contrast with the NT News letter-
writers, who emphasise them – unsanitised difference is clearly present.
And while there is clear concern about government attempts to 'manage'
long-grasser behaviour (in this example, with a fence designed to deter
them) there is no attempt to transform the behaviour into sanitised difference (e.g. emphasising the cultural rules of long-grasser camps) as
activist narratives tend to. Instead, the contradictions of the contact zone
are laid bare as both the 'anti-social' behaviour of long grassers and the
discriminatory behaviour of the government are acknowledged.

The quote above mentions the all-too-human smell at the back of
the shops. One of the NT News letter-writers quoted earlier claimed
that long grassers camped at the shops use 'the nearest tree or shrub' for
their toileting. There is, in fact, a public toilet block behind the Tiwi
shops that could potentially offer a solution, but it is permanently locked.
The minutes of the consultation meeting are opaque about this, stating that '[the] Toilet Block is a big issue', without further elaboration.
A neighbour filled me in on the story. He reported that the toilet block
behind the Tiwi shops was continuously filthy as the level and type of use
outstripped the maintenance and cleaning provided. It was frequently
vandalised despite the anti-crime measure of a 'supervised graffiti' project
on its outer wall. Eventually the Darwin City Council installed a large
padlock on the metal doors, and only the sports clubs that used the oval
had a key. Soon, there were whispers of racism, because most of the sporting club members were White, and the long grassers Black. One day, a
council worker arrived and blowtorched the doors closed so no one could
use them. They remained fused shut – a shrine to the awkward stalemate
of the post-settler state.

Book-Up

During the consultative meeting to discuss the upgrade of the Tiwi shops,
the proprietor of Tiwi Supermarket was strangely silent. Given the concern shown by the Diabetes Australia representative for the welfare of

her clients, one might think he would be equally concerned about the potential for his 'legitimate' customers to be scared off by long-grasser behaviour.[35] His silence may be explained by another peculiar arrangement of this part of this contact zone that relates to long-grasser banking practices.

As I have mentioned, the White residents of Tiwi buy little from the local shop, preferring the better quality and cheaper food on offer at the large supermarkets in the adjoining suburb of Casuarina. What probably keeps Tiwi Supermarket afloat is the steady business of long grassers who prefer to use a 'book-up' system of credit not available at larger outlets. Rather than paying up front for food, clothes and alcohol, long grassers take what they need and the shop employees keep a record of their purchases. On the day the customer's unemployment or other welfare benefits are paid, the shop owner deducts the amount they owe directly from their account. This usually involves the shop owner having possession of the long grassers' ATM cards and PIN numbers. It is unclear whether this is a requirement set by shop owners or a long grasser preference, given the difficulty of keeping track of small possessions such as bank cards and remembering PIN numbers when living in the open and often intoxicated.

This unorthodox financial system means they can purchase what they want, when they want, without having to handle money, with as much credit as the shop owner is willing to give them. Does this arrangement leave them at the mercy of the shop owner? It certainly does. Is this exploitative? If it is not exploitative by definition, it is certainly vulnerable to gross misuse. Is it legal? Definitely not. Yet it occurs, as demand for the service is met with clandestine supply.[36]

I first saw the book-up system when I worked at Utopia, a collection of outstations three hundred kilometres north-east of Alice Springs, in 1998. Everyone would use the book-up system at the local shop, although I do not recall whether their bank cards and PINs were held by the shop owner. I did notice the long list of people displayed at the front of the shop with figures beside their names denoting the size of their bad debts usually running in the hundreds, probably reflecting larger purchases of washing machines or bicycles (but not alcohol in this case, as it was a 'dry' community). I noticed too that my beloved weekend hunting trips with the families I had become friends with seemed to always incorporate a visit to the next closest store, at a cattle station homestead nearly two hours' drive away down dirt tracks. Having accumulated a bad debt at the local store, they would cancel their accounts, and organise for their government benefits to be paid at the next store (a massive administrative feat for people with only conversational English). I did not discover what would happen if and when they accrued a bad debt at that store too.

I had heard of this happening at the Tiwi shops and other urban shops from numerous sources, but I found it officially recorded in the decisions of the Northern Territory Licensing Commission. The commission has jurisdiction over any outlet selling alcohol in the Northern Territory. They regularly respond to complaints regarding the sale of alcohol to intoxicated persons and the 'book-up' of alcohol, both of which are illegal. A decision handed down on 24 February 2005 regarding Tiwi Supermarket concerned five complaints much like this one:

> **Complaint 4:** About 12.10 P.M. on Thursday 8 July 2004, an employee of the Tiwi Supermarket sold liquor, being one 4-litre cask of Buronga Ridge wine, seven 375ml cans of Melbourne Bitter beer and six 375ml cans of Jim Beam and Cola, to Mr Ignatius Narjic by way of utilising a credit facility known as 'book-up' in that the purchase was recorded in a book retained for the purpose of recording grocery purchases and Mr Narjic's debit card was retained by the store. His PIN was also known by the storekeeper from previous grocery transactions. (NT Licensing Commission 2005)

The decision regarding this case and the four others like it was to suspend Tiwi Supermarket's liquor licence for five days – the longest suspension ever given by the Licensing Commission. Another decision about the supermarket in the neighbouring suburb of Alawa described the book-up system employed by the proprietor, Mr Lim, in detail:

> Although he denies allowing liquor to be booked up, he does allow Aboriginal customers to book-up groceries and non-liquor purchases. He keeps the [debit] cards of all those who book-up groceries, in envelopes in a shoebox at the till, *and the respective PIN numbers are kept written (in Chinese) on the backs of the envelopes.* He keeps the cards as security for the food accounts. From time to time he swipes the cards to check if they are in sufficient credit to authorise payment of his accounts, in which case he then processes the debit to the customer's card and pays himself. He goes into the shop each Sunday morning and routinely tries them all. (NT Licensing Commission 2003; emphasis in original)

Although no less illegal, the effort of recording the numbers in Chinese as a form of security is touching. Perhaps the gesture stems from Mr Lim's fear of exposure and is really a defensive strategy designed to make him look better in case of official scrutiny. However, it could also point to a real concern for the security of his customers' accounts, reflecting a sense of professional and personal responsibility. More than once in urban shops and bottle shops I have seen a clearly drunk Indigenous person (reeking of alcohol, slurring their words, unable to stand upright let alone walk straight) refused service at the checkout, sometimes in a gruff way, but sometimes gently, almost like a friend, as the employee may well feel from their daily interactions with that person, both drunk and sober. When seen up close, the affective and financial ties that bind long grassers to shop employees often exceed labels such as 'exploitative' or '(neo)colonial'. Choice, desire and even love inevitably enter the frame, complicating prior knowledge about Indigenous disadvantage that White anti-racists bring to the contact zone.

Sorcery

I have explored how long grassers are seen by varying non-Indigenous actors in the urban landscape. But how do long grassers see themselves? The impulse to know what 'Indigenous people themselves' think is a central pillar of the knowledge system shared by White anti-racists. Often, Indigenous people who are called on to perform indigeneity say things that White anti-racists already believe, which can be satisfying for all parties (see Chapter 5). But in the contact zone, where the discourse of anti-racism meets radical difference, the results of asking what Indigenous people think can be unpredictable and confusing.[37]

Take, for example, another report on the long-grasser issue, this one not commissioned by government but a product of the Indigenous health research institute where my study was based. 'Yolngu Long Grassers on Larrakia Land' was a collaborative project conducted by two Yolngu[38] researchers from Galiwin'ku (a north-east Arnhem Land community on Elcho Island); a linguist and a teacher, both with decades of experience in Arnhem Land; and an anthropologist from the institute. Forty-three long grassers were interviewed in their first language. The reasons they gave for living in the long grass were complex, ranging from the inability to afford a flight back to their home community after accessing medical treatment, to a desire to escape disputes and conflicts in their community, to an enjoyment of the 'freedom of living in the long-grass' (Maypilama et al. 2004: 3–4). However, the report makes it clear that fear of sorcery is the main reason people flee their communities and end up living in the long grass:

> Fear is probably the most common reason given by people for why they have left East Arnhem Land to live in the long-grass in Darwin. There is almost universal fear of galka' – sorcerers/assassins – among the Yolngu, and is particularly the case at Galiwin'ku [community in north-east Arnhem Land]. Some people may have been accused of sorcery, while others fear being accused. Some people are frightened of being contracted by sorcerers to

perform assassinations and are threatened with violence if they refuse to perform sorcery. People who are accused of being a galka' will run away in fear of their lives. It is important to understand that when a person dies, someone will almost always be accused of having caused that person's death. As long as there remain questions about how someone has died, others will live in fear of being accused and of being the victim of bayarra' [payback]. Some people living in Galiwin'ku are so afraid of galka', and so tired of arguments and violence, that they stay inside their houses all the time, and won't go out. Many people are frightened of the suicide, violence, mental illness and uncontrolled anger back at the 'mission'.[39] These people said they feel much safer in Darwin. (Maypilama et al. 2004: 11–12; emphasis in original)

In contrast to the prominence given to sorcery in this report, only one of the forty-seven long grassers who were interviewed for research commissioned by the NT Government mentioned sorcery (Memmott and Fantin 2001: 71),[40] and anthropologist Bill Day mentions 'alleged' sorcery in a home community only once in his dissertation on Darwin long grassers (Day 2001: section 9.9).[41] This is an example of the great discrepancies that arise in the contact zone. Are long grassers better understood as the victims of colonial displacement and institutional racism, or the victims of their own ruthless countrymen and their own 'backward' culture? How do anti-racists respond when an Indigenous-controlled research project tells us that the major cause of Indigenous homelessness is beyond our control? An anti-racist may argue that the contemporary proliferation of sorcery is a product of the colonial establishment of settlements that brought different clans into uncomfortably close proximity; but for most, even the mention of sorcery strays too close to Orientalist depictions of Indigenous people, either romanticising their difference or denigrating their primitiveness (see Chapter 2). It is this inevitable troubling of anti-racist beliefs that makes them visible, offering a window into the inner workings of the Australian post-settler state.

One evening soon after I read this report, I stood with a friend outside the shops of the nearby suburb of Jingili waiting for our gourmet take-away pizza. A long grasser who must have spied my friend rolling a cigarette came stumbling towards us.[42] He was about fifty and seemed friendly, with a grey beard, dirty clothes, and reeking of alcohol. In one hand he held a can of beer.

'You got two dollar?' he asked.
'Nah, mate, nothing', I replied.
'You gimme tobacco?'
'Sure'.

My friend pressed a wad of tobacco into his hand. As he skilfully rolled a cigarette with his free hand I asked him, 'Where you from?'
'Maningrida'.
'Why you in town?'
He answers without hesitation, 'Ah, for drinking! No grog in Maningrida'.

We all chuckle, and he wanders off into the darkness behind the shops, where presumably he is camped.

Now, this man was from Maningrida, not Galiwin'ku (although there are merely 150 kilometres as the crow flies between the two communities), but I was struck by the contrast between what I had learnt in the Indigenous-authored research report and what he told me. Did this indicate that the attribution of itinerancy to sorcery was fanciful and wrong? And does this imply that the authors of the report are pandering to the desires of anthropologists to elevate to the status of 'culture' something that is merely alcoholism? Or maybe, as some anti-racist Whites might argue, he was 'just saying that', and I was naive to expect him to tell the true cultural reason for his exile from his home community to a complete stranger, and a White one at that. Maybe he was pandering to my expectations, performing the 'drunken Blackfella' that the White locals of Darwin expect him to be. And what about my part in the performance? Long grassers don't approach just anyone – racist White locals can be dangerous.[43] Maybe it was our young appearance, or our colourful clothes bought from local markets, that signalled to him that we were a safe target for humbugging.[44] My use of Aboriginal English also showed my willingness to venture a little way across the cultural divide. His honesty (if he was in fact being honest) provided me with an opportunity not to be shocked, displaying my tolerance and understanding of addiction, or my knowledge that there would be other, deeper reasons behind his stereotypical reply. These multiple, intersecting performances are characteristic of the dense racial politics of the contact zone.

Notes

1. A 2001 study of long grassers in Darwin by a consultant anthropologist listed the major characteristics of this social group as follows:
    1. People who do not pay for accommodation.
    2. People who have a visible public profile: they socialise, shelter, drink, and argue/fight in public.
    3. Perceived by some to exhibit anti-social behaviour at times.
    4. Perceived by some to be at risk and needy.

    5. Have low incomes, a substantial part of which is spent on alcohol.

    6. Generally have few possessions, minimal clothes and bedding.

    7. Generally conform to a 'beat' of camping, socialising and resource places.

    8. Most do not have any immediate intentions of returning to home communities.

    (Memmott and Fantin 2001: 38)

2. By labelling the group of people who express certain views about long grassers as 'racists' I do not mean to dismiss them, but to parse out the variety of discourses circulating in the contact zone. For literature that pays more ethnographic attention to this group, see for example Cowlishaw 1999; Hartigan 2005; and Moran 2009.

3. Alternatively, for a minority of activists, long grassers are the ultimate symbol of political resistance, defying White liberal sentiments to live a free bush life wherever they like, refusing to be hidden away from public view in remote communities, and demanding, through the presence of their deviant black bodies, a reckoning with the colonial past.

4. To be sure, experiences of radical difference certainly exist in the southern Australian metropoles of Sydney and Melbourne (where the bulk of anti-racist discourse is generated), but to the average southern White anti-racist they are often fleeting, lasting the length of a meeting or conference, and confined to official and symbolic settings. In the north, with a much larger proportion of Indigenous people, who are themselves more likely to be 'cosmetically apparent' (Huggins 1998: 141) as Aboriginal or Torres Strait Islander, experiences of radical difference are not hard to come by, and importantly, are experienced *routinely* as part of everyday life, both professional and personal.

5. Note that the political geography of Australia is, in this respect, the reverse of that of the United States, with a progressive 'South' and a frontier-like 'North'.

6. See http://www.reconciliationaustralia.org/ and http://www.antar.org.au/. See the Introductory chapter for discussion of my use of the term 'anti-racist'.

7. Mary Ellen Jordan's book *Balanda: My Year in Arnhem Land* (2005) is an example of this kind of transformation.

8. All statistics in the following paragraphs derive from Reconciliation Australia and Auspoll 2012. The data from this survey is likely to be representative of the views of the wider population. The distribution of gender, age, income, and education levels in the sample is proportional to the general population. The main concern with their method is that it is an online survey and may therefore under-represent those without internet access. In addition, those who are antagonist or indifferent towards Indigenous issues may decline to participate and those that are enthusiastic about them may be more likely to participate. This may lead to an overestimation of the size of the 'anti-racist' category and an underestimation of the 'conservative' category.

9. The discourse of 'do-gooder' has been debated and critiqued in Australian anthropology for decades; see Rowse 1990.

10. On customary law and the Australian state, see Douglas 2006. On 'environmentality', see Agrawal 2005.

11. Most Indigenous and non-Indigenous people have jobs that are ultimately funded by the government, and the Northern Territory receives five times the amount of federal funding of the other states per capita in an attempt to account for the extreme disadvantage of Indigenous people in remote communities. Critics of the Northern

Territory government often argue that the generous public facilities available in Darwin (such as a free outdoor wave pool and a second free outdoor complex with giant waterslides) come at the expense of the people the extra money was meant for – remote-dwelling Indigenous people (Lea 2008).

12. 'Tribes' is now considered anachronistic, and terms such as Aboriginal nation, language group or cultural group are used instead.

13. This postwar urban expansion of Darwin (the population increased 9-fold from 5,000 in 1947 to 46,000 in 1974) was cut short by Cyclone Tracy, which flattened much of the town and the northern suburbs on Christmas night, 1974. Despite the evacuation of the vast majority of residents, the massive reconstruction that followed again lured people to Darwin and the population recovered its size in barely two years (Heatley 1986; Lea 2014).

14. Although the effect of those social policies is a kind of multiculturalism we might celebrate, at the time they were aimed at preventing the development of 'colour consciousness' among Darwin's 'half-caste' population that might arise from residential segregation. Government policy of the time saw their future in full assimilation with the White community (Wells and Rowse 2005: 128).

15. In 2006, Australia as a whole had a population of 22.3 million, 2.6 per cent of whom were Indigenous.

16. Most of this information is informed by statistics on income, education, home ownership, and so on. The exception is my comments about the degrees of non/Indigenous ancestry, which reflect only my local knowledge. Australia data collection on 'ancestry' is still in development. The 2001 question found that most Indigenous people claimed 'Australian' ancestry, along with 35 per cent of the general population. The question did not identify non-Indigenous people who claim Indigenous 'ancestry' (Kunz and Costello 2003). Unlike the United States or New Zealand, where you can have multiple ancestries (US) or gradations of Indigenous ancestry and identity (NZ), in Australia the only reliable information classifies people as Aboriginal, Torres Strait Islander, Aboriginal *and* Torres Strait Islander, or non-Indigenous.

17. I do not mean here to criticise the Australian Bureau of Statistics who go to great lengths to include Indigenous people in all types of social situations in the 5-yearly Census, even employing anthropologists to assess their efforts (see Sanders 2004). On the policing of long grassers, officers from four different authorities seek to stop long grassers camping illegally and/or creating a 'public disturbance': the police, parks officers (if they are camping on government land), council staff (if they are camping on council land) and the Community Patrol (an Indigenous-run service).

18. When I was visiting one dry community, an hour from another Territory town, I was told community residents would pay the $360 demanded by taxi drivers to drive them on the unpaved road into town to spend their welfare money on alcohol, and drive them back. Presumably they made the money back through selling some of the alcohol at an exorbitant price to other residents.

19. For more information on the Letterstick Band, see http://www.skinnyfishmusic.com.au/Indigenous_roots/ls_band.html.

20. 'Mob' is an Aboriginal English term for a group of people, usually a cultural, language or clan group.

21. Most famously for forcing the withdrawal of a British military base on Melville Island in 1829, after five years of warfare, and for being the first to capture Japanese prisoners on Australian soil in the Second World War. I do not know whether the

Gidjingarli songwriters were aware of this existing association between the Tiwi people and warriors.

22. Music and lyrics by Terence Wilson. Thanks to CAAMA Music for permission to reproduce the translation here. Sincere thanks to Dulcie Malimara for translating the song and Bill Day for facilitating this. An-mujumburr is the familiar or 'bush' name of a relative of the songwriter.

23. Skinnyfish has since become hugely successful, largely due to the international super-stardom of Elcho Island singer-songwriter Geoffrey Gurrumul Yunupingu.

24. Yet another layer of interpretation is the translation process itself, kindly done for me by Dulcie Malimara with the help of her friend, anthropologist Bill Day. Perhaps, aware of her White audience, her translation of the words 'sick' and 'cry' sought to portray the song as anti-drinking, and thus comparable with liberal morality.

25. The term 'long grass people' has been in use for well over a decade (see Day 2005b; Langton, Morris and Palmer 1998). As homeless Indigenous people in Darwin readily self-identify as long grassers, I use the term without quotation marks from this point on.

26. See Day 2001: 160–66, for an account of contemporary long-grass life. For other accounts, see Sansom 1980; Heppell and Wigley 1981; Memmott 2000; and Fisher 2012. Tiwi long grassers consider the Tiwi shops to be an important place. This was illustrated when a Maningrida man who had been active in the long-grasser movement died of throat cancer. A ceremony was held for him at the Tiwi shops: 'Although the Darwin City Council has permanently locked and barred the public toilets at the Tiwi shopping centre, this did not deter the campers from organising a smoking ritual at the centre the day following Sandy's passing. Smoke wafted into the shops as the surviving "Warriors" sang traditional laments accompanied by didgeridoo and clap sticks' (Day 2005a).

27. A database search of the Northern Territory News performed on 9 Nov. 2005 found that only one other suburb (Nightcliff) was mentioned in as many articles and letters that also mentioned 'itinerants'. Although to a degree it is merely Tiwi's share of a generalised 'problem', there might be more long grassers in Tiwi than other suburbs because of the proximity of the hospital, the Aboriginal hostel, many camping places along the coastal reserve, and the services available at the Casuarina shopping centre. Official reports blame long grassers in part on the high rates of hospitalisation in the Indigenous community, with family members accompanying the sick person to town or coming to visit them (Maypilama et al. 2004: 3; Memmott and Fantin 2001: 71). The solution to the problem of lack of accommodation near the hospital, namely the long-established Daisy Yarmirr Aboriginal Hostel, is sometimes perceived as the cause of further problems. Remote community visitors staying at 'Daisy Y' may attract their drunken long-grasser relatives, who rely on them for support, to the surrounding long-grass camps.

28. See also http://longgrass.tripod.com.

29. For analyses that argue that the long-grasser 'problem' is a function of insufficient housing stock, see Holmes and McRae-Williams 2009; and Taylor, Walker and Marawili 2011.

30. A colloquial Australian term, the 'drover's dog' is tough, ugly, and not easy to make wince.

31. In 2003, the Northern Territory government introduced its own innovative programme to deal with the long-grasser 'problem'. The progressive Labor government, emboldened by its historic election win in 2001 after twenty-seven years of

Conservative Party rule by the Country Liberal Party (CLP), developed the 'Itinerant Strategy', a name later changed to the more melodic 'Community Harmony Strategy'. In a stroke of postcolonial genius, it was proposed to use a large part of the $5.25 million allocated to the strategy to fund the Traditional Owners (TOs) of the Darwin area, the Larrakia Nation, to run the programme. With the aim of curbing 'anti-social behaviour' (a term encompassing begging, public drunkenness, public defecating, fighting and sleeping in public spaces), signs explaining the traditional Larrakia laws governing visitors from other Aboriginal lands were erected throughout Darwin. The Larrakia Nation was funded to employ teams of 'Larrakia Hosts' in Community Harmony Project T-shirts who would operate in the city and suburban markets popular with tourists, negotiating with long grassers to cease their anti-social behaviour and access services or return to their home communities (with the cost of their flight deducted from future welfare payments), and providing information to tourists.

32. Evidence that attendees were Indigenous could have been Indigenous surnames, or the use of collective pronouns (e.g. 'our people') by some speakers to refer to Indigenous people, or the deferral by non-Indigenous people to the Indigenous person/s present to offer an 'expert' opinion.

33. Field Notes, 5 Sept. 2005: 4, 91.

34. Field Notes, 9 May 2005: 4, 28.

35. I, for one, have had to wait some distance away until a noisy altercation between long grassers had moved away from the shop doors. I did not personally find it alarming or particularly inconvenient – like other White anti-racists in the contact zone, familiarity with radical difference greatly lessens fear and anxiety – but others may have.

36. Compare with Carter's description of an informal pawnshop acting as 'in an unorthodox sense, a community resource' for an Aboriginal community on the south coast of New South Wales (Carter 1988: 67). Note that the practice of holding bank cards and PIN numbers in shops can reflect a need to protect oneself from one's kin, rather than the inability to keep track of the card. In shops that do not sell alcohol (the case in 'dry' remote communities, but not in the Tiwi shops), women can then use their pension to buy food and circumvent relatives who demand the money for other reasons. Although I do not have the space to explore this here, there are striking similarities between the 'book-up' system and the Basics Card introduced with the Northern Territory Emergency Intervention.

37. I allude here to the related long-standing anthropological tradition of asking how 'natives think', most famously by Lucien Lévy-Bruhl and Marshall Sahlins.

38. 'Yolngu' means 'person' in the language of the Indigenous people of north-east Arnhem Land.

39. Galiwin'ku and many other remote Indigenous communities were established as missions, most being handed over to Indigenous control in the 1960s and 1970s (other communities were established as government ration stations or cattle stations). See Chapter 6 for further exploration of mission history in contemporary anti-racist discourse.

40. Note that a further fifteen people did not answer the question.

41. Bill Day's work was mostly with people from Maningrida, and it may be that sorcery is more prominent in other communities.

42. While visitors and those new to Darwin are generally troubled by these approaches, above all concerned that they might appear racist if they refuse to give money (especially if approached in front of other anti-racist Whites) longer-term residents learn

to be comfortable refusing to give money. Some will say, 'I don't know you', as a way of showing there are other *known* Aboriginal people to whom help would readily be offered.

43. There have been recorded instances of young Whites assaulting long grassers; see, for example, Watt 2002 and probably many other cases that are not recorded.

44. 'Humbugging' is an Aboriginal English term for begging (to strangers) or repeatedly asking a known person for something.

Chapter 4

WELCOME TO COUNTRY

The Welcome to Country (WTC) ceremony and its twin, an Acknowledgement of the Traditional Owners (Acknowledgement), have become prominent anti-racist rituals in Australia. These rituals are rich in meaning: they are simultaneously symbols of colonisation and dispossession; of recognition and reconciliation; and a periodic focus of political posturing. This chapter analyses the multiple meanings of WTC ceremonies, from 'national psychic Band-Aid', to individual political statement, to continuous Aboriginal tradition. In particular, I explore the politics of belonging elicited by WTC and Acknowledgement rituals. Welcome to Country ceremonies have been criticised by political conservatives because they challenge their mode of belonging and make them feel unwelcome. In contrast, those who support the ceremonies describe them as deeply moving. I argue that widespread enjoyment of these rituals among White anti-racists is explained because they paradoxically experience belonging through a sense of not belonging. I suggest that WTC and Acknowledgement rituals can most usefully be thought of as a device to encourage reflection on belonging. This approach would acknowledge the challenge to White belonging posed by WTC rituals and keenly felt by conservative Australians. It would suggest a more productive response to conservative attacks than that currently offered – a response that seeks a path towards mutual understanding between anti-racists and conservatives, and between Indigenous and non-Indigenous Australians.

Introductory Acknowledgements

I will begin with three 'Acknowledgements'. The first is the University of Canberra's suggested script for an Acknowledgement of country, available on their website. The wording is attributed to the United Ngunnawal Elders Council, an organisation set up by the Australian Capital Territory Office of Aboriginal & Torres Strait Islander Affairs (ACT Government: Community Services 2012):

> I wish to acknowledge the traditional custodians of the land we are meeting on, the Ngunnawal people. I wish to acknowledge and respect their continuing culture and the contribution they make to the life of this city and this region. I would also like to acknowledge and welcome other Aboriginal and Torres Strait Islander people who may be attending today's event.

The second Acknowledgement is one I give myself on occasion, appending it to a conventional Acknowledgement:

> I would also like to acknowledge my own and your own ancestors and all the diverse places they were born in and journeyed to. I acknowledge the injustices committed by many of our ancestors who journeyed to new lands, as well as the injustices that caused many to journey from their homes. I honour the courage it takes to make a new life in a new place, and to welcome newcomers. I also acknowledge the ancestors that we share with others in this room, whether those shared ancestors are hundreds, thousands, or tens of thousands of years in our past.

The third Acknowledgement is that adopted by the former conservative premier of the southern Australian State of Victoria, Ted Baillieu, as an alternative to a conventional Acknowledgement. Soon after taking over office from the Labor Party premier Steve Bracks in 2010, he controversially removed his predecessor's policy that required government ministers to acknowledge Traditional Owners (TOs) when making public speeches. Ted Baillieu's updated Acknowledgement is as follows:

> Can I particularly acknowledge all of those, past and present, including our Indigenous communities, whose love of this land has made this a place we treasure and a state we all seek to nurture. (Bolt 2011)

Few Australians would be unaware of the 'Welcome to Country' ritual, particularly since Prime Minister Kevin Rudd decided in 2008 that the first sitting of the Federal Parliament each year would begin with a WTC from a Traditional Owner of Canberra, the nation's capital. Over the past three decades, the practice of inviting a representative of a local

Indigenous group to 'Welcome' the audience onto Aboriginal country has become commonplace in many public forums, including academic and professional conferences, and all kinds of events held by governments and educational institutions. Guidelines on WTCs produced by various government departments advise that a major sporting event or the opening of a new hospital ward also require a 'Welcome'.[1] A WTC is conducted by an elder and is usually a short speech, but for larger events can include dance, music or even a smoking ceremony (when culturally significant plants are burnt on stage to produce smoke).

The twin ritual of a WTC is an Acknowledgement. This is where a non-Indigenous person (or an Indigenous person who is not a TO) acknowledges that the current location of the audience is regarded as ancestral country for a particular Aboriginal or Torres Strait Islander group, and acknowledges the elders of those TOs.[2] An Acknowledgement is done either in response to a Welcome, or in place of a Welcome when the event is too small to warrant a WTC, or when a planned WTC does not eventuate.

The Welcome to Country ritual is now firmly engrained within some segments of Australian society, including government, university and non-government sectors. It has accumulated a mass of protocols, explicit and implied. Hundreds of WTCs and thousands of Acknowledgements are likely to occur every day in Australia, and many Australians who speak in public or organise events have incorporated it into their routine. As I will discuss, it has become a key site of Indigenous recognition by mainstream Australia, a cause of anxiety for some event organisers, and a periodic focus of political posturing. This chapter will explore the varying and diverging meanings of the rituals, but focus on their function as White anti-racist 'speech acts' (Austin 1962) that perform identity work for White anti-racists who wish to address and overcome the legacy of colonialism. As an audience appreciatively watching a WTC ceremony or someone that acknowledges Traditional Owners, non-Indigenous people position themselves as 'anti-racist'. Alternatively, rejecting or mocking a WTC or Acknowledgement can establish the viewer as a 'conservative', or a 'racist'.

However tempting these categorisations are, I argue that the meaning of WTC and Acknowledgement rituals extends far beyond a political insignia. In fact, the reason why they are so effective at parsing out political positions is because they are potent commentaries on 'belonging'.[3] The three Acknowledgements I began with are emblematic of conflicting approaches to belonging. The first is a conventional Acknowledgement of the Traditional Owners. The second is an addendum that extends Acknowledgement of Traditional Owners to encompass non-Indigenous origins and ancestors. Baillieu's third welcome emphasises affect and nurture, not traditional ownership, as a basis for belonging, and positions Indigenous people as one group among many. A Welcome penned by another person on the conservative side of politics, that we will discuss below, does not mention Indigenous people at all.

The two 'unconventional' Acknowledgements share a concern to include non-Indigenous people within their ambit. However, I will argue for an important distinction between a defensive Acknowledgement that excludes Indigenous ownership, such as Baillieu's, and an inclusive Acknowledgement of non-Indigenous origins and precursors that coexist with Indigenous ownership, such as mine. An inclusive Acknowledgement can make explicit the unease that Acknowledgements express and generate about sovereignty, belonging, and the provisional unity that is the Australian nation. It can encourage constructive social commentary on the contradictions stitched into the fabric of post-settler Australian society: issues of origins and ownership, inhabiting and belonging, love and labour, a distinctive indigeneity and a common humanity.

Origins and Meanings

Before going further, a word about origins. Some believe the WTC was adapted from the Maori *powhiri*, a ceremony to welcome visitors that includes speeches, singing, a gift to the host and the pressing of noses (*hongi*) (Grant McCall, pers. comm., 14 March 2009). This traditional ceremony has been institutionalised in New Zealand in recent decades, and its function in the bureaucratic domain mirrors the WTC (see Levine 2011).

Anthropologist Katherine Lambert-Pennington (2007) reports that the Welcome ritual emerged in the 1980s, and spread in the 1990s due to encouragement from the Council for Aboriginal Reconciliation. Another origin story emerged in early 2010 when there was widespread coverage of the WTC following comments by the then Australian opposition leader (currently Prime Minister) Tony Abbott that such ceremonies are 'tokenistic'. At that time, actor Ernie Dingo and performer Richard Walley claimed they organised the first WTC ceremony in Perth in 1976. As founders and members of the Middar Aboriginal Theatre, they performed it at the request of visiting Maori and Cook Island dancers after consulting their elders, who advised it was appropriate (O'Brien and Hall 2010). Walley claims the practice spread to the Northern Territory in the 1980s when the Australian Tourism Commission asked a member of the theatre to perform one in Alice Springs. These accounts are all reasonably consistent within each other, suggesting an introduction in the mid-1970s and a subsequent spread.

Other accounts emphasise that a Welcome to Country can be conceptualised as a 'continuous Aboriginal tradition'. Across Australia, a variety of traditional rituals existed for visitors approaching a place, and for receiving visitors into one's country. Anthropologist David Martin, for example, sees elements of the 'classical' rituals performed on 'those unfamiliar with and to the particular tract of country – rubbing on underarm sweat, spraying water into lagoons, calling out to ancestral spirits, speaking in the right language for that country – not so much to welcome the strangers, but to protect them from possible harm from the unfamiliar spirits of the country' (Martin, pers. comm., 27 May 2009). Another common ritual complex for visitors and 'welcomers' was the use of extended silence, whereby visitors would camp on the border of the tract of country and wait for long periods for people associated with that country to acknowledge them (Sutton 2003). Comparable customs are described by the non-government organisation Reconciliation Australia and in anthropological literature (Kirton and Timothy 1977; Reconciliation Australia 2010).

It is appropriate here to mention the origin of this chapter. My enquiry into WTC rituals started as an attempt to help a friend. She is a medical doctor in South Australia and a board member for an outer metropolitan Division of General Practice. Each of their board meetings begins with an Acknowledgement of the Traditional Owners. Although there are undoubtedly living descendants of the tribe they acknowledge, there is no active community. In this case, the Acknowledgement of TOs is 'a memorial'. My friend found it troubling to acknowledge a tribe now presumed to be extinct in the absence of any meaningful engagement with Indigenous people, and wanted some scholarship to bring to a discussion with her fellow board members about whether the Acknowledgement should continue, and what other action they should be taking.

When I sent out an enquiry to the Australian Anthropological Society 'listserv' in 2009 asking for material on this topic, very little published work was suggested (Lambert-Pennington 2007; Everett 2009).[4] However, many anthropologists shared their personal views about WTC ceremonies. In the time since I sent out this call, controversies about Welcome to Country ceremonies have periodically surfaced in the Australian media. My analysis of these rituals draws on these recent debates, the scant academic work on this issue, the email responses to my query, and the research at the centre of this book.

My fieldwork at the Darwin Institute of Indigenous Health did not focus on Welcome to Country or Acknowledgement rituals. While I witnessed plenty of them in the course of my research, I rarely mention them in my field notes.[5] They were so much a part of the landscape of anti-racism that they escaped my critical attention. However, WTCs and Acknowledgements can be understood as an example of the work that White anti-racists do to create and maintain their identities and remain intelligibly 'anti-racist' to Indigenous and non-Indigenous observers. As I have explained, I use the term 'anti-racism' not as an evaluative label identifying people that act in ways that counter racism, but as a culture, discourse and identity, most prominent in educational, academic and bureaucratic settings, that certain people within these settings invest in. This investment may wax and wane over time, but where it exists, it tends to produce a range of behaviours that allow White anti-racists to be recognised and to recognise each other. The job of remaining visibly anti-racist is made difficult because (as discussed in Chapter 2 and explored further in Chapter 6) whiteness itself is a stigma within the spaces of Indigenous affairs, spaces where there is a deliberate attempt to invert colonial power relations.

In this chapter, I approach WTC and Acknowledgement ceremonies as 'anti-racist speech acts' that maintain White identities and manage White stigma by questioning White belonging. I weave discussion of the manifold and conflicting meanings of the rituals into a broader argument about White anti-racist 'performances' and political contestations between conservative and progressive commentators.[6]

Anti-racist Speech Acts

Interpreting Acknowledgements as 'White anti-racist speech acts' draws on an understanding of identity as *performed* through linguistic and non-linguistic means, following sociologist Erving Goffman (1959). He considers a range of subjectivities, from sailor to monarch to woman, to illustrate how people create particular impressions of themselves and how others read those impressions. His analysis of the way we present ourselves to others allows for a complex combination of conscious and unconscious gestures and words, intentional and inadvertent slips in the performance, and the ways that groups maintain their performance of a shared identity.

As I discussed in the Introduction, his use of 'backstage' and 'front stage' are helpful for understanding anti-racism. Backstage, the audience is forbidden and group members can freely interact without the pressure of staying in character. The front stage is the focus of this chapter. Much work goes into ensuring that the (literal or metaphorical) stage looks and sounds consistent with anti-racist subjectivities, whether it is a seminar, conference, or academic publication. A WTC is but one example of the many factors that an anti-racist must keep in mind.

For instance, the number of Indigenous presenters at an event should be at least equal to the number of non-Indigenous presenters – a stage full of White people discussing Indigenous issues is a bad look. However, if some of the people on stage that appear 'White' are in fact Indigenous, any overt, whispered or unspoken criticism from the audience is not a concern, as any such criticism simply portrays the critic as ignorant at best, and racist at worst, for assuming that a pale-skinned person is not Indigenous. Non-Indigenous dark-skinned people are intermediate in their visual impact – better than a White person, but not as good as an Indigenous person. Gender balance is important too – ideally, Indigenous men and Indigenous women should be equally represented. The appearance of White women on stage is slightly better than White men. If there are questions taken from the audience, the facilitator will be keen to call on any Indigenous people that raise their hand to speak, to show they are creating a space where Indigenous voices are heard.

Listing these concerns as I have just done may create the impression that I am trivialising or mocking these efforts, particularly as mocking and trivialising are major pastimes of the conservative press (of which more later). Let me make it clear that I respect the intentions of those who make these efforts, and I recognise that the outcomes of those efforts, for example greater Indigenous participation, are both tangible and important. It must also be stressed that White anti-racists are not constructing these complex algorithms of representation in a vacuum. They are responding to the concerns expressed by Indigenous people (see, for example, Moreton-Robinson 2000; Smith 2012). Making explicit this knowledge of 'how to be an anti-racist' seems somewhat distasteful on the page, although it is acceptable to talk of these things, if obliquely, in conference planning meetings. The techniques required to privilege Indigenous voices are employed tacitly on the 'backstage', and are not for consumption by a public audience.

There are a limited number of people who feel comfortable speaking from a stage to a large audience, and many of those people who are Indigenous are inundated with requests to speak or serve on committees or contribute to publications (particularly in a city the size of Darwin). Consequently, they are liable to refuse a request to speak publicly if it comes from someone they do not know well (particularly as most requests to speak at events, aside from WTCs, are unpaid). If event organisers succeed in producing an appropriate list of presenters on the programme, a Traditional Owner to perform the Welcome to Country, the right balance

of indigeneity, gender, professional background or whatever else is relevant to the event, this is itself an indication of the merits of the organisers.
It demonstrates their ability to recognise what was required, and that their
personal ties to the Indigenous speakers are sufficient for these busy people
to agree to participate. This is, however, far from the end of the story.

In my experience it is not uncommon for speakers to fail to turn
up, or to leave unexpectedly. When these speakers are Indigenous these
absences are most often explained to the audience as 'family issues', or
sometimes 'cultural issues'. With the high rates of illness, death, incar-
ceration, violence and other stressful life events suffered by Indigenous
families, this is not surprising. However, I am interested here in how the
failure of an invited Indigenous presenter to turn up is an opportunity for
White people to further display their anti-racism. This example below
was from a workshop on Indigenous health research I attended. The main
facilitator was an older White man who had a senior position; and Kylie,
who held a mid-level role, was scheduled to present a session:

> He introduces the other facilitators, noting that Kylie had to leave soon
> after arriving this morning: 'She's had some urgent family matters she
> needs to attend to, they were unexpected. She will hopefully join us later
> in the day and we wish her well with her family'.[7]

Through Kylie's absence, the facilitator is able to demonstrate his ability to be culturally sensitive and to be flexible enough to accommodate
Indigenous cultural needs whenever they arise. He is also able to counter
racist generalisations about the unreliability of Indigenous people with
his unselfconscious gesture of sympathy, wishing her well on behalf of all
of us. The mainly White audience had an opportunity to *not* react, to not
blame or judge. Through our neutral listening, we all perform the 'white
ally' (Aveling 2004a). His explicit comments act to silence (but also,
paradoxically, highlight through demonstrating the need to silence) the
ideas that are certainly not voiced, and perhaps barely thought: musings
of whether Kylie really had a family emergency, or perhaps was disorgan-
ised enough to be double-booked, or behind in her paid work, or offended
at being asked to be a 'token black' by the organisers; or maybe she has a
gambling habit and went off to the casino. Some of these imaginings raise
the possibility that her absence is a snub to the organisers, undermining
their implicit claims to have meaningful relationships with Indigenous
people – *because if that were true, Kylie would care enough to attend*. It is
this smoulder of inchoate musings that necessitates the facilitator's careful words. A WTC ceremony similarly plays into this field of racialised
performances.

A similar set of performances was evident at another workshop where a scheduled Indigenous presenter was not able to attend. The main facilitator, again a White man, apologised to the audience as he began the section on Indigenous research methodologies: 'Today I'm the default presenter; it was just not possible for it to be otherwise this morning'.[8]

Effectively, he is apologising for being White, at least in this context. Another Indigenous co-facilitator sits beside him as he clicks through the power-point slides. I am sure he is aware of the negative visual impact of a White man speaking authoritatively about Indigenous knowledge systems while the Indigenous woman next to him remains silent. One can only imagine that he implored her, she whose identity was better suited to the task, to read out the notes accompanying the slides instead of him when the scheduled presenter failed to turn up. But for whatever reason (lack of confidence? lack of familiarity with the material? resentment that she was being asked just because she was Indigenous?), she has declined.

The effort of organising, of trying, but of calmly accepting when it all goes wrong, is also the performance of anti-racism. Unsuccessful anti-racism is perhaps the most common form of anti-racism, perhaps its highest form. It is accepting responsibility and not getting angry, of avoiding blame, of submitting to White stigma, to the inevitability of one's oppressiveness. The 'hidden transcript'[9] goes something like: *Although I am a non-Indigenous person presenting on Indigenous research methodologies, it is not as it seems. I have not sought this role, and I know I shouldn't be here. I'm only here because the Aboriginal people that could present, that in fact co-authored the document I am reading, are not here, for reasons it is not my business to question.* In the contact zones of post-settler colonial Australia, where identity-maintenance is a perennial occupation, even the smallest event is imbued with a range of racialised meanings.

As demonstrated in these examples, White anti-racist people working in Indigenous affairs are often preoccupied with the way they appear to others – specifically, whether they appear to be dominating or 'speaking for' Indigenous people. White people working in Indigenous arenas inhabit an inherently problematic discursive space.[10] In navigating this 'dangerous territory', monitoring one's language is crucial. This quote is from a seminar where a non-Indigenous speaker was explaining how Indigenous organisations developed a comprehensive critique of research practices from the 1980s onwards: 'Aboriginal organisations had grown up – that's a patronising thing to say – had emerged as organisations, were taking control of research'.[11]

The speaker recognised that she had slipped up in using the phrase 'grown up', a phrase that subtly suggests she is in a position of 'parent' to Aboriginal 'children'. Some may think she was being over-vigilant – that

'grown up' is a neutral phrase – but in the context of a White person talking about Indigenous people in public, she was right to expect that at least
some of the audience might have taken offence – either Indigenous people,
or non-Indigenous people on their behalf. Whether or not some people in
the audience would have been offended is beside the point. Through the
opportunity to show her sensitivity to the *possibility* of offence, publicly
admitting her tendency to oppression (in this case through being patronising) and substituting an unquestionably neutral term ('emerged'), she
manages to exhibit her anti-racism. Her slip-up and consummate recov-
ery demonstrate anti-racist attributes that might otherwise be difficult to
exhibit.

This discussion illustrates that WTC and Acknowledgement rituals are
political statements that provide a non-Indigenous person with an opportunity to demonstrate and reinforce an anti-racist identity. An event
organiser who chooses to schedule a WTC is displaying their symbolic
recognition of Indigenous rights. Individual speakers who begin with an
Acknowledgement make a similar personal statement of their anti-racist
credentials. As a political statement, an Acknowledgement can act as a
challenge or an accusation. For example, once the first speaker at a conference does an Acknowledgement, the other speakers in that session must
decide whether to follow suit. For some in an audience, the absence of an
Acknowledgement can make the opposite political statement (whether
or not this is the intent of the non-Acknowledger) – this person does not
recognise Indigenous sovereignty or does not respect Indigenous culture.

I have described how identity maintenance forms a backdrop to White
anti-racist speech acts, so that the failure of an Indigenous person to be
present for a WTC is both a challenge to White anti-racist identities and
an opportunity to bolster them by exhibiting cultural sensitivity. This also
applies at a collective level in the form of intra-community politics that
White anti-racists must negotiate. WTC ceremonies are a key site where
these complexities can play out. As some of those who have organised
WTC ceremonies will know, a WTC can transform from a hopeful political statement into a political nightmare. Contestations among those identifying as Indigenous over traditional ownership of land and over group
membership can make organising a WTC a major exercise in diplomacy.

The dispute between the 'one-n' Ngunawal and the 'two-n' Ngunnawal
Traditional Owners of Canberra is perhaps the best-known example. One
anthropologist told me how a Canberra TO, in order to deflect accusations that she is not Ngunawal, 'started using a new term the Ngunnawal-
Ngambri tribe so non-Aboriginal people have to choose carefully which
name they are using or be co-opted into one side of the dispute'.[12]
Organisers of a WTC at Latrobe University in Wodonga in late 2009

were not careful enough to avoid a public conflict. The WTC for a prominent annual oration erupted into anger when Indigenous members in the audience, who believed the speaker was not a Traditional Owner, loudly interrupted. The controversy concerned Gary Murray, a Melbourne-based academic who is described by *The Border Mail* as a 'Dhudhuroa man' but who himself identifies as a member of the Dhudhuroa, Wamba Wamba, and Dja Dja Wurrung nations. The article reported that 'Campus executive director Lin Crase said it was unfair on the university to be expected to make the right call when Aboriginal people were still divided' (Conroy 2009).

The requirement for Welcomes at many kinds of events has led to the emergence of the WTC ritual as 'an industry'. Several anthropologists who responded to my email enquiry discussed the 'welcome economy'. Traditional Owners who do WTCs in capital cities can be called upon to do them numerous times a week. Two respondents reported that TOs were paid $500 for a Welcome, making them a reasonable source of income. My preliminary research found that the rate was not so generous. NSW Health, for example, pays only $100 for a Welcome; to earn $530, a smoking ceremony is required (NSW Health 2005). More recently, Wurundjeri elder Ian Hunter, a TO of the Melbourne region, complained in the media that the Wurundjeri Council (an organisation he was not affiliated with) was charging up to $850 for a WTC (Masanauskas 2012). Whatever the rate, it is clear the interdependence of city TOs and the academic and bureaucratic classes constitutes an intercultural space par excellence (Merlan 2006).

Tokenism and Conservative Critique

The material I have discussed above, while empirically sound, may be profoundly discomforting for White anti-racists. Revealing the backstage manoeuvrings that support front stage performances can appear to belittle these efforts and provides fodder for conservative commentators, concerns of which I am well aware. However, attempts to conceal these efforts, for example by pretending that Indigenous communities do not have internal divisions or factions, creates its own problems.

The New South Wales health department guidelines on WTCs offer some advice to this effect, suggesting they have had some experience of community conflict. In the event of a dispute over traditional ownership, they recommend 'acknowledg[ing] "all the traditional owners of this land" without naming those people' (NSW Health 2005: 4). This careful approach lays bare some of the contradictions of the practice. By covering over the contemporary disputes over traditional ownership, we present a more 'deserving' subject of Acknowledgement (the anonymous Traditional Owner) at the expense of acknowledging the reality of contemporary Indigenous life, which includes contestations over identity, land affiliation and representation.[13]

Obscuring internal community politics may also invite criticism from conservative commentators. It is likely that a conversative writer such as Keith Windschuttle, editor of Quadrant magazine, would consider NSW Health's Acknowledgement of anonymous TOs to be evidence that the ritual is tokenistic (Windschuttle 2012). Tokenism was a central platform of the public criticism of WTC/Acknowledgement rituals in the wake of Ted Baillieu's decision to make an Acknowledgement of TOs non-mandatory for Victoria's government ministers. Tim Wilson, policy director for the right-wing think tank the Institute of Public Affairs (later appointed by Tony Abbott as the inaugural 'Freedom Commissioner' at the Human Rights Commission), was reported as supporting Baillieu's new policy because 'obsessive acknowledgement can only belittle and undermine the intent of such statements' (Masanauskas and Gillet 2011). Although Wilson's statement is couched in the language of care, many of the 299 comments on the online version of the article are anything but concerned with the efficacy of Acknowledgements in honouring Traditional Owners. Instead, respondents react to the perceived affront of a WTC or Acknowledgement, claiming that Indigenous people are unduly privileged by the government, that they should be grateful for what Western culture has brought to them, and that as 'Australians' it is insulting to be welcomed to their own country (ibid.).

From a different perspective, anthropologist David Trigger has expressed similar concerns about tokenism. He notes that 'not repeating an Acknowledgement (and sometimes not arranging a Welcome) is to try to avoid tokenism. My view is the repetitive Acknowledgements from speakers at a conference is embarrassingly tokenistic and trivialises the important issues at stake' (Trigger, pers. comm., 29 May 2009). A refusal to participate in the Acknowledgement ritual can be a silent protest against 'the hypocrisy underlying an "Acknowledgement" that simply enables whitefellas to publicly position themselves in relation to the "idea" of recognising Aboriginal interests' (Trigger 2009).

While the language of Trigger's concerns about tokenism is similar to that of Tim Wilson, the effects of the two statements diverge. A key difference is the site of their utterance and reproduction. Claims of tokenism in the national conservative newspaper the Herald Sun are a dog-whistle to those who object to the discomforting effect of a WTC and who feel disadvantaged by symbolic and material efforts to address Indigenous disadvantage. Similar claims uttered in the backstage of White anti-racist identity formation, such as a personal email or academic journal article, aim to deconstruct the Acknowledgement's function as a 'White anti-racist speech act' and reveal the discourses of belonging and non-belonging that lie behind it. I will return to this point in the final section of the chapter to argue that opening up these questions of belonging, while inherently risky, is crucial for developing mutual understanding across political and racial divides.

White Anti-racist Narratives and Their Critics

Two groups of Australians have strong feelings about WTC and Acknowledgement rituals. One group are anti-racists, both non-Indigenous and Indigenous, who strongly support these rituals. For example, the former premier of Victoria, Steve Bracks, has stated: 'The thousands and thousands of times I started my speech with an Aboriginal welcome, I always felt very strongly about it' (ABC Online Indigenous News, 19 May 2011). One respondent, commenting on a piece by Indigenous writer Luke Pearson discussed below, argued that an Acknowledgement, like an apology, was the minimum owed to Indigenous people: 'The Aboriginal people – undeservedly – endured the equivalent to apartheid. Outright genocide in places, stolen generation… The list goes on. A symbolic "Acknowledgement" just like the long-awaited "SORRY" is the least we could offer. It doesn't cost a penny and it shouldn't hurt. Anyone who lacks that basic degree of genuine goodwill doesn't deserve to live on this Land'. Another comment discussed the importance of the ritual for reconciliation: 'I believe we can never have a better future for all Australians unless we acknowledge our past and at least show our Indigenous fellow citizens some empathy, compassion and respect'.[14]

These themes point to the function of WTC/Acknowledgement rituals as a kind of 'national psychic Band-Aid' in the same vein as former prime minister Kevin Rudd's apology to the Stolen Generations.[15] The acts of colonial dispossession and violence that founded the settler colony and the racist regimes that followed have created transgenerational psychic wounds among the Indigenous population (Atkinson 2002). These acts mean Australia suffers from a permanent need to transcend the role of perpetrator and smooth over the unheeded calls for Indigenous sovereignty to create a cohesive, caring national narrative (Moses 2011). The Reconciliation Movement as a whole was an important attempt in this direction. The WTC ritual, along with Kevin Rudd's apology to the Stolen Generations, may be the movement's greatest success stories (Johnson 2011).

In responding to the first WTC ever heard in the Australian Parliament on 12 February 2008, Kevin Rudd declared: 'Let this become a permanent part of our ceremonial celebration of the Australian democracy, incorporating the ceremonial of the dreaming from antiquity into the ceremonial of this great democracy' (Rudd 2008). Following Lattas (1993), Everett argues that Rudd's gesture of incorporation serves 'not only to unite the nation, but to appropriate Aboriginal primordial links to the land which cannot otherwise be claimed by the Australian state' (Everett 2009: 55). The WTC ritual is one example of a 'rhetoric of inclusion and reconciliation which [i]s realised symbolically through representations of Aboriginality as accessible and enjoyable cultural forms' (ibid.: 56). WTC rituals are critiqued here as appropriating indigeneity for the benefit of White Australians and the post-settler state while claiming to be inclusive. There is a clear tension here between inclusion and co-option that I will shortly return to.

Another aspect of the therapeutic effect of WTC rituals is enjoyment. Everett describes how '[s]pirited applause, much head nodding and warm smiles are common responses from white audiences to these speeches', particularly when they incorporate Indigenous languages (Everett 2009: 61).[16] Everett, Hart and others suggest that what is enjoyable about WTCs is not (just) the quality of the oration or dance, or the pure pleasure of proximity to the exotic. The nature of a WTC as a symbolic statement of Indigenous ownership means non-Indigenous people can enjoy Indigenous culture and presence without feeling threatened by Indigenous sovereignty. This perhaps explains why WTCs are predominantly a feature of urban Australia, where native title claims are both most unsettling to non-Indigenous Australians and most unlikely to succeed (Hinkson 2003: 302–3). The claims of Indigenous ownership made in a WTC are usually wholly symbolic, with little chance of achieving legal reality.

Nevertheless, from the point of view of TOs, a WTC can be a quasi land claim. In the case of the Darug people of Sydney, who have been unsuccessful in their native title claims, Everett argues that 'the making of symbolic land claims is an important way to publicly make their claims known and gain some recognition of the cultural foundation of those claims from Australian society' (Everett 2009: 58).

In combination, these complementary roles of quasi land claim and symbolic statement of ownership create a paradox: 'The welcoming that occurs is done *by* those whose claims to prior ownership of that place have already been denied *to* those who already inhabit that place and do not recognise the claims of others [that is, non-Indigenous Australians as representative of the Australian state]' (ibid.: 57). A WTC ceremony performed at a political event and described by a journalist illustrates this paradox: 'The elder actually said: When you give me my country back, then I'll welcome you to my country. Oblivious to the subversion, a succession of politicians and dignitaries took to the microphone and thanked them for the welcome. What a farce. No one had noticed the politicians breezily not noticing the actual words of the ceremony' (Shepherd 2011).

It is useful to consider recent theories of settler colonialism here. Cultural theorist Lorenzo Veracini argues that the founding principle of settler colonialism is the desire for Indigenous people to 'go away', to cease to exist and make room for the settlers. He identifies 'a recurring need to disavow the presence of Indigenous "others"' as the centrepiece of settler colonial thought (Veracini 2011: 2). Further, the desire for Indigenous disappearance is not only expressed through conventional means of physical or cultural genocide, but also through equality, recognition and reconciliation. These processes, which are generally seen as positive, ultimately act to assimilate Indigenous people into mainstream society: 'sanctioning the equal rights of Indigenous peoples has historically been used as a powerful weapon in the denial of Indigenous entitlement and in the enactment of various forms of coercive assimilation' (ibid.: 8).

Indigenous studies scholar Victor Hart echoes Veracini's argument when he considers WTC rituals to be a form of 'epistemological violence': 'the violence comes from knowing that Welcome to Country is an iteration of terra nullius mythology where Blackfellas can appear at the beginning of the event (i.e. the beginning of history) and then conveniently disappear whilst Whitefellas do their serious "business"' (Hart, pers. comm., 15 April 2009). Kristina Everett documents one instance when Darug TOs refused to 'conveniently disappear' at an event in Sydney. During a re-enactment of a frontier scene when settlers shot natives, Darug 'natives' remained on the stage long after their cue to leave: 'Voices speaking Darug language kept calling from the shrubbery, and a parade of dancers appeared moaning, groaning, clutching their stomachs, their heads, their hearts and then "dying" on the lawn of Old Government House', causing intense embarrassment to those present (Everett 2009: 62). By disrupting the narrative set by the WTC ritual – welcoming, then exiting – the Darug people exceeded and thus revealed the limits of recognition provided by the post-settler state (see Chapter 5).

Affronting White Identities

For those who hold generally conservative views, intense feelings of discomfort do not only occur when WTC ceremonies take unexpected turns. This group of Australians feels intense discomfort at any form of WTC or Acknowledgement.[17] Although progressive commentators, like one cited above, believe that an Acknowledgement 'shouldn't hurt', for many conservative Australians they do.

In the terms I have discussed here, it is the function of WTC and Acknowledgements as a 'national psychic Band-Aid' that is the most irksome for conservative Australians. For conservative commentators such as Andrew Bolt, the suggestion that there is anything to heal or apologise for is abhorrent – the only thing that requires an apology is the besmearing of Australian governments and the populace by accusing them of racism. To people like Bolt, WTC ceremonies are an insult to the Australian state and people and a racist mechanism of division. As the byline of an article he wrote in the *Herald Sun* succinctly puts it: 'Welcome to Country ceremonies are racist and anything but welcoming to non-Aborigines who were born right here'. He argues that WTC ceremonies and Acknowledgements 'betray the principles which gave life to the society in which we are so blessed to live' and offers an alternative wording, acknowledging 'that we meet on land that is yours, mine and every Australian's' (Bolt 2010).

Bolt is concerned here that WTC and Acknowledgement rituals make certain Australians feel unwelcome and leave their contributions to Australian society unacknowledged. A Welcome makes Bolt and his supporters feel unwelcome because their sense of belonging is severely threatened by the presence of Indigenous claims. Bolt responds with a universal gesture that acknowledges all Australians and does not give any special status to Indigenous people. This is similar to Baillieu's welcome, quoted in the opening of this chapter, although Baillieu does mention Indigenous people, if only as a subset of all Australians who 'love this land'.

Responding constructively to such critiques is a challenge for antiracists. It is tempting to respond to Bolt's accusation of racism in kind. Indigenous writer Luke Pearson provides an example in his response to Ted Baillieu's decision to make an Acknowledgement non-compulsory for Victoria's government ministers. His comments reiterate the function of a WTC as an 'anti-racist speech act' and view the accusation of tokenism as a positive attribute:

> Any Minister who doesn't want to perform an Acknowledgement of Country is saying that they have such contempt for Aboriginal people, accurate Australian history and modern Australian values that they refuse to make even the smallest gesture of goodwill and respect. They don't care that Aboriginal cultures are the oldest living cultures on Earth … They do not care about the massacre sites that are scattered across their State. They

do not care about the Stolen Generations, Aboriginal Deaths in Custody or about 'Closing the Gap'. They do not care about their own failure to provide adequate services and outcomes for their Aboriginal constituents, or for the many Victorians who support their State moving from oppression to respect, and from ignoring their Aboriginal history to celebrating it. These politicians do not respect Aboriginal people anywhere in Australia, or the millions of Australians who believe that this tiny gesture is not only essential, but nowhere near enough. It is a TOKEN gesture. It is meant to be a symbol of respect and understanding. (Pearson 2010)

While I have sympathy for Pearson's position, I do not think that this response is sufficient. By focusing on an Acknowledgement as a performance that positions the speaker as someone who cares about Indigenous people, Pearson accurately describes the ritual from an anti-racist perspective (similar to the analysis I offered above), but he fails to respond adequately to the source of conservative critiques. Pearson effectively rallies to the cause those who are already anti-racist, and invites them to share his view that those who do not wish to perform an Acknowledgement are essentially racist. Many of the hundreds of online comments on Baillieu's WTC decision strongly object to the contention that they are racist if they support him, and some make the counter claim that WTC ceremonies are racist because they divide Australians into 'Indigenous' and 'non-Indigenous' categories (Masanauskas and Gillet 2011). We are left with a stalemate: two camps calling each other racist.

Acknowledging Discomfort

In concluding this chapter, I want to suggest an alternative response to these critiques. This response must begin with the acknowledgement that a WTC ceremony raises difficult questions about settler belonging and the unfinished business of social justice for Indigenous people. Some contributors to the debate recognise that this is the whole point of the rituals. For example, one comment on Luke Pearson's article argues that 'acknowledging the Traditional Owners of any part of Australia is common courtesy and a mark of sympathy and respect. If it makes Mr Ballieu uncomfortable it is probably doing its job as well... those who do feel uncomfortable probably should. That's the beginning of understanding'.[18] Stephanie Convery makes a similar point:

> The truth is, there *is* a disconnect between political symbolism and action on Indigenous issues in Australia. The recognition of traditional owners, the welcome to country, is essential if only because it draws attention to

this disconnect. It reminds the non-Indigenous listener of the fact of their colonial heritage, of the continued existence of Indigenous people and culture, and their direct relationship to everyone who calls themselves Australian. Or at least, it should. (Convery 2010)

This reminder is precisely what Bolt wants to avoid; and precisely what White anti-racist Australians want to embrace. For conservatives, belonging depends on denying any claims to Indigenous sovereignty (whether real or symbolic); for anti-racists, belonging depends on continually being reminded of such claims.

We return here to the concept of White stigma, that I will explore further in Chapter 6. White belonging is a source of stigma for anti-racists: their very presence on the Australian continent stands as a constant reminder of Indigenous dispossession. The unsettling effect of a WTC or Acknowledgement ritual is experienced as satisfying because it affirms existing discomfort. *You do not belong here, you came here without consent,* the WTC tells us. *You need to be welcomed because you have made yourself welcome.* For conservatives, this subtext is highly offensive because it stigmatises White identity and negates their mode of belonging. For anti-racists, this speech act, whether received from an Indigenous speaker or self-spoken, has the effect of acknowledging and thus lessening the White stigma already keenly felt. Through stigmatising whiteness in a collective and public fashion, the White anti-racist paradoxically finds a more comfortable mode of belonging to the settler state.

White anti-racists can be dismissive of conservative anxieties about WTCs because they experience them as affirming their sense of belonging, and also because the act of dismissing them sets them apart from the 'racist' White people they seek to distinguish themselves from. But dismissing as racist those who feel uncomfortable with WTC ceremonies will do nothing to promote understanding of Indigenous issues among those I identified as 'conservatives' in Chapter 3 – people who are likely to agree with Ted Baillieu and make up a significant minority of Australians. Instead, anti-racists should be prepared to engage with the discomfort that WTC ceremonies can induce.

Through engaging with these anxieties, we have a better chance at addressing them. In public conversation with Michael Williams, Director of the Aboriginal and Torres Strait Islander Studies Unit at the University of Queensland in 2009, David Trigger suffixed an Acknowledgement of TOs with an acknowledgement of 'the strength of purpose, skills and tenacity of the generations of settlers and migrants from Europe, Asia and elsewhere who have historically created the society into which I was born' (Trigger 2009).[19] In this way he sought to take the lead from a

Nyungar TO who explained in a Welcome that non-Indigenous people can eventually 'belong' to the country, 'provided Aboriginal "protocols" are understood and followed' (Trigger 2008: 307). I will leave aside the question of whether non-Indigenous people can 'belong' to the country,[20] and focus instead on the idea that WTC and Acknowledgement rituals can open up such questions.

In supplementing an Acknowledgement of TOs with an acknowledgement of settler and more recent migrant contributions, one could argue that Trigger is mimicking Bolt and downgrading the importance of TOs. However, while Bolt's defensive gesture is designed as a criticism of the WTC ritual which he openly says should be abolished, Trigger's Acknowledgement and, for that matter, mine, are intended as *a device to encourage reflection on belonging*. In our case, settlers and migrants are mentioned as an addendum to an Acknowledgement of TOs, not as a replacement.

To be certain, including settlers within the bounds of an Acknowledgement risks downgrading the recognition of Indigenous people (symptomatic of the wider challenges of reshaping White and Indigenous identities discussed in the Conclusion). It undermines the function of the ritual as an 'anti-racist speech act', and threatens one's own recognition as an anti-racist. As I see it, this risk is worth taking. The alternative is to suppress, and thus strengthen, the highly charged emotions of belonging and non-belonging that these rituals engender. Both anti-racists and conservatives would prefer to conceal these challenges to White belonging: anti-racists would prefer not to mention settlers, and conservatives prefer not to mention TOs, or mention them only in passing.

This alternative approach to the Acknowledgement ritual may be slowly gaining ground. My own addendum quoted in the opening of this chapter was inspired, in fact, by Acknowledgements I have heard given by Indigenous academic Professor Ngiare Brown. The University of Canberra official welcome, which is attributed to the United Ngunnawal Elders Council website, also suggests a similar addendum. Their website advises: 'You may wish to add, "I acknowledge the ancestors, kin and future generations of all people present"'.[21]

These examples of WTC and Acknowledgement rituals highlight their function as 'a device to encourage reflection on belonging'. When such incorporative gestures are made without the defensive note of Andrew Bolt, they enhance this effect. I consider this to be the most constructive meaning that can be gleaned from WTC and Acknowledgement rituals. They create an opportunity to consider who 'belongs' in any given part of Australia. To make the most of this opportunity, the contradictions inherent in WTCs and Acknowledgement performances must be acknowledged, and not played down.

White anti-racists would usefully recognise the role that these rituals play for them, as well as the threat the rituals pose to others who are not invested in an anti-racist identity. Conservatives should accept that national pride is not a zero-sum game: one can acknowledge Indigenous traditional ownership while maintaining pride in the achievements of settler and migrant Australians. A reluctance to acknowledge Indigenous prior occupation and continuous links to land reflects an insecure mode of belonging to the nation. At the heart of these debates are deeper questions about who has entitlement to occupy this continent, and the plight of the descendants of those who witnessed the first wave of European settlers over two centuries ago. Both the popularity of the Welcome to Country ritual, and the ongoing controversy it produces, show that anxieties about belonging remain central to Australian identity.

Notes

1. I have even heard a Welcome to Country delivered at the start of a radio programme, implying that a physical place to welcome a physical audience to is not necessarily required. See http://www.abc.net.au/rn/awaye/stories/2009/2680820.htm.

2. The argument made in this chapter that WTC ceremonies challenge the sense of belonging for non-Indigenous Australians may also apply to Indigenous Australians who are not Traditional Owners of a particular area. However, this possibility is beyond the scope of this chapter.

3. Some key works on 'belonging' and Australian identity include Gelder and Jacobs 1998; Hage 1998, 2003; Moreton-Robinson 2003; Moran 2005a, 2005b; and Elder 2007.

4. Papers relating to this topic published and found since then are Kowal 2010; Cowlishaw 2011; Dempster 2007; Merlan 2014; and McAuley 2009.

5. The only explicit mention of Welcome to Country ceremonies in my field notes is a colleague suggesting that Indigenous people think 'you shouldn't do the welcome to country thing. Some of them say, "well it doesn't mean anything, you shouldn't just do it"' [Field Notes, 21 Sept. 2004]. The fact that only a critique of WTC ceremonies struck me as worth recording demonstrates how normalised they were as a part of anti-racist experience.

6. The terminology of 'progressives' and 'conservatives' refer to Australians that identify with views that are typically classified as left-wing or progressive (such as pro-choice and collective bargaining), and right-wing or conservative (such as reducing welfare and reducing tax), respectively. Views in relation to Indigenous issues are particularly relevant here: 'progressives' are likely to support land rights, reconciliation, affirmative action and compensation; 'conservatives' are likely to oppose them. In this chapter they are used as heuristic categories that are necessarily generalising.

Individual Australians may see themselves as conservative on some issues and progressive on others, or may identify with both or neither of those labels. As explained in Chapter 3, 'progressives' are a large group of Australians within which 'anti-racists' are a subset.

7. Field Notes, 16 Sept. 2004. Note that Kylie's main employment as a senior project officer was with another organisation. Her role here was to discuss a policy she had helped to develop for the research organisation running the workshop. She was not specifically paid for this but it would have been seen as part of her job.

8. Field Notes, 19 Jul. 2004.

9. Scott uses Orwell's short story 'Shooting an Elephant' to argue that the 'hidden transcript' of domination is that the powerful are as imprisoned by oppression as the oppressed. They differ from the oppressed in that when they defy their transcript they risk 'only ridicule' rather than violence. In this context, my work explores the hidden transcripts of the liberatory discourses of the powerful (Scott 1990: 10–11).

10. Muecke describes how his right to speak at a 'Black Literature' conference in 1986 was questioned: 'It seems to me that I already knew as I wrote the paper for that conference that the only Aboriginal response would be one that challenged my right to speak, which is also my right to listen, to move around, to speak at conferences, and so on. Even though I was talking only on my own terrain [about the experience of publishing Indigenous people's stories], the political and performance aspects of my own speech had led me into dangerous territory' (Muecke 2005: 48).

11. Field Notes, 20 Sept. 2004.

12. This person requested to remain anonymous. Personal communication, 26 Apr. 2009. See also Dauth 2011.

13. Such contestations are documented in the anthropological literature. See, for example, Adams 2002; Sanders 2004; Batty 2005; and Tonkinson 2007.

14. Comments made by 'Sonny' and 'Confused2' (ABC 2010).

15. The apology, performed the same day as the first WTC to occur in the Australian Parliament, concerned Aboriginal and Torres Strait Islander people who were removed from their families into state institutions for much of the twentieth century (Human Rights and Equal Opportunity Commission 1997). For scholarship on the apology, see for example Mookherjee et al. 2009; Moses 2011; Johnson 2011; and Short 2012.

16. Another example of enjoyment is provided by another comment on the ABC online page mentioned earlier: 'I like the practice of paying my respects to local people. When it first came into common practice I was a little embarrassed to do it but it felt good and right to do, so I continued. When I spoke at an international conference at an overseas venue a few years ago I automatically paid my respects to the local people. It was interesting to see how it lifted everyone's spirits up, people commented later on what a lovely practice it was and what a nice society Australia must be to acknowledge each other respectfully.' Bunyip, http://www.abc.net.au/unleashed/2722866.html.

17. On the online poll of the biggest-selling national newspaper that usually presents a conservative viewpoint, 65 per cent of 2,500 voters agreed with the statement that 'Ted Baillieu was right to reduce the Acknowledgement of Aboriginal land owners at official events'. http://www.heraldsun.com.au/news/premier-ted-baillieu-drops-compulsory-aboriginal-welcome/story-e6frf7jo-1226058528404. This suggests that a large minority of Australians, if not a majority, are uncomfortable with Acknowledgements.

18. Comments on Pearson 2010.
19. Trigger's separate citation of settlers and migrants raises the question of how the two categories are defined. Trigger and Mulcock (2005) argue that 'settlers' are those that can trace their ancestry to the early migrants to Australia, and 'migrants' are those who have arrived more recently or are descended from these recent arrivals. However, the temporal marker of 'recent' arrival is far from clear. I tend to subsume the category of migrants into 'settlers', perhaps as I am interested in those Australians that see themselves as 'settlers' in Aboriginal land, whether their ancestors arrived on the First Fleet or they arrived last week. However, this distinction warrants further analysis.
20. Trigger (2009) argues that non-Indigenous people may be able to acquire a form of indigeneity 'through birth in the country, birth of forebears here, and/or a sense of emplaced identity with the land, the cities, the suburbs'.
21. http://www.canberra.edu.au/blogs/dvce/2010/07/16/welcome-to-country-and-acknowledgement-of-country/.

Chapter 5

MUTUAL RECOGNITION

꘎꘎꘎ • ꘎꘎꘎

It was the job of many institute employees to collect all kinds of data about Indigenous people – accounts of illnesses experienced, exercise habits or cigarettes consumed, samples of bodily fluids (mostly blood and urine), nasal swabs, eye or ear examinations, as well as qualitative accounts of experiences of health care services or understandings of child development. 'Participation' was a common topic of corridor conversations. Most projects had lower than expected numbers of participants. While senior researchers were generally supportive of their staff's efforts and resigned themselves to lower numbers, this could threaten the integrity of their data set and hence their ability to produce meaningful results. Team meetings of projects in the data collection phase would often brainstorm new ways to increase data collection that fell within the bounds of their existing ethical approval. Researchers working on different projects compared participation rates in the tea room and debated the merits of seeking ethical approval to approach Indigenous people in their homes ('door-to-door recruitment') rather than wait at the health centre for potential participants to show up, or hire a bus to ferry people to the clinic.[1]

Rates of participation were not just a matter of whether a project was able to produce meaningful results to improve Indigenous health and to produce scientific publications (both important end points for researchers). Like many other aspects of working in Indigenous affairs, failure or success in attracting research participants affected the subjectivities of White anti-racists. We saw in Chapter 2 how low participation rates could be a trigger for unravelling remediable difference and unleashing fears that addressing disadvantage may be an extension of the colonial assimilationist project. As one researcher put it, 'if it hasn't been taken up well and the community don't own it, well do they really want it?' From this perspective, research projects are an imposition on Indigenous communities – a hindrance rather than a help.

Low rates of participation can raise other questions about anti-racist identities, less dramatic but equally disturbing. Did Indigenous people decline to participate because the tasks requested by researchers were culturally inappropriate; or because the processes for obtaining consent were intrusive? Were some community members unhappy that a member of a competing family was recruited to assist with data collection? Or perhaps community members were not comfortable around the researcher and avoided him or her? These and other possible scenarios show how low rates of participation might threaten anti-racist identities.

One way of managing these implicit accusations was for researchers to point the finger themselves. In one discussion about participation, a researcher proposed that health screenings at a community be organised by clan groups of Indigenous people on behalf of Institute researchers: 'The best thing is to get clan groups to tender for it. Like for a screening, to get fifty people screened you pay them $10,000 if they get the job done in three months. And you need to pay people for their participation too'.[2]

This comment, made in a research meeting by a project officer with a decade of experience in remote community nursing, was met with vague murmurs of assent. It is a reasonably radical suggestion that remote community members (where the average level of Western education is low) can be trained to conduct something as specialised as a health screening with a level of independence and precision that warrants the remuneration she suggests. Paying research participants is another sticky issue – ethics committees frown on what they see as 'inducements' to participate for the wrong reasons. In the semi-public context in which the comment was made, however, any questioning of the comment would put the questioner in danger of being construed as a racist. For why else would one argue that remote Indigenous people are not capable of running a health screening? The comment provided an opportunity for the speaker and those listening (who on this occasion were all non-Indigenous) to be *recognised* as anti-racist.

To discuss the recognition of White people is at odds with the bulk of the recognition literature that focuses on minority groups.[3] This is doubtless because state recognition of *White* people is rarely an issue. Indigenous people and minorities must struggle for equal rights and special measures, granted or withheld by dominant political structures, while White citizens are unmarked by race and seen as 'normal'. However, the concept of recognition is a broad theme reaching beyond the strictly 'political' to explore how identities, epistemologies and ontologies are shaped by relations with the state and through interpersonal encounters. For centuries, philosophy has considered the basic acts of recognition that make human society possible. In the words of political theorist Patchen Markell, life is a constant stream of call and response: 'Who are you? Who am I? Who are we? In answering these questions, we locate ourselves and others in social space, simultaneously taking notice of and reproducing relations of difference and identity' (Markell 2009: 1).

In this wider sense of recognition, White people are 'recognised' in their everyday encounters. We can think of recognition as the mechanism of White privilege. In stores, classrooms, on public transport, in the justice system, and countless other settings, White people are recognised as 'normal' and receive different treatment to non-Whites, usually preferential.[4]

White anti-racists, however, are invested in particular forms of recognition that differ from everyday White privilege. As we have seen in the chapters so far, many anti-racists wish to be recognised as 'good' White people that differ from the 'racist' norm. This chapter shows how White anti-racists and Indigenous people recognise themselves and each other through a series of intersecting performances. It has been well established in the literature that Indigenous people are subject to conditional recognition by the state and the dominant majority. This chapter shows that White anti-racists are also conditionally recognised. A range of behaviours can be interpreted as manoeuvres to stay within the bounds of the space of recognition or negotiate its boundaries.

I first outline the problem of recognition in liberal democracies, arguing that this problem is constitutive of liberal thought. Liberal inclusion has contained exclusions since the beginning. Recognition and inclusion of non-White, non-male, non-propertied others has occurred cumulatively and has often involved creating exclusions from exclusions: in early twentieth-century Australia some Indigenous people could be granted citizenship, but only under specific circumstances.[5] Claims for wider Indigenous recognition in Australia were first based on the recognition of equality – of sameness – but since the late 1960s have shifted to the recognition of essential difference. This mirrors a global shift that has been theorised as the rise of the 'politics of recognition'. Anthropologists and political theorists have used the concept of 'conditional recognition' to describe how difference is circumscribed in the process of being recognised. The paradox (or, in Povinelli's terms, the 'cunning') of recognition is that minorities must submit to external and always partial definition in order to access rights from dominant states (Povinelli 2002b).

Recognising Difference

The problem of recognising difference within modern democratic states can be traced to the origins of liberal thought. Liberal theorists of the seventeenth and eighteenth centuries such as Locke, Voltaire, Rousseau, Kant, Hume and Jefferson all argued for democratic government that represented the interests of the people. Their ideas of equality among 'ordinary' men were radical at the time and led to modern liberal democracies. However, many groups of people were excluded from the civil rights offered by these governments, including slaves, women, minority religious and ethnic groups, and colonised peoples.

The exclusion of Indigenous peoples by the Australian government is a case in point. Although Indigenous people were officially considered British subjects by virtue of their birthplace, and were included in the creation of the 'Australian citizen' in 1948, they were excluded from voting by the newly formed Commonwealth government in 1902 (a right only reinstated in 1962). A plethora of further exclusions of 'aboriginal natives' (along with 'natives' of Asian and Pacific countries) in various pieces of state legislation created second-class citizens who did not enjoy the rights of 'normal' citizenship (Chesterman and Galligan 1997). Myriad pieces of legislation enacted in the early decades of the last century placed Aboriginal movements, employment and marriages under state control.

For example, in Western Australia in 1944, an act came into effect that allowed Aboriginal people to apply for a 'Certificate of Citizenship', exempting them from Aboriginality and entitling them to full citizenship rights. This certificate could be granted provided that a magistrate was satisfied that they had not had any contact with other Indigenous people and had led a 'civilized life' for the preceding two years; that full citizenship rights were 'desirable for and likely to be conducive to the welfare of the applicant'; and that the person was fluent in English, had no communicable diseases, and was 'of industrious habits ... good behaviour and reputation ... and reasonably capable of managing his own affairs'.[6] In this shopping list of citizenship we see the multiple qualifications on which exclusion can be based. Rather than exclusions and inequality being unfortunate and temporary obstacles to the project of modernity, some scholars argue that liberalism is constitutively exclusive. Uday Mehta analyses Locke's *Second Treatise of Government* to explore the possibility that exclusion is 'an aspect of [liberalism's] theoretical underpinning and not merely an episodic compromise with the practical constraints of implementation' (Mehta 1999: 48).

Those many groups denied the rights initially granted to propertied men have fought for equal rights from the nineteenth century to the present. For the majority of that time, these battles have been fought on the grounds of 'sameness'. That is, Indigenous and other subjugated peoples argued that they were equal to White men and thus should be treated the same way. The early phases of the Aboriginal rights movement in the 1920s and 1930s that fought against discriminatory laws and practices provide examples. Fred Maynard, president of the Australian Aboriginal Progressive Association (formed in 1924 in Sydney) wrote in a letter to the then prime minister: 'Our people have ... accepted the modern system of government which has taken the place of our prehistoric methods and have conformed to the same reasonably well when the treatment accorded them is fully considered. We are, therefore, striving to obtain full recognition of our citizen rights on terms of absolute equality with all other people in our own land' (Attwood and Markus 1999: 68). Acceptance on the grounds of sameness was tied to the obsolescence of Indigenous culture ('our prehistoric methods'), a reference to the epistemology of racial hierarchies (Stocking 1968; Anderson 2002).

By the 1970s, the language of the Indigenous movement in Australia had changed. As the battles for formal equality were progressively won, the discourse of difference became more prominent. Rather than arguing for *equal* treatment on the basis of sameness, arguments were made for *special* treatment on the grounds of difference (Stokes 1997; Rowse 2000; McGregor 2011). Today, 'difference' is the dominant discourse of Indigenous social justice. In this discourse of difference, 'social inclusion' (the most recent policy buzzword) is tied to the maintenance of cultural distinctiveness rather than its obsolescence – a deliberate rejection of the racial hierarchies of an earlier scientific era (McGregor 1997, 2011). As I argued in Chapter 2, indigeneity as unique and inalienable difference is intrinsic to the belief system shared by many White anti-racists.

This discursive shift reflects global cultural movements. As scholars as diverse as Slavoj Zizek, Stuart Hall, Judith Butler and John Gray have theorised, the collapse of universalism in the second half of the twentieth century has created a seemingly variegated landscape of power (Zizek 1993; Hall 1994; Butler 1997; Gray, Bagramanian, and Ingram 2000).

Knowledge and identities are now presumed to be culturally specific, leaving liberal nation-states and transnational organisations to chart a course to peaceful coexistence without the benefit of a transcendental rationality. In contrast to earlier attempts by Western states to govern minorities, contemporary approaches must value cultural difference and recognise the impact of the colonial past. Scholars are divided, however, on whether these new relationships between more empowered minorities and more sympathetic states offer a positive progression in the history of liberal governance, more of the same, or a turn for the worse.

This political terrain has been explored through 'the politics of recognition' (Taylor 1994; Fraser 2000; Povinelli 2002).[7] Charles Taylor describes the politics of recognition as the result of a tension in liberal values between 'universal dignity' and 'authentic identity'. The principle of universal dignity leads to equal citizenship, 'an identical basket of rights and immunities' (Taylor 1994: 39). In contrast, the politics of authentic identity require that one's distinctiveness be recognised and preserved. Measures to help disadvantaged minorities based on 'universal dignity' will act to improve the universal human rights of each member of the group, while measures based on 'authentic identity' will seek to maintain group distinctiveness over time.

On the surface, it may seem relatively simple to allow people to maintain differences through generations without threatening basic 'universal' values upheld by dominant society. But when the merits of difference from the norm are acknowledged, relativist tensions immediately slip in. If, in order to preserve a Quebecois identity (to use Taylor's example) Quebec forbids children from non-Anglophone families from attending English schools and hence from learning English, will they not suffer unnecessary difficulties in life from being denied a chance to learn the 'universal' language?

In addressing this tension, political theorist Will Kymlicka (1995) argues for a distinction between 'external protections' and 'internal restrictions'. External protections grant cultural and linguistic minorities special rights not available to others (such as university quotas), exemption from universal obligations (such as military service), and a degree of autonomy. This is necessary for the equal enjoyment of life for cultural minorities. Internal restrictions that limit the right of minority group members to exercise their own freedoms, however, should not be tolerated in a liberal society. These basic freedoms include a measure of autonomy, choices between worthwhile options, and the right to dissent or opt out of the minority group. For liberal democracies, cultural distinctiveness is at once a prerequisite for individual freedoms and a potential threat. The difficult task of a liberal majority is to judge which cultural norms are necessary for the survival of a minority culture and the freedom of its members, and which impinge upon freedom and choice (Kymlicka 1995: Ch. 3). The result is that some differences of minority groups are recognised and valued, while some are ignored or suppressed. This process has been conceptualised as 'conditional recognition', or alternatively, as a 'space of recognition' into which the subaltern must fit.

The anthropological literature provides some useful examples of conditional recognition. Li shows how recognition of Indigenous groups by international conservation NGOs in Indonesia depends upon their traditional cultural practices being compatible with conservation principles (Li 2003: 388; Li 2007). Cowlishaw describes how a government-funded cattle station that aimed to provide employment came undone because Indigenous people did not sufficiently distinguish public from private: 'inappropriate' use of station vehicles resulting in their destruction was a turning point in government support for the cattle station (Cowlishaw 1999: 246–47). Povinelli argues that Indigenous 'customary law' is recognised by Australian common law on the proviso that Indigenous practices are not 'repugnant' to Australian law. She concludes that the 'cunning of recognition' is in the state requirement that Aborigines be different enough to deserve special consideration (such as Indigenous land rights), but not different enough to lie outside of Australian law. If customary law was radically different to common law, it would 'shatter [its] skeletal structure'. Indigenous people have to be different enough to be recognised as such, but not so different that they are too alien to be recognised (Povinelli 2002).[8] This is another iteration of the concepts of remediable difference and radical difference set out in Chapter 2. Remediable difference falls within the bounds of conditional recognition, and radical difference lies outside it.

Anthropologist Anna Tsing provided a vivid example of inhabiting spaces of recognition in the figure of the tribal elder. Her study of international environment NGOs and locals in Southern Kalimantan, Indonesia, features Yuni, Musa and Sumiati, a family of 'tribal elders' who are largely responsible for the success of the village in attracting numerous development projects. She describes a photograph of Yuni at a development conference that took place in the village. In the photograph he appears 'serious and neatly dressed but awkward, innocently out of place, standing as if on display between the audience rows' (Tsing 1999: 171). In this image, we see Yuni inhabiting the 'space of recognition' shaped by development discourses, a space that constructs him as 'the open, desiring subject of an imagined modernity yet with the untutored simplicity of tradition in his background and breeding. He is a tribesman longing for change' (ibid.).

This and other accounts suggest the politics of recognition are constituted by the creation of spaces (both abstract and material) where subalterns can be recognised and receive the resources associated with recognition. The processes of creating and inhabiting a space of recognition, for instance as a tribal elder, are contested and constantly negotiated, featuring both complicity and resistance, and result in the formation of new identities. Tsing calls this theatre of recognition 'the field of attraction', and sees her anthropological project as one of fleshing out 'the longings, the broken promises, the erotic draw, and the magic … that makes the tribal elder emerge as a politically active and creative figure' (Tsing 1999: 167). As we will see, the recognition of Indigenous subjectivities at the institute is a similarly charged 'field of attraction'.

Another way to approach this 'field of attraction' is as a site of multiple interpellations. As philosopher Louis Althusser described it, interpellation is the mechanism by which an ideology (a set of dominant ideas) constitutes concrete individuals as subjects. The classic example is the policeman calling out 'Hey, you!' in the street. The person that turns to see if they have been called (or perhaps starts running) is in that moment 'interpellated' as a subject, in this case as a potential criminal. A friend similarly interpellates you as a subject by calling your name, reaching out to shake your hand; or if they do not yet know you, assuming you have a name and asking what it is (Althusser 1971). The field of recognition can be understood as a site of multiple interpellations, where subalterns are interpolated as oppressed and powerless people needing and worthy of assistance. The creation of spaces of recognition and the process of inhabiting these spaces are two distinct but interrelated processes. Subalterns can refuse these spaces, or exploit and transgress them, ever testing the limits of recognition.[9]

Reconceiving the politics of recognition as the politics of *mutual* recognition requires a key conceptual shift here. At the same time that minorities seek recognition of their distinct cultures and interests, certain members of the dominant group seek recognition as anti-racist subjects. To take Tsing's example, just as tribal elders are interpellated as powerless and deserving, donor and development workers are interpellated as compassionate, generous and anti-racist. In both cases, those seeking recognition must fit the spaces allocated to them in order to remain recognisable, but may simultaneously push the boundaries of recognition.[10] White anti-racists at the institute seek to be recognised (by Indigenous people and by other White anti-racists) as culturally sensitive, mindful of the structural and historical oppression of Indigenous people, respectful of Indigenous difference, and, above all, *not* racist or assimilationist.

My use of the term 'mutual recognition' does not imply symmetry in power relations. White anti-racists have the choice of seeking recognition as 'anti-racists' or fading into the 'invisibility' of dominant whiteness (McIntosh 1990).[11] Conversely, most Indigenous people have no choice but to grapple with the conditional space of recognition on offer.[12] The main argument of this book, however, is that the recognition of White anti-racism powerfully shapes the way Indigenous disadvantage is conceived and addressed. The 'voluntariness' of these processes does not undermine their importance.

An example of mutual recognition illustrating both sides of this interpellative field is found in Vincanne Adams' study of Nepalese Sherpas that explores relationships between Sherpas, tourists, mountain climbers and development workers. Western tourists grant recognition to Sherpas as skilful mountain climbers of unlimited endurance with an unquenchable desire to please, and Sherpas form themselves, more or less, to fit these spaces of recognition. In a simultaneous process that has received less attention, Sherpas create spaces in which Westerners can be recognised as what she calls 'patrons', with Westerners shaping themselves accordingly. She tells stories of Westerners hosting visiting Sherpa friends for extended visits to the West, and complex relationships of sponsorship that begin with a tourist visit and continue for decades. She explores how aspects of Sherpa culture, particularly Tibetan Buddhism and Shamanism, have shaped the processes of 'seduction' through which Sherpas keep Westerners in their orbits (Adams 1996).

The model of recognition I elaborate in this chapter comprises four interconnected and constantly negotiated processes: spaces of recognition are created for Indigenous people, who inhabit them, and spaces of recognition for White anti-racists are created, and inhabited by them. The focus of this account is how White anti-racists inhabit spaces of recognition. However, because White anti-racists seek recognition partly by recognising Indigenous people, I also discuss the construction of Indigenous spaces of recognition.

In the remainder of this chapter, I explore scenes from the institute as an interpellative field of attraction where intersecting performances of indigeneity and anti-racism are staged. I first consider how Indigenous people are recognised as either 'authentically' different Indigenous people – what I call the 'authentic Indigenous voice' – or self-improving, entrepreneurial Indigenous subjects. Drawing on Povinelli's insight that knowledge about Indigenous people is most powerful when it is least informative, I show how White anti-racists seek recognition by refusing to define indigeneity. I then turn to micro-negotiations between institute researchers that define and shift the limits of recognition of anti-racism.

Indigenous Subjectivities

A key site where Indigenous subjects are recognised at the institute is its website. At the time of my fieldwork the relevant page described the support provided to Indigenous staff in this way:

> The Institute established the Indigenous Support Unit to provide a framework for enhanced representation, support and participation of its Indigenous staff and students. The Unit meets regularly to promote the involvement of Indigenous staff in all Institute activities and provides targeted professional development opportunities for its members.
>
> The group provides an understanding of local Indigenous history and culture to ensure our research outcomes will be readily accepted by Indigenous communities, and ultimately, to improve the health of Aboriginal people. This is particularly important, as despite numerous initiatives and programs to improve the health of Indigenous people living in remote communities, there are still major ongoing health problems and disadvantages in health care. This failure to improve Aboriginal health often stems from a lack of awareness or knowledge of distinct cultural, language, environmental and economic differences between remote Aboriginal communities and urban Australia ...
>
> The Institute actively fosters participation and collaboration with Indigenous people throughout the research process. Our aim is to have optimal Indigenous involvement in the design, conduct and participation of research projects that focus on Aboriginal health. Indigenous employees, particularly in research roles, and strong linkages with Indigenous communities are key components of what makes the Institute a unique research organisation.

There are three parts to the narrative of this passage. Indigenous staff are: (1) committed both to enhancing their 'professional development opportunities' and to 'improv[ing] the health of Aboriginal people'; (2) unlike White researchers, they possess 'knowledge of distinct cultural, language, environmental and economic differences between remote communities and urban Australia'; and (3) their role is to have 'optimal ... involvement in the design, conduct and participation of research projects'. These elements of the narrative illustrate the space of recognition for Indigenous people at the institute.

The Indigenous people who fit the space of recognition described in this passage have a Western education and aspire to more of it. They are motivated by a desire to improve the health of their communities and Indigenous people in general. They believe public health measures can improve Indigenous health provided that the institute's 'lack of awareness' of Indigenous culture is remedied with their own cultural and community knowledge. It is expected that the benefits they accrue through their recognition – employment, social status, respect from White researchers – will be used to further help their communities by acting as role models to other Indigenous people, and by encouraging their children and families to further their own education. They also offer an understanding of Indigenous protocols and concerns that are opaque to many White people.

The first aspect of this space is an aspiration for self-betterment. I call this mode of recognition the 'self-improving Indigene'. Individual Indigenous people who are recognised are those who apply any benefits they receive, including knowledge about being healthy, to the betterment of themselves and their families. What is demanded of Indigenous people is a version of the 'entrepreneur of the self' emblematic of late liberalism (Rose 1999: 164). Noel Pearson has become synonymous with the idea that Indigenous people will seek to 'take responsibility' for self-improvement once the 'poison' of welfare dependency is remedied (Pearson 2000, 2007).[13]

The second aspect of this space of recognition is the possession of unique cultural knowledge. Indigenous people may have to display aspirations for Western forms of improvement to be recognised, but it is their distinctly non-Western identity that makes them 'Indigenous people' in the first place. I call the authority derived from this aspect of the space of recognition the 'authentic Indigenous voice'. Indigenous people hold exclusive rights over this voice, which is presumed to be unified and collective. In meetings, seminars and workshops, White anti-racists will commonly suffix their statements with 'but it would be good to hear what an Indigenous person thinks about this'. They might utter the accusatory 'how many Indigenous people are here?', suggesting that a discussion of Indigenous health is unlikely to be constructive, or even ethical, without Indigenous people present and contributing. In a particularly stark example, an entry on a Darwin-based opinion website about Indigenous policy proclaims: 'Some people say the answer is blowing in the wind, but it's not. Just ask any Aboriginal person what should be done, and they will tell you! There's the answer!' (Troppo Armadillo 2004). When an Indigenous person does speak, they are rarely questioned or challenged, and their comments are generally followed by a respectful silence.

It is 'non-cosmetically apparent' – usually meaning White-skinned – Indigenous people at the institute that push the boundaries of this aspect of the space of recognition.[14] Those who know that the speaker is Indigenous will treat their comments as utterances of the authentic

Indigenous voice, and listen respectfully. Those who do not know them may not display a similar reverence. Such Indigenous people may choose to state their indigeneity explicitly, especially when they are in an unfamiliar context where few people are aware of their identity. But when they are in a known setting, such as an institute seminar, they are unlikely to do so,[15] perhaps knowing that a failure on the part of some White people to recognise the authentic Indigenous voice can only reflect badly on them, making them appear ignorant or even racist (because they assumed that a pale-skinned person is not Indigenous).

The third element of the passage quoted above promises that Indigenous people at the institute will be 'optimally involved' in every aspect of the research process. In the final paragraph the overall logic of the narrative is laid out: if Indigenous people are themselves researchers, their links to remote communities and their unique Indigenous knowledge will remedy the faults of previous research and lead to health improvement. The Indigenous person recognised in this space is a melding of the authentic Indigenous voice and the self-improving Indigene. This melding mirrors the resolution of Orientalism and remedialism in 'remediable difference' discussed in Chapter 2. Within the dominant belief system among White anti-racists, the space of recognition created for Indigenous people to inhabit (or refuse, or deform) requires them to be culturally distinct – authentic – and to use this distinctive knowledge to improve themselves and their kin.

The White anti-racist who seeks to improve Indigenous health must foster both self-improving Indigenes and authentic Indigenous voices. There are numerous techniques for achieving this. Research projects seek the 'optimal Indigenous involvement' of Aboriginal people in all aspects of their projects, ideally through Indigenous chief investigators or co-investigators, and organise training and support for the Indigenous employees they attract.

The authentic Indigenous voice is also captured through the processes of consultation and participation. An early and widespread manifestation of this is 'community consultation', an assemblage of techniques aimed at extracting the wishes of the community. It has involved the creation of racialised para-professional positions such as 'Community Liaison Officer' or 'Cultural Consultant', and rituals such as the community barbecue. In recent years, techniques to foster the participation of Indigenous people in health research have proliferated. Some are borrowed from other fields, particularly international development. Participatory Action Research (PAR) was one popular method, with PAR experts regularly flown in to Darwin from southern capitals to conduct workshops at the institute.

Such techniques of inclusion have been critiqued by Australian authors and internationally by development studies scholars (Sillitoe 1998; Peters-Little 1999; Cowlishaw 1999; Cooke and Kothari 2001; Cornwall and Brock 2005; Mosse 2005a; Kowal, Anderson, and Bailie 2005; Markell 2009; Sullivan 2011). A common element of these critiques is to question the implicit assumption that the individual and collective wishes of Indigenous people neatly map onto either the priorities of international development or the efforts to 'close the gap'. This assumption reflects the precarious fusion of the authentic and the improving that forms the space where Indigenous people are recognised.

Anthropologists of postcolonial situations have described subaltern subjectivities as a similar double-act of ancient and corrigible. Langford, for example, explores how contemporary constructions of Ayurvedic medicine are at once modern, serving powerful discourses of Indian nationalism, and non-modern 'traditional' and 'cultural' knowledge. She describes how the trick of 'tak[ing] on forms of the modern while simultaneously retaining the promise of redemption from the modern' generates tremendous discursive power (Langford 2002: 17). In the example recounted earlier, Tsing describes how environmentalists construct villagers as both living in complete harmony with their environment and requiring assistance to learn how to live sustainably (Tsing 2005: 263). In an Australian case, Batty (2005) considers Indigenous people who lead Aboriginal organisations in Central Australia. This group of Aboriginal people exemplifies both the self-improving Indigene and the authentic Indigenous voice, as they are required to demonstrate their connections to 'traditional Aboriginal culture' alongside advanced management skills.

The contradictions at the heart of this space of recognition are illustrated in Adams' description of Western representations of Nepalese Sherpas:

> To be a Sherpa in the eyes of a Westerner meant to be in need and, equally important, to be amply *deserving* of aid … to be different in all the ways the West desired – exotically spiritual and unfailingly hospitable, yet endlessly needy – different enough to warrant a tourist visit and warrant being 'saved' by the West. It also meant being similar to the West in all the ways the West desired – to want to become educated in schools where English was the medium of instruction, and to develop a consumer need for things the West could provide, including medicines, Western Ph.D.s and Mercedes-Benzes ('proof' of successful development for both many Sherpas and Westerners). (Adams 1996: 16–17)

This combination of exotic difference and Western aspirations produces remediable difference. As explored in Chapter 2, this particular construction of difference ensures both the 'deserving neediness' of subalterns and the benevolence of White anti-racists. An interesting feature of Indigenous difference, as recognised by White anti-racists, is its deliberate ambiguity.

Ambiguous Power

In *The Cunning of Recognition*, Elizabeth Povinelli discusses a media article about a prominent Indigenous arts bureaucrat. The article describes her as a 'city power broker' in charge of many staff and a large budget. Her job clearly demonstrates she is self-improving, but space is devoted to highlighting her authentic Indigenous voice. It notes her 'particularly Aboriginal view of the political geography of this nation' and that in her work directing festivals and funding programmes 'she has meticulously followed the diplomatic protocol of ancient Australia' (Jobson 1997, cited in Povinelli 2002b: 58).

Povinelli argues the article pointedly does not explain the content of these ancient protocols or how they might be applied in the corporatised modern art world:

> This referential non-specificity is not the result of a lack of knowledge or the failure to report it. Rather, 'ancient protocol' is experienced as maximally symbolic at exactly the moment when it seems minimally determinate. This semiotic hinge allows readers to fantasize a maximal variety of images of the deserving Indigenous subject at the very moment the description of the content of the social geography reaches zero. (Povinelli 2002b: 58)

This analysis suggests that it is not the content of Indigenous knowledge that commands the authority of the authentic Indigenous voice. Rather, it is the possibility of power and mystery contained in oblique references. The discourse of Indigenous health abounds with non-specificity. Lutschini's review of the term 'holism' in the academic literature of Aboriginal health found it was represented as immutably Aboriginal and embodied by Aboriginal people, as opposite to a Western/biomedical approach, and as essential to improving Aboriginal health. Beyond these essential and oppositional generalities there was intense confusion over the content of the term.[16] Lutschini argues this non-specificity is detrimental to the cause of improving Indigenous health, but others would see it as instrumental on the part of Indigenous people. Muecke suggests that a refusal to specify the content of Indigenous knowledge is a deliberate strategy in the face of White demands to speak, a 'judicious silence' that preserves Indigenous power through gesturing towards the 'great wealth of culture [that] lies below the surface' (Muecke 2005: 111).[17]

At the institute, the 'semiotic hinge' of unspecified Indigenous knowledge is a source of power, in line with arguments of Povinelli, Langford and Muecke. However, there are two differences in emphasis. First, specific knowledge of Indigenous difference is freely circulated at the institute, so that the work of depopulating the content of Indigenous knowledge is more visible than in other contexts. Second, while Muecke argues that evacuated Indigenous difference is instrumental for Indigenous people, at the institute it is also instrumental for White anti-racists, facilitating their recognition.

While the website blurb quoted above glossed over the 'cultural, language, environmental and economic differences' that the institute's Indigenous staff promise to overcome, the content of these differences is spelled out in formal and informal channels. Formal ethical guidelines advise the translation of consent forms into Indigenous languages. Warnings are passed between researchers to make sure community meetings are generously catered to accommodate large family groups, to record the multiple names of each research participant if you want to find them again, and to ensure people are not asked personal questions when their classificatory siblings are present. Some institute staff with more experience or with a degree in Indigenous studies or anthropology may be wary of 'gratuitous concurrence', whereby an Aboriginal person agrees with whatever is being asked. A semi-official document photocopied for new staff called 'How to Stay Out of Trouble when Visiting Remote Aboriginal Communities' explains pertinent aspects of Indigenous remote community life, and advises how researchers should conduct themselves, recommending that neat and modest clothes be worn, that researchers ring the community multiple times to check that they will be met at the landing strip, and that they head to the council office immediately to announce their arrival.

The institute is a space where Indigenous difference is far more substantiated than in the general public sphere. Therefore, it is more noticeable when Indigenous knowledge is evacuated of content. Attaining this indeterminacy provides opportunities for White anti-racists to be recognised. White anti-racists inhabit the space of recognition by defending the right of Indigenous people to enjoy their 'semiotic hinge', to use Povinelli's term. It is this identity work that is prominent at the institute, where most Whites know something about Indigenous culture and lifeworlds.

At a seminar on Natural Resource Management and Health, in the midst of a passionate plea for Indigenous knowledge systems and processes to be recognised by the 'Western system', a researcher stressed that this Indigenous knowledge would not be specified:

> We need to have equity in different knowledge systems. And this doesn't mean that we write down the cultural knowledge they have – knowledge in the public domain is often misused ... It's more than just responsibility, or identity, but I won't talk about it. We are not interested in mapping the structures of traditional knowledge ... their decision-making structures are intact.[18]

Within the context of the seminar, this appeal was not aimed at anyone in particular, but rather at the unspecified 'public domain'. This unspecified plea for non-specificity is one mechanism by which White anti-racists can be recognised.[19] White anti-racists are likely to be satisfied with non-specificity and even desire it, embracing Indigenous knowledges especially when they are at their most symbolic.

Recognising Anti-racism

White anti-racists at the institute performed complex and intersecting verbal manoeuvres in order to remain recognisable as 'anti-racists' and avoid the discursive territory of 'racism'. The previous chapter illustrated ways that White people perform anti-racism in relatively public forums, such as self-correcting language that could be interpreted as patronising or judgemental. In more private 'backstage' settings, such as meetings between researchers, performances of anti-racism were deliberated and refined. A common focus of deliberation was the definitions of racism and anti-racism. While the recognition of White anti-racists requires these terms to be clear, the boundaries between what is racist or (neo)colonial, and what is anti-racist or decolonising, are contested and always shifting. To remain recognisable, anti-racists must monitor the boundaries of anti-racism and participate in their ongoing negotiation.

The example below is from a conversation about a proposal from outside the institute that named the 'Tribal Council' as the Indigenous organisation that would oversee the research project. These researchers are discussing the term 'tribal council', which sounds antiquated to their ears. Jenny suggests that the non-Indigenous authors of the proposal are ignorant of the Indigenous organisations they should be collaborating with:

> Jenny: Is there really a 'Tribal Council'? It doesn't really have that ring of
> authenticity does it? It doesn't sound real, it sounds like a hypothetical
> guess.
> Annette: Down south though they have been going back to calling them
> 'tribal councils'.
> Kevin: They are still calling them that?
> Annette: They have gone back to doing it, and the proposal might be from
> down south.[20]

The use of a suspiciously archaic (thus potentially 'colonial') term
rings alarm bells for these researchers, and threatens to push the proposal's author beyond the boundaries of recognition as a fellow anti-
racist. Interestingly, the techniques of establishing authentic anti-racism
are aural: it is the 'ring' or 'sound' of 'tribal council' that threatens to
reveal its racist implications. For these anti-racists, 'tribal council' has the
timbre of colonialism.

However, Annette offers a clear entry point for the proposal's author to
retreat back within the boundaries of anti-racism. Perhaps, she suggests,
we are merely out of date, and the phrase 'tribal council' is not colonial
after all, but freely chosen by Indigenous people in southern Australia
who have reclaimed the colonial title for their own purposes. White
anti-racists are always ready to readjust the boundaries of anti-racism and
retune our ears so that 'tribal council' no longer grates.[21]

Another conversation where the boundaries of anti-racism were negotiated related to the issue of participation that this chapter opened with.
Here, the topic was informed consent. Rosie conducted a project in one
remote community. While the standard practice in Indigenous research is
to obtain written informed consent from each research participant, Rosie
became concerned when she observed that some community members
wanted to participate in the project but did not want to sign the consent
form, saying 'I'll talk to you, no worries, but I won't sign the form'. Rosie
took her concerns to a community member, an Indigenous woman with
'a lot of experience dealing with White people', who had agreed to be
an advisor to the project. Rosie told the advisor she wanted to share her
concerns about the cultural inappropriateness of written consent with
the institute's ethics committee and negotiate an alternative process for
obtaining consent. Rosie continues the story:

> Rosie: ... And she [the advisor] was adamant that we didn't. She said,
> 'Don't tell [people at the institute in] Darwin that there's Blackfellas here
> who won't sign the piece of paper – they will sign it, they can understand
> it'. So we recorded something on audiotape [in the local language] to play
> to people.
> Author: It probably said, you **will** sign the form... [general laughter]

Rosie: I think it might have.
Steve: It's the welfare experiences from the past, people are worried that the forms might get put up on a wall at conferences.
Tamara: I don't sign anything I don't have to.
Rosie: Also at the council, the council chairman was offended when I asked him to sign [a consent form] – 'we've already said yes' was his perspective.[22]

The two different spaces of Indigenous recognition discussed in this chapter provide two readings of the observed reluctance of Indigenous people to sign consent forms. A reading privileging the authentic Indigenous voice would interpret it as cultural difference, and press the ethics committee to allow more culturally appropriate forms of indicating consent, such as verbal responses. If we read the situation through the prism of self-improvement, we might conclude that Indigenous people are reluctant to sign forms because of ignorant distrust of the bureaucratic processes designed to protect them. In that case, the appropriate course of action would be to educate them about informed consent and their rights to refuse, withdraw from or complain about a research project. The reluctance to sign forms can be read as a difference to be respected, or as a deficit to be remedied.

Rosie's telling of the story suggests to me that she agrees with the first reading of the situation. She was concerned that written informed consent might not be culturally appropriate in her research site, and she was willing to discuss this openly with the ethics committee, exposing her project to potential criticism and even revocation of ethical approval.

The figure of the project advisor, a remote community woman with some Western education, offers yet another reading of the situation. Rather than a desire to educate the ethics committee about Indigenous cultural values, or a desire to educate Indigenous people about their legal and moral rights as citizens, the project advisor appears primarily interested in deflecting notions of her countrymen as primitive. The hidden transcript of her narrative I alluded to in my contribution to the discussion might go like this: *Don't tell those cosmopolitan people in Darwin that blackfellas out here are too ignorant and afraid to sign a form – they will sign it.* This is another version of the improvement narrative, but without the aura of gentle tutelage and self-realisation. It is a narrative that White anti-racists are uncomfortable with, as seen in our nervous laughter when I parodied the authoritative tone I imagined was in the taped message. The discomfort produced by this reading of the situation marks the disruption of remediable difference. The project advisor's authoritarian methods raised the possibility that this project, and all such projects, may be neocolonial, and specifically assimilationist, imposing their practices and epistemologies on Indigenous people. This implies, to echo Chapter 2, both that Indigenous people need changing and that White anti-racists must change them (with the help of forthright Indigenous project advisors). In one stroke, the boundaries of recognition shift, threatening to make White anti-racists and deserving Indigenous people unrecognisable.

The conversation suggests that Rosie (who did not speak the local language, and thus did not know what the tape said) suspected that the advisor might be bullying the research participants into signing the form. While the advisor's actions appear to be in conflict with Rosie's reading of the situation (i.e. Rosie sees 'not signing forms' as a cultural difference to be respected), any unease she might have is countered by happiness that the project advisor took an active interest in the problem she faced, and implemented an 'Indigenous' solution. Rosie's recognition and endorsement of the authentic Indigenous voice enhances her recognition as an anti-racist, even if that voice is dissonant with her own view of the situation and threatens mutual recognition on a broader scale.

Other researchers participating in the conversation performed different aspects of anti-racism. Steve displays his understanding of the historical roots of Indigenous distrust of forms. Tamara identifies with this distrust. In doing this she refuses to recognise it as 'cultural difference' at all, but a rational concern shared by 'moderns' such as herself. The comment may contain a subtler accusation of racism aimed at those who think it is silly to be afraid of forms.

Another fruitful context where anti-racists at the institute were recognised was the drafting of community reports. The technology of the community report has emerged in the last fifteen years in response to criticisms that researchers took research data from communities without providing any meaningful benefits in return. A 'community report' is now a standard research output, and savvy research projects will use DVDs and Facebook pages as more 'culturally appropriate' means of communicating with their audience. One research project in which I conducted participant-observation produced multiple reports for fifteen different communities based on templates that the project team had developed. The Indigenous researcher on the team had significant input into the language used in the template. In a series of discussions, members of the research team debated whether the language used in the report was culturally appropriate or patronising. This excerpt is in the first person, as Danielle and I worry together about the report:

> I'm looking over the community reports again with Danielle. Our boss Janice has made comments on the draft. She has asked that we find another simpler word for 'infrastructure' (we puzzle, perhaps 'services', and then

decide to leave out the word altogether as the report does not include data on infrastructure anyway). On the margin of a subsequent page that says '14 taps were good, 27 were no good', Janice has written: 'Simple English does not mean baby English or incorrect grammar. Change this and the rest of it'.

Danielle changes 'no good' to 'not functioning'. She explains why she initially used the phrase 'no good' and similar phrasings elsewhere in the report. 'When I looked at the report I thought, 'who is going to be reading that?' It seemed really patronising. But then I realised that Malcolm [the Indigenous researcher on the project] had written the template that way and I thought, 'well who am I to tell him how he should write it?'

At a meeting later in the week, Malcolm is absent. Janice, the head of the team, tells us, 'I don't see why there should not be plain correct grammatical English. Part of the feedback documents is an educative process. I don't think it helps if our feedback process teaches people to speak incorrectly. They are more likely to listen to it if it is clear and correct'. I felt a bit ashamed that I did not pick this up and allowed this patronising, incorrect, bad-example language to go through without commenting on it. 'Did I endorse patronising people?', I wonder guiltily.[23]

This scenario presents multiple, shifting performances of anti-racism that illustrate the contingency of recognition. For Danielle and for me, this situation creates confusion about the kind of performance that is expected. One possibility is that in the act of performing respect for Malcolm's cultural knowledge, we were seduced by Malcolm's authentic Indigenous voice that misrecognised Indigenous people as sub-literate. Worse, did we unknowingly coerce him to make the document look stereotypically 'Aboriginal'? Have we been taken in by our own patronising fantasies of what Indigenous people want to hear? Or are Janice, Danielle and I seeking recognition from each other when we change the language so we appear *not* to be patronising Aboriginal people? Perhaps Malcolm is just trying to do his job, and the 'patronising' language is appropriate, catering to Indigenous culture and low levels of Western education in the target audience? Do we just need to get over our discomfort (initially overridden by Danielle but rekindled by our boss Janice) and stop being prudish about the low levels of literacy and community preferences for Aboriginal English? Or in a third scenario, perhaps Malcolm is unconcerned about the report sounding patronising because he knows that no Indigenous will be interested in reading it? Perhaps the communities' participation in the project is the greatest performance of all? Or yet another possibility, maybe his 'dumbing down' of the language reflects internalised racism on his part and in the target communities?

Maybe he expects that Indigenous people will expect the language to be simple because they are used to being patronised by White people? If that is the case, is Janice right in insisting that the truly anti-racist course of action is an educative process in standard English and self-respect?

This surfeit of questions demonstrates the complexity of mutual recognition. In explicit and implicit debates over language, and over autonomy and coercion, White anti-racists attempt to stay within the bounds of recognition or shift its borders. White anti-racists are forever at risk of going beyond the bounds of recognition into the territory of colonialism, 'racism', or assimilationism. Concurrently, Indigenous people must inhabit the space of recognition of self-improvement – a space cast from an amalgam of remedialism and Orientalism, and demanding both the authentic Indigenous voice of the elder and the modern efficiency of the entrepreneur. On both sides, these spaces are prisons *and* vehicles of change: spaces of confinement *and* potential mobility.

Notes

1. Data quality was a parallel issue that also generated much discussion, from the performance of various brands of glucometer in extreme heat and humidity to the problem of 'gratuitous concurrence' (discussed later in the chapter) whereby Indigenous people agree with whatever a survey is asking out of politeness, lack of interest or to end the encounter as soon as possible.
2. Field Notes, 29 Nov. 2004.
3. This literature is discussed in the Introduction and Chapter 6.
4. There is a large literature on everyday White privilege. See, for example, Bonnett 2000; Dyer 1997; and McKinney 2005.
5. This phenomenon has been explored by a strand of political theory influenced by Walter Benjamin, Carl Schmitt and Giorgio Agamben as 'the exception'; see Agamben 1998.
6. WA Parliament 1944: section 5, cited in Chesterman and Galligan 1997: 132.
7. This work draws on earlier feminist scholarship on the 'politics of difference'; see, for example, Young 1990. For other important accounts of the politics of recognition, including in Indigenous contexts, see Fabian 1999; McNay 2008; Markell 2009; Bhabha 2011; and Barker 2011.
8. In a related argument at the international level, Stoczkowski (2009) describes UNESCO's struggle to distinguish between 'good' cultural heritage that should be preserved, and 'harmful traditions' (including honour killing, forced marriage and female genital mutilation) that should be outlawed.
9. Work that has informed my understanding of how Indigenous people inhabit the spaces of recognition created for them includes Michaels 1988; Beckett 1988, 1994; Keen 1988; Thiele 1991; Attwood and Arnolds 1992; Anderson 2003; Muecke 2004; Peters-Little 2006; Paradies 2006; Healy 2008; and Cowlishaw 2011.

10. In related work, Tania Li draws on Stuart Hall's use of positioning and Laclau and Mouffe's concept of articulation to describe the struggles to expand and contain who counts as 'Indigenous' in Indonesia (Laclau and Mouffe 1985; Hall 1994, 2002; Li 2000, 2007).

11. I discuss 'Whiteness Studies' in chapters 2 and 6.

12. Although, as noted in the Introduction, the Indigenous population nationally is highly diverse with many Indigenous people 'passing' as White in their everyday interactions, this is less the case in the Northern Territory where the vast majority of the Indigenous population are visibly recognizable as such.

13. For critiques of this position, see for example Martin 2001; Altman 2009; Pholi, Black and Richards 2009; and Kowal 2012b.

14. The term is Lillian Holt's. On the limited space of the contemporary recognition of Indigenous people, see Conklin 1997; and on the history of the 'savage slot', see Trouillot 1991. The politics of authenticity and indigeneity continue to attract scholarly attention. A few key and recent examples include Paradies 2006; de la Cadena and Starn 2007; Kauanui 2008; Cattelino 2010; Buchanan and Darian-Smith 2011; and Griffiths 2012.

15. Although they may do it subtly by, for instance, referring to Indigenous people as 'we' rather than 'they'.

16. Lutschini (2005) argues that this confusion was compounded by a refusal to engage with the mainstream literature on holism because of the desire to present an opposition to non-Indigenous concepts. For an example of the highly symbolic in North American Indigenous health discourse, see Minde and Minde 1995, and for an examination of how the indeterminacy of definitions of 'health' and of 'the right to health' operate in a general context, see Greco 2004.

17. Langford (2002) describes a similar efficacy of indeterminate Indian knowledge about Ayurveda.

18. Field Notes, 22 Oct. 2004.

19. Another example of this occurred at a Whiteness Studies conference I attended, when a White anti-racist was asked to talk about the 'power' that inspired her interest in studying the Indigenous realm. She replied, 'I can't speak about Indigenous power … I am silenced, but in a positive way. I can't say what it is … but it's the source of what is provoked in me by the Indigenous people I work with'. Unspecified Indigenous knowledge is prominent in this account.

20. Field Notes, 16 Sept. 2004.

21. In recent years the term 'Indigenous' has come to been seen by some as racist because it homogenises Indigenous people around the world, with the preferred term being the more specific 'Aboriginal and Torres Strait Islander'; see, for example, Tatz 2001b. However, this move has not been entirely successful, with the term 'Indigenous' retaining its acceptability in many forums. Currently some are advocating that the term 'First Nations' (borrowed from Canada) should replace 'Aboriginal and Torres Strait Islanders'.

22. Field Notes, 26 Aug. 2004.

23. Field Notes, 12 Oct. 2004.

Chapter 6

WHITE STIGMA

In the history of Australian Indigenous affairs, 2 December 1972 is an auspicious date. The election of the progressive government led by the late Gough Whitlam heralded a change in Aboriginal policy. The new prime minister declared that his aim was to 'restore to the Aboriginal people of Australia their lost power of self-determination', marking a decisive move away from previous 'assimilation' policies that intended to absorb Indigenous people into mainstream society (Whitlam 1973: 12). The following year, the Federal Department of Aboriginal Affairs was established, taking over the administration of Aboriginal affairs from various state authorities. It was a move applauded by Indigenous leaders and non-Indigenous advocates alike. Influenced by intellectuals such as C.D. Rowley (1972a, 1972b), the guiding policy of the new department was 'self-determination' for Indigenous Australians, defined as 'Aboriginal participation in making policies, and in decisions about their progress that affect them, and about their future' (Australian Bureau of Statistics 1973: 971). The new department initially focused on supporting the formation of Aboriginal organisations that could run autonomous Aboriginal communities, and on promoting Aboriginal land rights.

The shift to self-determination was influenced by decolonisation movements, the United States civil rights movement and the burgeoning international Indigenous rights movement, all three of which gained serious momentum in the 1960s. A by-product of this shift was to radically change the role of non-Indigenous people who sought to participate in

Indigenous development. No longer in charge of Indigenous advancement, White anti-racists were now cast as partners and supporters (Rowse 2002: 110–30; Niezen 2003).

As I discussed in Chapter 2, a striking feature of White anti-racist discourse in the self-determination era is a reluctance to claim any agency in the process of Indigenous improvement: to suggest that Whites are 'helping' Indigenous people can be taken as an accusation of paternalism.[1] White anti-racists prefer to think of their role as temporarily supporting Aboriginal people to reach their own goals until such time as White help is no longer needed. Indeed, the 1975 annual report of the Department of Aboriginal Affairs declares that once Aboriginal organisations have overcome their teething problems and ceased to depend on White advisors and employees, 'the department itself should disappear' (Batty 2005: 214).

The desire for self-effacement is still common among White anti-racists. My study of this group revealed a paradoxical agency: the will that wills its own demise. Many White anti-racists justified their work in Indigenous health by expressing their desire to train an Indigenous person to replace them. As we saw in Chapter 2, one downplayed her role as 'mere facilitation' of Indigenous people's wishes.[2] Another woman said, 'I'm not wanting to drive the process at all, I want to give the process away'.[3]

This chapter explores two aspects of White anti-racist subjectivity: a highly ambivalent attitude towards one's own agency, and the willingness to suffer hardships without complaint.[4] These two related features of White anti-racist subjectivities – self-effacement and suffering – are rarely discussed in the academic or popular literature, yet they are crucial to understanding the limits and possibilities of current approaches to Indigenous disadvantage. I supplement my discussion of self-effacement and suffering with a detour through scholarship on fractured German identities, international development workers and North American anti-racist activists – all cases that illuminate aspects of Australian White anti-racism.

One way to approach the analysis of these reluctant agents is to consider their place in the 'fantasy space' of the Australian post-settler state. Drawing on Zizek's (1993) concept of the 'fantasy scene' (where the subject is constituted through desire for the 'Thing'), Ghassan Hage argues that the fantasy of the nation serves as an object of desire for White nationalists. For most White Australians, any move to include migrants and Indigenous people threatens 'the imagined national home', the 'fantasy space in which the nationalists' very being as desiring subjects is staged' (Hage 1998: 73).

Povinelli's work suggests that Indigenous social justice (what she explores as 'liberal multiculturalism') acts as a parallel, liberal fantasy space for Australians who reject White nationhood. Anti-racist Australians, who are genuinely troubled by Indigenous suffering, support Indigenous welfare programmes as well as the recognition of past wrongs and the limited forms of land rights offered by the state. Her work demonstrates how anti-racists partake in a 'fantasy of liberal capitalist society' where Indigenous subjects are called upon to perform authentic difference without offending liberal sensibilities (Povinelli 2002).

In this chapter, I extend Povinelli's insights to interrogate the ideal future imagined by White anti-racists, a future when Indigenous people are lifted out of disadvantage to participate fully in Australian society, statistically equal to, but culturally distinct from, other Australians. This imagined future is the logical outcome of remediable difference, the concept I discussed in Chapter 2. Using the language of that chapter, White anti-racists who seek to change the structural determinants of Indigenous health and support Indigenous self-improvement hope to 'close the gap'. Closing the gap in this way promises to erase unsanitised difference and produce healthy but recognisably Indigenous subjects with sanitised difference intact. Within this fantasy space, previous failures of the state to close the gap between Indigenous and non-Indigenous statistical outcomes are attributed to the lack of Indigenous control. To succeed, state programmes must be led by Indigenous people in the spirit and the letter of self-determination.

Why should this anti-racist fantasy space require that White agency be diminished to the point of disappearance? In this chapter I argue that applying the concept of 'stigma' to White privilege is a novel and productive approach to understanding these aspects of White anti-racist subjectivities. White stigma acts as a barrier to the broader goal of constructing ethical White subjectivities fit for the post-settler state. Overcoming this barrier necessitates a range of behaviours and beliefs, including self-effacement and suffering, that are otherwise difficult to explain. This analysis of White stigma complements the argument of Chapter 2, offering another tool for understanding how the construction of White anti-racist subjectivities necessitates remediable difference and copes with its failure.

Below I illustrate how self-effacement and suffering manifest themselves at the Darwin Institute of Indigenous Health. As we have seen, White anti-racists who work at the institute live in the regional capital of Darwin, but regularly travel to remote Indigenous communities where the bulk of the institute's research is conducted. It is when White anti-racists venture into these spaces that they are most troubled by the stigma of privilege.

Stigma and Whiteness

Stigma is a sociological concept developed most famously by Erving Goffman in his book *Stigma: Notes on the Management of Spoiled Identity* (Goffman 1963). To the Greeks, the term meant a physical mark on a slave or criminal to indicate their blemished status to the public. Goffman suggests that the modern concept of stigma is an attribute that acts as 'an undesired differentness' (ibid.: 5) from the 'normal' category that the viewer had anticipated. A stigma must induce a decrease in the estimation of the viewer, from a more highly esteemed category of 'normal' to a lesser category: a stigma is 'deeply discrediting' (ibid.: 3). The stigmatised identity must be managed through a variety of mechanisms, and if possible, by passing for 'normal'. Another set of managing activities involves 'in-group purification', where there is an attempt to remake the stigmatised identity by ridding it of its undesirable attributes (ibid.: 108).

White stigma is a controversial concept. For the sake of the argument, Indigenous people, who are usually stigmatised themselves, would be taken as the 'normal' category.[5] From the point of view of Indigenous people, the mark of white skin causes the (Indigenous) viewer to reassign the person viewed to the category of 'White'. In contrast with categories usually associated with stigma (like disabled, homosexual or drug user), 'White' is not generally seen as inferior or sub-human, but associated with privilege, education and wealth.

However, within the norms of anti-racism, whiteness is also associated with a host of negative characteristics, such as exploitation, colonisation and imperialism, and general dominance over non-White people (Bonnett 2000), what we might call 'negative Occidentalism' (see Chapter 2). In the particular sites where the anti-racist fantasy space is the dominant imaginary, such as the institute, whenever whiteness is made explicit it is seen as something to be avoided, diminished and counteracted. When White anti-racists are interpellated as white (see Chapter 4), this is generally experienced as a stigma, whether the Indigenous people present explicitly denigrate whiteness (a relatively uncommon occurrence) or not. White stigma must then be managed by White anti-racists to minimise its impact on their work and lives. More broadly, White anti-racists must work to build a White subjectivity that transcends its stigmatised attributes. This hypothetical, ethical White subjectivity would be a perfect fit for the anti-racist fantasy space. Once it is achieved, White anti-racists could finally be confident in their ability to address Indigenous disadvantage without endangering the Indigenous subjects they seek to benefit.

Some models of stigma specify that only a group with less power than the dominant group can be stigmatised, thus disallowing the concept of White stigma (Link and Phelan 2001). Goffman, however, does not make such a stipulation. His conception is more relational and contextual. He argues that 'the normal and the stigmatised are not persons, but rather perspectives. These are generated in social situations during mixed contacts by virtue of the unrealised norms that are likely to play upon the encounter' (Goffman 1963: 138). White stigma is therefore possible in the minority of spaces where the 'unrealised norms' associate White privilege with negative attributes.

The norms of some academic circles, such as 'whiteness studies' scholarship, provide many examples of White stigma. Within this progressive discourse, the mechanism of colonisation and continuing oppression of Indigenous people and minorities is attributed to whiteness (Moreton-Robinson 2005). White anti-racists are in constant danger of inflicting further injury on non-White people, even as they attempt to do the opposite (Ahmed 2004). What White people can 'do' about their whiteness is the source of much debate. Can it be refused or even abolished? Or is it resistant to all efforts to evade and escape it? (Roediger 1994; Probyn 2004; Aveling 2004a, 2004b). The existence of whiteness studies itself is a cause of consternation of many whiteness studies scholars. The introduction of an important early collection suggests that 'maybe this should be the last book on whiteness' (Fine et al. 1997: xii). A paper by a prominent Australian scholar of whiteness studies announced her withdrawal from researching Indigenous people after she concluded that her White privilege is an incontrovertible barrier to conducting 'decolonising' research (Aveling 2012). Whiteness operates within this discourse as a stigma: an undesirable attribute to be managed, or if possible, disappeared.

The concept of stigma itself does feature in some whiteness scholarship, but only as a figment of paranoid, racist, White imaginations. Stigma always appears as 'perceived white stigma' whereby White people feel that their whiteness disadvantages them in the postcolonial, post-civil rights, post-apartheid era (Gallagher 1997; McKinney 2003; McDermott 2006). This is seen in the context of an 'emerging crisis of white identity' that Michael Omi predicted would occur as demographic shifts and immigration mean that Whites will soon be a minority in the United States (Omi 1996: 181; see also Winant 2004; Kaufmann 2005).

Whiteness studies scholars tend to view White stigma as a calculated fiction, a defensive gesture on the part of White people who see their unearned privileges beginning to erode as non-White groups gain political power. Underlying much of this work is an assumption of misrecognition. Whites, hungry to maintain their power at all costs, mistake justice for persecution. It is implied that if these White supremacists, mainstream college students and others who contest their apparent stigmatisation finally recognise their persisting privilege, they will stop feeling stigmatised and join the ranks of White anti-racists who actively seek to reduce their privilege and its detrimental effects on non-Whites.

The White anti-racists I am concerned with readily acknowledge their privilege, do not perceive their position as stigmatised, and only rarely and reluctantly complain of unfair treatment on the basis of race. As Hughey notes in his study of White anti-racists in the United States, White anti-racists differ from other Whites in that they are aware, perhaps hyper-aware, of their whiteness (Hughey 2012).[6] This would not inoculate them from criticism from some scholars who are likely to interpret the experiences and behaviours of White anti-racists at the institute as the disguised efforts of closet racists to maintain their threatened privilege (see, for example, Zajicek 2002; Niemonen 2007). As I have discussed at various points in this book, I abstain from this evaluative approach to anti-racism and instead consider anti-racism to be a culture, discourse and identity worthy of anthropological attention. Before exploring how 'stigma' can elucidate White anti-racists' tendencies to self-effacement and suffering, I consider a parallel project analysing progressive German identities.

Perpetrator Identities: Australian Anti-racists and 'Non-German Germans'

Historian Dirk Moses has drawn on Goffman's treatment of stigma to explore the problem of German identity in the long shadow of the Holocaust (Moses 2007b). He argues that Germans in post-Holocaust Germany are marked with the stigma of the perpetrator that has been passed down by their forebears. He draws on Luhrmann's concept of the 'traumatized social self' to explain how the German group identity has been transformed by the revelations of Nazi atrocities and is 'now associated with failure, moral inadequacy, embarrassment and guilt' (Luhrmann 2000, 185; cited in Moses 2007a: 55).

Many German intellectuals today defend the national collective identity from such negative associations, arguing (for example) that Germans born after the end of the war cannot be held responsible for the events of the Holocaust. A minority, however, contend that every generation of Germans must come to terms with the events of the Nazi genocide and their country's role in it. Events such as the construction of the Holocaust memorial in Berlin in the late 1990s (completed in 2003) highlighted the contrast between the defenders of German identity, a group Moses calls

'German Germans', and those that believe further identity reconstruction is needed, a group he calls 'non-German Germans' (Moses 2007a, 2007b).

'Non-German Germans' attempt to create a new German identity by strongly identifying with the victims of the Holocaust and with Jewish culture, and by rejecting all they identify as 'typically German'. Many will recall the moment when they realised the extent of Nazi atrocities as the point when the German national identity was indelibly sullied (Moses 2007a: 62). They are vigilant in detecting residues of racism and fascism in their government and compatriots. They may also distance themselves from older family members who were alive during the war, or fabricate a family history of Nazi resistance.

These behaviours can be understood as strategies of 'stigma management' aimed at developing a 'new German group self' (Moses 2007b: 155). In contrast, 'German Germans' reject the stigmatisation of German identity by distancing the Nazi era from the narrative of the nation. They regard the efforts of non-German Germans to call them to account as a form of persecution (Moses 2007a: 58), a similar phenomenon to the 'perceived stigma' that whiteness studies scholars have identified.

In Australia, a similar national divide was revealed in the so-called 'history wars' (Macintyre and Clark 2003). Since the 1970s, progressive historians have worked to document the frontier wars of European occupation; the numerous forms of oppressive state control of Aboriginal lives; and most recently, the removal of Aboriginal children from their families and into institutions in the name of assimilation (see, for example, Reynolds 1987; Haebich 2000). One of the most controversial debates has centred on whether the institutionalisation of Aboriginal children 'for their own good' amounts to cultural genocide (Tatz 2001). In a statement commonly cited to support this view, the Western Australian Commissioner for Native Affairs and key assimilationist thinker, A.O. Neville, posed a rhetorical question at a 1937 conference: 'Are we going to have a population of one million blacks in the Commonwealth or are we going to merge them into our white community and eventually forget that there were any aborigines in Australia?' (Commonwealth of Australia 1937: 11).

Unsurprisingly, conservative intellectuals have been critical of these attempts to expose the 'fantasy space' of White nationhood devoid of its original inhabitants. For their work exposing the poor treatment of Aboriginal Australians by the state, progressive historians are accused of perpetuating a 'black armband' view of Australian history (Blainey 1993).[7] It is historically and morally wrong, the conservatives argue, to portray settler society in wholly negative terms as invaders and destroyers of Aboriginal societies (Windschuttle 2002). Like 'German Germans', conservative thinkers seek to defend national identity from defilement. Like 'non-German Germans', White anti-racists seek to generate new forms of national identity by exposing the unpalatable aspects of perpetrator history, so persuading White Australians to distinguish themselves from their (biological and social) ancestors.

For Australian White anti-racists, the pollution of the perpetrator is both more distant and more proximate than in the German case. The perpetrators of dispossession and child removal are temporally and genetically distant from contemporary anti-racists, while most young adult Germans have grown up with at least one grandparent who lived through the Second World War. Some White Australians of Anglo-Saxon origin may wonder whether their ancestors participated in dispossession, or know that they did, but for most anti-racists it is an identification with the nation and with whiteness that generates stigma, rather than with their immediate ancestors. 'We have benefited from Indigenous oppression' is the general claim that can be made on behalf of migrants to Australia as well as the descendants of early settlers.[8]

The pollution of the perpetrator is more proximate, however, owing to the persistence and visibility of the victims, the Indigenous population. The suffering of the Jews in Nazi Europe is a historical fact, but the suffering of Aboriginal people is a prominent reality, regularly gracing national newspapers. While the issue of German stigma is illustrated primarily through debates about history and memory, Indigenous Australians stand as living testimony to the genocidal crimes of White society, their shorter lives an organic barometer of colonial oppression.

My aim here is not to judge whether the subset of White Australians in question (or Germans for that matter) feel badly enough, too badly or too good about themselves. I am interested in the effects of a negative collective self-view among White anti-racists who seek to recognise and ameliorate the effects of colonisation through their work in Indigenous communities. For White anti-racists, the colour of their skin marks them as 'colonisers'. If we are to see this ascription as a stigma, it is a stigma of a special, highly contextualised form. It is a voluntary stigma, applying only to those White people who accept responsibility for the effects of colonisation on Indigenous people.[9] It only takes effect when these White people are engaged in Indigenous issues, usually in the context of paid employment, but also through activism, education and personal encounters. For most White anti-racists at the institute, the bulk of their daily lives in Darwin (where Indigenous people make up only 10 per cent of the population) takes place within the cradle of White privilege. Only upon entering specific spaces such as the institute or remote communities does the stigma of whiteness come into play.

Development Desires

Before we explore the workings of stigma management in the Northern Territory, it is useful to reflect on the White anti-racist self-concept presented in the social science literature on international development workers. This extends the discussion in the Introduction, where I suggested that the study of international development workers had great relevance to the study of White anti-racism in post-settler states. As social groups, international development workers and professionals in Indigenous affairs greatly overlap (and many institute employees had spent some time working in international development).[10]

Critical accounts of development workers build a picture of normative White anti-racism – what White development workers are like, and what they should be like. As we will see, the imperative to 'help' the marginalised and suffering is seen as an exercise in narcissism – a desire to cultivate a morally unblemished bourgeois identity. I will argue that this critique of the self-loving development worker reveals a normative belief that 'good' development workers should hate themselves, should seek to remove their oppressive, stigmatised presence from the scene of development and disappear. Two studies are the focus of analysis here: Paulette Goudge's *The Whiteness of Power*, which focuses on Nicaragua, and Barbara Heron's *Desire for Development*, which discusses development workers in Africa (Goudge 2003; Heron 2007).[11] Both authors are ex-development workers who conducted interview research with fellow development workers. Both believe that development is a tool of global dominance of the North over the South, and that development workers are continuous with and similar to the missionaries and colonial administrators of the past.

The White development workers that Goudge and Heron interview are similar to the White anti-racists I studied at the institute, as I argued in the Introduction using quotes from one of Heron's interviewees, Carol. Most members of both groups actively sought out work with marginalised people because they wanted to improve the lives of those less fortunate than themselves. Both groups approached their work armed with a (more or less) sophisticated critique of colonialism and geopolitics. They all believed that colonisation and imperialism are the causes of inequality and poverty, and saw their role as facilitating the empowerment of local communities to identify and address their own priorities.

Goudge and Heron consider the lofty goals articulated by many White anti-racists as sustenance for their narcissism. Goudge argues that the manifold forms of privilege White anti-racists enjoy means their presence can only reinforce oppression, even as they seek to dismantle it. Heron similarly argues that development work is geared towards the creation of bourgeois White feminine identities. White 'desire for development' is the desire to construct moral White subjectivities (similar to my argument in Chapter 2). Drawing on critical race theorists, Heron argues that through these attempts to help the less-fortunate masses that can never quite attain whiteness, the bourgeois subject can at once attest to their morality while affirming their superiority (Bhabha 1994; McClintock 1995; Cooper and Stoler 1997). In this rendering, White anti-racism is no less racist than racism, and is constituted through narcissism – it is all about us.

The answer Heron offers is for White development workers to keep in mind that they are inextricably implicated in global systems of oppression, and to understand that their desire to 'help' those in the global South is an expression of White bourgeois identity (Heron 2007: 151). Following these guidelines will prevent an array of narcissistic feelings, including the desire to help, good feelings about helping, and desiring friendship or love with the subaltern. However, there are two sets of emotions that are set apart from these 'bad' narcissistic ones and commended: pain, and the desire for disappearance.

First, the question of pain is important in both accounts. Goudge notes disapprovingly that White anti-racists get upset when recounting how co-workers or strangers abused them for being 'white imperialists'. She is approving of one woman who dismisses her own hurt feelings (after being berated by a co-worker) because the woman understands 'where and why such reactions to her might originate' (Goudge 2003: 84).[12] Goudge does not think White anti-racists should complain about bad treatment. Instead, we should welcome these painful experiences as tools to help us remain aware of our privilege. We *should* be treated badly considering our complicity in (neo)colonial oppression. As well as feeling good when we are treated badly, we should feel bad when we are treated well, such as when we are offered the best food and lodgings. Heron argues that bourgeois subjects must experience disintegration – 'a dissolution of unifying narratives of a moral self' – in order to form a *'more moral* position of accountability' (Heron 2007: 154–55, emphasis in original).[13] This disintegration is painful, but necessary to counter the oppressiveness and false morality of the anti-racist position.

Second, both authors see the solution in removing the White anti-racist from development. Truly anti-racist development workers should admit *they should not have been there in the first place*. Any reluctance to do so is due to a narcissistic attachment to their bourgeois identity (Heron 2007: 136–39). The proper place for White anti-racists is in their home countries in the North, working to challenge the system of racial dominance at its heart, and reduce its impact on the South by personally consuming less.

The normative anti-racist that emerges from this literature is one who knows that their desire to help is narcissism in disguise; who feels the pain that is inflicted on the subaltern by their presence and the broader development enterprise; and who resists rather than reinforces a White bourgeois identity, ultimately by disintegrating their sense of self and removing themselves from the scene of development.

Compared to the White anti-racists that Goudge and Heron describe, the White anti-racists who work in Indigenous Australia appear, on the whole, more politically sophisticated, with a greater understanding of the link between White privilege and Indigenous disadvantage. This could be a product of their location in a post-settler colony that makes their role as beneficiaries of the dispossession and oppression of Indigenous people more difficult to deny or obfuscate. As a result, quite a number of them embodied the normative White anti-racism of Goudge and Heron (while those authors could only find one or two who fitted the bill). As we will see, Goudge's and Heron's prescriptions for pain and disappearance are adopted by some White anti-racists at the institute. I argue that the reason these therapies are recommended by scholars and adopted by anti-racists is their efficacy in managing the stigma of whiteness.

Mercenaries, Missionaries and Misfits

White anti-racists need to manage White stigma in an attempt to create a White subjectivity that can help Indigenous Australians without harming them. Like non-German Germans, one way White anti-racists manage their stigma is through criticising other Whites, including other White anti-racists. In the German case, the figure of the arrogant anti-Semite typifies the stigmatised identity. For White anti-racists, the assimilationist intent on making Indigenous people White is the paradigmatic symbol of disdain. It is extreme, however, for a White anti-racist to accuse him/herself or a colleague of being an assimilationist – akin to an accusation of cultural genocide. At the institute, stigmatised whiteness is more commonly encapsulated in the classificatory system of 'missionary, mercenary or misfit', the most widespread trope of self-critique among White people working in the Indigenous arena.

This triumvirate has been used to refer to White people working in a variety of development contexts the world over. It is always cited as a piece of insider knowledge, a local joke. Two cross-cultural consultants from Alice Springs in Central Australia tell us that 'there is a tired old saying in the NT [Northern Territory] that the kardiya [white people] who come from South to work with yapa [Indigenous people] are either mercenaries, missionaries or misfits' (Price and Price 1998), while the author of a *New Canadian Magazine* article about development workers recalls 'a person from Oxfam told me there are three kinds of people who do this type of work' (Silverman 2005). Four other books have used this title (T. Hall 1996; Loney 2001; Patterson 2006; Warah 2008), as well as an Australian Medical Association conference on Indigenous health held in Darwin in 2002.

Veteran development anthropologist Jock Stirrat has explored this lexeme in the context of international development. He identifies 'mercenaries, missionaries and misfits' as employees of international development agencies, employees of non-government organisations (NGOs), and disillusioned development workers, respectively. He argues that those in the 'development business' claim to be in it 'just for the money' as a defence mechanism against the guilt of earning so much and the uncertainty of their impact on the lives of the poor. The title of 'missionary' is applied to the NGO worker who 'is motivated by a sense of duty and obligation. This may derive from some sense of guilt at the poverty of the developing world; it may derive from a particular political agenda or it may be fuelled by some romantic dream. No matter what, the outcome is the same: a sacrifice of self in the pursuit of some greater goal' (Stirrat 2008: 412). As will we see, it is this latter category of development worker that most closely resembles the White anti-racists at the institute and that they find the most problematic. Stirrat sees both the mercenaries and missionaries as working towards the transformation of the subject of development into a modern post-Enlightenment individual with the ability to transcend the social ties that bind her to hierarchy, dependency and powerlessness. These two categories are opposed to the misfits, the development worker who no longer believes in development but cannot fit into Western life, and remains trapped in a cycle of overseas postings.

The aforementioned cross-cultural consultants – a Warlpiri woman who is now a Northern Territory member of parliament, and her White husband – explain how the categories apply in Indigenous development:

> The mercenaries are fairly straightforward. Self enrichment at the expense of naïvely trusting and tolerant yapa [Indigenous] communities … Then there are the missionaries, the old, Christian and conservative and the new, rationalist and radical, out to change the world. Many of the old are exhausted and burdened by self doubt. The new are energetic and

confident … Feminists, environmentalists, various brands of socialists, anti-nuclear activists and others all come with burning, youthful zeal … Misfits turn up in all groups of course. In the North they become 'colourful characters' and find a ready acceptance in yapa [Indigenous] communities. (Price and Price 1998)

All three of these tropes were present at the institute. White researchers are the first to show suspicion of their colleagues' motives, and interpret any hint of self-interest as a sign of exploitation. Indigenous communities are portrayed as victims of those who purport to help them, 'inundated' with interest from White researchers clamouring for their involvement in an effort to secure easy research funds from funding bodies eager to support Indigenous projects.[14] White researchers accuse their colleagues and themselves of 'build[ing] their careers on people's ill-health',[15] while hiding their selfish motives by 'cloaking what we do in good intentions'.[16] The mercenary is a prominent trope of White stigma, managed through criticising others and anticipating suspicion of one's motives from colleagues. The second discourse of the misfit surfaces in light-hearted quips about us 'mangy collection of odd-bods' who work in Indigenous health.[17] The third trope of White stigma, the missionary, is the most complex and compelling.

In the narrative above, mercenaries and misfits, along with the 'old' missionaries, are hangovers from the colonial frontier. What one might call the postcolonial frontier is inhabited by what they call the 'new, rationalist and radical' missionaries. Some White anti-racists at the institute also critique themselves as 'new missionaries':

One hundred years ago people from our societies went away and became missionaries, and that is how they got their raison d'etre for being good. I think now what people do is, in the last twenty years or thirty years … people from southern states, not everyone, but a certain group of people have got their raison d'etre from coming up to save the black man. If necessary, from himself as well. And they would have been missionaries three or four generations ago, and they've now become 'people who work in Aboriginal health'. Now that's reasonably denigrating, but I think that's the way to understand it, myself probably included in this.[18]

The charge of 'missionary' is a serious one to make against a White anti-racist. In other texts where progressive Whites are accused of being 'like missionaries', this serves as reproof enough, with no further elaboration required (Henkel and Stirrat 2001; Niezen 2003).

In Australia, Christian missions were set up around the country in the nineteenth and twentieth centuries, with regions parcelled out to various denominations. From the turn of the last century until the 1970s (and in some cases the early 1980s) these missions served as the main arm of government administration in most parts of Aboriginal Australia (Swain and Bird Rose 1988). Typical representations of missions in the public sphere focus on their role in 'the suppression of Aboriginal cultural practices and languages' through 'engaging in practices such as forcibly separating Aboriginal children from their families in order to maximise control over the child's education into Christian ways and beliefs' (Australian Museum 2006). Comparing someone to a missionary implies they are imposing their belief system on Indigenous people, and that their failure to respect Indigenous culture will have deleterious effects (recall here the discussion in Chapter 2 of anti-racists' fears of 'imposing' their beliefs and desires on Indigenous people). Taking this view, the 'new missionary' uses secularity as a guise behind which lurks the imposition of values, just as the 'old' missionary used Christianity.[19]

Whether missionary or mercenary, White anti-racists appear destined to inflict harm on Indigenous people by exerting power over them, either for blatant self-gain or out of misguided superiority. As this stigma acts as a serious obstacle to realising the anti-racist fantasy space of imagined future equality, stigma management is required. At the institute, the predominant method of countering White stigma is to minimise White agency. If White intervention in Indigenous lives is by definition damaging, then it follows that the less White people are doing, the less chance of injury to Indigenous subjects.

In the professional development courses I have run with White professionals in Indigenous health, participants are asked to choose, from a range of quotations, one that particularly resonates with them. This quotation from an Indigenous person commenting on what White people can 'do' about racism is always strongly endorsed, 'You don't have to do anything to help me. You don't have to do anything to help my people. Just be there. As soon as you say you want to help me, that puts me down. Always remember that' (Mellor 2004: 64).

The popularity of this quotation is instructive for what it tells us about the desires of White anti-racists. This unnamed Indigenous person promises that by 'just being there', it is possible for White anti-racists to be of use to Indigenous people. To be 'helpful', White people must not act, and must not declare that they want to act.[20]

Statements that similarly minimise the agency of White anti-racists are often made by institute researchers. One researcher stated that her role was 'supporting individuals, giv[ing] them the capacity to do what they see fit ... providing opportunities for self-determination'. She constructs her role as not following her own volition, but supporting

Indigenous people to follow theirs. As discussed in Chapter 2, another colleague stressed that when she was a nurse in a remote health clinic, 'I was merely just facilitating what [the Aboriginal health workers] had been doing for a long time'.[21] Such tame language is needed to diminish the stigma of White agency. Like Anna, whom I discussed in the Introduction, this woman referred to White people who try to assist Indigenous people to make decisions as 'contaminants', unfailingly biasing the process towards their own desires, despite all efforts to be neutral.[22]

I witnessed another group of colleagues at the institute brainstorming a term for 'White people who worked in Indigenous health'. Terms like 'altruistic' and 'helper' were tried and rejected, and no term was found. The next day, a colleague approached me to tell me that she and a few others had come up with the perfect label: 'White Helpers on Indigenous Projects – WHIPS!' (Kowal and Paradies 2005: 1353). The irony of the acronym was intentional, and exemplifies both the persistent stigma of whiteness and the constant need to attenuate it. While we try to establish a position of neutral assistance, we cannot escape our role as 'whips', instruments of discipline and castigation.

The task of managing White stigma requires constant vigilance, as one colleague explained: 'Constantly, constantly, constantly, you are thinking: "Am I not seeing the Indigenous side to this". You know? And often that will have nothing to do with it. But you are always thinking, "Is this an Indigenous issue?"'[23] Another colleague felt 'you have to question yourself every step of the way … you're not so confident any more'.[24] The constant possibility that one may be imposing one's beliefs or otherwise harming Indigenous people requires the White anti-racist to remain, in Goffman's terms, 'self-conscious and calculating about the impression he is making' (Goffman 1963: 14).

Another related device that attempts to resolve the problem of White agency is to claim to be the least of all possible evils, the 'good-enough White anti-racist'. As one researcher put it, 'I think that if I don't do this job, maybe someone else will do it who does not care about Indigenous issues at all'.[25]

The few White anti-racists that Goudge and Heron approve of in their accounts of international development workers come close to the White anti-racists I have described. Carol, the interviewee discussed in the Introduction, is praised by Heron for problematising her agency and admitting that she does not 'know how to deal with having power by virtue of [her] race' (Heron 2007: 96). Carol described her efforts 'not to impose herself' by remaining silent as much as possible (ibid.: 103). Her ultimate goal was 'to live a life that is as harmless as possible', pointing towards the inherent *harmful*ness of the White anti-racist that must be self-managed with vigilance (ibid.: 135).

As well as self-vigilance, White anti-racists deal with the problematic nature of their agency with the self-assurance that it is only temporary. This is expressed in what I call the 'five years' time' discourse. For White anti-racists, 'the ultimate endpoint is to be out of a job', either because the statistical gaps have finally yielded to reasoned intervention, or because Indigenous people are filling all the positions. White anti-racists take up positions on remote communities (as town clerks, sport and recreation officers, health promotion officers, clinic managers, or store managers) with the intention of mentoring a local worker so that 'in five years' time' they will be happily redundant and able to hand over to the 'now suitably skilled' Indigenous person.[26]

The strategies discussed thus far are aimed at recognising the stigma of whiteness in the hope that through self-vigilance, the anti-racist will be less likely to act 'White', or that their damaging influence will be temporary. In addition to these strategies, White anti-racists at the institute also creatively engage in constructing new identities beyond the missionary and the mercenary. Unsurprisingly, these efforts are marred by ambivalence.

One colleague told me that she had been discussing the 'three Ms' with her workmates: 'You know the three Ms? Well, we think there is one more: Motherers'.[27] Another colleague describes her attitude to working in Indigenous health as 'like being a mother; it's unconditional love'.[28] To conjure the figure of the mother as an alternative White anti-racist identity is a complex move. It is clearly meant to depart from the other 'three Ms', especially missionaries. Paradigmatic mothers differ from paradigmatic missionaries in that they are women, and their love is unconditional, not tied to religious affiliation or the task of improving souls. Although this feminised and secularised concept goes some way to overcoming the White stigma inherent in existing tropes of White anti-racism, it is still a deeply ambivalent category (Jacobs 2009). The researcher who suggested the '4th M' intended the category of 'motherers' to be as problematic as the other three categories. The most obvious problem is the use of a mother–child analogy for the relationship between White anti-racists and Indigenous people, positioning the latter as passive charges. Although maternal authority is perhaps softer and kinder than paternal authority, it is authority just the same.

To escape the stigma of authority, a final strategy for White anti-racists is to divest themselves of power altogether (if only discursively). This was a factor in the pleasure that many colleagues experienced when going on hunting trips or attending ceremonies in remote communities, activities to which they brought little knowledge or aptitude. A doctor working at the institute expressed this explicitly as an attempt to invert dominant power relations: 'I am trying to counter the whole power thing that comes from being a doctor. If I go there with the doctor hat on, people treat me a certain way. But if I go there with my community development hat on, people are completely different. Out bush I am the kid and they are the absolute experts'.[29]

In refusing the professional expertise of 'the doctor hat' and adopting the subservient role of White 'kid' to Indigenous 'absolute experts', White anti-racists can remedy their excessive and pathological power over Indigenous people and thus counter White stigma.[30] As a child, the White anti-racist cannot exploit Indigenous people. This relief is a good part of the pleasure Whites feel in those (unusual) moments where they are in the care of Indigenous people.

To be hunting in a remote place, knee-deep in mangrove mud, totally reliant on your Indigenous host to find your way back to the car, and then to direct you down barely visible tracks through the bush, back to the dirt road; to be in the middle of a lively discussion in a language you do not understand, reliant on translation; to make halting attempts to speak a few words of language and be heartily laughed at; to hand over control of important possessions on demand – the driver's seat of your car, your bank card for the purchase of camping supplies. In these moments we feel the unadulterated delight of cross-cultural exchange and the relief of oppressiveness shed, if only temporarily.

The stigma of whiteness is resolved most completely, and most fantastically, through the figure of the child. The child does not wish to impose her beliefs, nor is she able to do so. The fascination of the child with the 'other' hides no agenda of self-interest or exploitation, and is not suspect. The epitome of innocence and powerlessness, the figure of the White child realises the ultimate goal of White anti-racists: the inversion of colonial power relations. Through this imaginary inversion, the White anti-racist is cleansed of stigma. The White anti-racist that most comfortably inhabits the anti-racist fantasy space is neither overbearing father nor tender mother, but fervent child.

Disappearing Subjects

The attempts of White anti-racists to manage White stigma through self-effacement can only be partially effective. As various scholars of whiteness have argued, even the most vigilant White anti-racist will find it impossible to transcend their privilege. Ultimately, the indelible stain of White stigma denigrates the moral worth of White anti-racists, and precludes their ability to help Indigenous people. As I have argued, since the 1970s White anti-racists have increasingly taken up the challenge of Indigenous studies and whiteness studies to recognise their role in the dispossession and oppression of Indigenous peoples. From the point of view of White anti-racists, this has been both the triumph and the tragedy of the self-determination era. Problematising the role of non-Indigenous people in Indigenous development was long overdue, but it can reduce White anti-racists to children, leaving them without sufficient confidence to accomplish the difficult tasks their work entails.

The picture that emerges from this analysis shows that the normative anti-racism implied in Goudge's and Heron's critiques is not the solution they hope for. The question that remains is why normative White anti-racism is based in the negation of its own possibility.

A psychoanalytic lens offers one answer. Following Zizek, Hage argues that the 'fantasy space' of White nationhood can never be realised because in the moment that it occurs, the desiring White subjects of that nationhood would cease to exist. The migrant and the Aborigine play the crucial role of scapegoat, providing a reason for the perpetual deferral of the perfect nation, and thus preserving its possibility (Hage 1998: 74).

Extending this argument to this case would imply that White anti-racist identities are constituted by the desire for the anti-racist fantasy space of imagined future equality, and would dissolve if its goals were ever achieved. For the White anti-racist who dreams of a world where Indigenous people are no longer oppressed, a scapegoat for the unrealis-ability of their fantasy space must be found. That scapegoat is the racist White state and the racist White people who populate it – a category that is forever threatening to include the White anti-racist herself. To preserve the possibility of the anti-racist imaginary of future equality, the 'good' perpetrator must always be in danger of betraying her exceptional status, reverting to type and ruining the very goal she purports to strive for. The torturous ambivalence of the white anti-racist may be a prereq-uisite for the existence of this subjectivity that requires her to be saviour and scapegoat simultaneously.

The fantasy space of white nationhood is encapsulated in A.O. Neville's racist hope that Aborigines would be absorbed into white-ness and we would 'eventually forget that there were any aborigines in Australia' (Commonwealth of Australia 1937: 11). The 'fantasy space' that ultimately animates White anti-racist hopes is the inverse of this vision. Instead of disappearing Aborigines, White anti-racists wish to disappear themselves. As we have seen, institute researchers enjoy anticipating their obsolescence at such time when Indigenous people are finally self-sufficient; they also muse about 'pulling out' of remote communities in order to more immediately remove their contaminating influence.[31]

When the anti-racist fantasy space fails to deliver a tenable construction of ethical White agency, the most soothing fantasy is the dream that colonisation never occurred. An ethical, unstigmatised identity is thus premised on an historical impossibility. Like the 'non-German German' who must 'endure a non-identity' (Moses 2007a: 70), a stigmatised identity may be inescapable for White anti-racists.

Alongside the existential suffering I have outlined, some White anti-racists at the institute endured other forms of suffering, including exhaustion, humiliation and discomfort. The remainder of this chapter focuses on these experiences that range from everyday inconveniences to more conspicuous indignities. Stigma management contributes to an explanation of these experiences, as the stigma of whiteness is temporarily alleviated in moments of suffering. But first, we must return to the institute to hear Patricia's story.

Stigma and Suffering

Patricia: What can I do Emma? I'm only one person. I'm not a missionary, I'm not a saviour.
Author: What are you then?
Patricia: I'm a workhorse, a donkey, a mule.[32]

I had caught Patricia in a vulnerable moment. As we sat in the sunny courtyard of the institute, she reflected on her experiences of a community-based health promotion project that had been her focus for over five years. While she lived in Darwin, she regularly made trips to a remote Aboriginal community of just one thousand residents on the north coast of Australia, where the project was based. Stepping off the plane was like stepping into another world, a world of great physical beauty and stark disadvantage.

Like the vast majority of researchers employed by the research institute, Patricia is a non-Indigenous Australian who sought to improve the social and health status of Indigenous communities. She believed that projects that were grounded in the local 'cultural landscape' had the best chance of making a real impact.[33]

The project she was working on appeared to reflect these principles. Despite this, it was not going as well as she had hoped. Utilising culturally appropriate community-development principles, she was supporting the development of a clan-based fishing business, an intervention that would hopefully improve nutrition and physical activity in the community, as well as economic independence. Although her community collaborators had initially been enthusiastic about the project, embracing the chance to access the skills and resources needed to start their own business, there had been little progression in recent months. 'I am totally zapped of energy', she told me:

> You know how it is, when you go out there, you have a list of ten things you need to get done and if you get two things done you are lucky and to get that done you have to do doglegs everywhere around the community … We buy the equipment, we facilitate training in stock storage, occupational health and safety, first aid, bookkeeping; we take them to talk to small businessmen in town. The boat just circulates around the family and there's no local business.[34]

Frustration and exhaustion are prominent emotions in this account and other 'backstage' conversations among White anti-racists working in Indigenous health. Patricia had followed the principles of self-determination and community development, and the wishes expressed by her Indigenous collaborators and advisers. She had strongly advocated with her bosses at the institute to harness their support for the notion that a small business could be a health intervention. Now she feels frustrated by the apparent lack of motivation among her Indigenous collaborators, which has prevented a demonstrable 'project outcome' (in this case a family business) despite her impeccable process and personal commitment.

In this narrative, Patricia plays the role of the suffering workhorse, doggedly soldiering on even when self-determination fails to deliver. While the tragic suffering of Indigenous people is the reason that anti-racist White people move from their metropolitan homes to the towns of the North, the suffering of anti-racists themselves is a common if unacknowledged feature of work in Indigenous affairs. My research found that suffering is an experience shared by many, whether the suffering relates to physical hardship, professional frustration, or suspicion and betrayal from Indigenous colleagues. Although these experiences are common, White anti-racists are unlikely to directly complain about it, instead speaking obliquely about the 'difficulties' of working in Indigenous affairs. Recognising whiteness as a stigmatised identity that White anti-racists continuously attempt to rehabilitate and make liveable makes this puzzling behaviour more intelligible.

One aspect of White anti-racist suffering is illustrated by the wide-spread and mundane belief that working in Indigenous health *should* be difficult for White people. Newcomers to the institute are told by their peers that research projects cannot proceed until trusting relationships are developed between community leaders and researchers, and that this process can take a long time. They are told that when planning visits to communities they should regularly phone to check that the proposed date is still convenient, and should expect that trips may be cancelled at the last minute due to ceremonies, funerals, or competing events run by government departments or NGOs. When research trips do go ahead, the high level of mobility in remote communities means that potential research participants may be absent, due to visiting family members or attending funerals elsewhere. Family rivalries within communities may mean that some families will avoid a research project that a competing family is involved in.[35] White anti-racists at the institute are alternately frustrated and sanguine about these difficulties as they learn to anticipate and manage them, seeing them as inherent to working with a disadvantaged minority group in a post-settler context.

Another important contributor to the difficulty of working in Indigenous health is the rigorous ethical approval process. There is general endorsement at the institute of the high level of suspicion that human research ethics committees show towards projects that are led by non-Indigenous people (which is the case for the majority of research projects). Indigenous-specific ethical guidelines state that non-Indigenous researchers must demonstrate that their motivations for doing the research are pure, for instance by describing how they changed their plans in response to Indigenous desires (National Health and Medical Research Council 2003).[36] These requirements are generally seen by White anti-racists as necessary to protect Indigenous people. As one colleague commented, 'It's certainly harder for us [White people] but that's the way it should be; it should be even more rigorous'.[37] I propose that within the belief system underlying this comment, difficulty for White anti-racists equates with safety for Indigenous people.

There are two ways that White stigma can explain suffering. The first is suggested by the equation above linking White suffering to Indigenous safety. The stigma of privilege puts White anti-racists in perpetual danger of oppressing Indigenous people, even as they actively try to do the opposite. The experience of suffering provides temporary relief from this self-imposed stigma. For if we are suffering, we take solace from the belief that we cannot be simultaneously causing harm.

We can apply a similar analysis to Patricia's frustration in the account above. Though she is clearly frustrated with the seeming inability of her

Indigenous colleagues to deliver, she focuses on the difficulties of her own position. Any elaboration of her Indigenous colleagues' shortcomings – *why* all the training and support she has provided has led to nought – remains unspoken. This may reflect more than mere politeness. If we read the episode through the prism of stigma management, it makes sense that her own suffering remains the focus. Although the project may have failed, at least the stigma of privilege has been lessened. Her suffering promises that she has remained true to the wishes of her Indigenous colleagues, and has done no harm.

Related to such frustration is the suffering of service. Becky Thompson's social history of White anti-racist activism in the United States includes much commentary on the physical and mental suffering associated with being an activist. As one of her interviewees comments, 'I don't know that we treat ourselves very well'. Others discuss the financial strain of donating money to many campaigns and supporting needy visitors, and the lack of resources in underfunded universities and NGOs. She comments that her interviewees did not complain about these hardships. Rather, the theme of suffering 'was the one most people baulked at, tried to avoid, and said they didn't understand'. Thompson does not attempt to explain this suffering, although two of her interviewees suggest 'White guilt' or the 'Protestant ethic' may be to blame (Thompson 2001: 348, 354, 360).[38]

A colleague at the institute talks about the hardships of staying at the community where she commonly works:

> I go there and sleep on the floor at the women's centre, I don't have a proper shower … When I stay there the old chooks [term of endearment for old women] come along too to keep me company, which is a big ask for them, to leave their other responsibilities. But you've also got to feed them, and it's hard to cook for six people out of a billycan and [with] no knife. The toilets at the women's centre when I went there last were disgusting; there was poo on the walls. So I went and bought them big mobs [large amounts] of cleaning materials out of my travel allowance.[39]

Similar stories of poor accommodation abound in tales of research field trips, along with complaints about the battered vehicles hired out at exorbitant rates by the town council, the poor range of food available at remote community stores, and the risk of being attacked by unrestrained dogs that roam the community. The threat of physical violence is perhaps the ultimate form of potential suffering. While the high rates of violence in remote communities are overwhelmingly incidents in which Indigenous people are both victims and perpetrators, occasionally White professionals, particularly nurses, are the victims of assault (including

sexual assault). Very few institute researchers have been victims of violence, and it is infrequently discussed, but there are a few shared stories
of individuals feeling threatened, such as one researcher who woke up in
(poorly secured) council accommodation to find an unknown man in the
room (luckily for her, he fled).[40]

The experience of shared suffering is prominent in the narrative
above. The 'old chooks' with whom my colleague has cultivated a strong
relationship are happy to put their own family responsibilities aside to
stay with her in the women's centre to ensure her safety. And while she
struggles to stay clean and well fed as she goes about her community
development work, my colleague knows that the poor conditions at the
women's centre are no worse and probably better than the state of the
locals' overcrowded houses.

The story had the effect of invoking sympathy and admiration for
her suffering, and for the Indigenous people who bear these poor living
conditions as a permanent arrangement. It also contained a kernel of
pleasure. This pleasure derives partly from a relief from White stigma
in the moment of suffering. The White anti-racist who engages in
cooking for six old ladies with one pot, or who cleans excrement off
toilet walls, clearly demonstrates her harmlessness. The pleasure of
the story also reflects the pleasure of the affective tie that is evident
between my colleague and the old women, a phenomenon which relates
to the second explanatory model linking White stigma and White
suffering.

This second model of stigma and suffering concerns the tendency of
White anti-racists to crave acceptance and love from Indigenous people.
The stigma of whiteness is lessened when we feel that we are loved by the
Aboriginal people with whom we work – if they love us, we cannot be so
bad. Just like our suffering, their love attests to our innocuousness. The
imperative to counter White stigma takes White anti-racists beyond an
Orientalist desire for 'the other' (Bhabha 1994), and into a realm where
we desperately seek Indigenous acceptance. This need makes White anti-
racists highly vulnerable to betrayal by Indigenous people, and liable to
endure instances of betrayal when they occur.

Patrick Sullivan's study of an Aboriginal organisation in the Kimberley
provides an example of this type of suffering. He describes how young
radical White employees were badly treated by their bosses: 'Whenever
confrontation surfaced between the [government] administration and
Aboriginal groups, these committed whites absorbed most of the aggression. This was partly because Aborigines themselves were frequently
exploitative, being so concerned not to allow the capture of their organisations by whites that they tended to use and discard them, always sure

that there were others to take their place' (Sullivan 1996: 115). The importance of White suffering in managing White stigma means these Aboriginal leaders can be confident that more White anti-racists who are willing to absorb Aboriginal aggression can always be found.

Geographer Rachel Slocum has argued that pain and humiliation is central to anti-racist politics. She defines pain as 'feelings of sorrow, sensations of blushing, tears and tightened throats as well as the anger from whites against other whites and non-whites against whites and the further sadness that such anger brings'. She describes how White anti-racists in the United States are subjected to 'harsh words' from both other White anti-racist activists and people of colour when 'someone failed to understand the analysis [that is, failed to accept the inherent oppressiveness of whiteness] or when they wanted to prove their anti-racist credentials'. In one meeting of the anti-racist organisation she studied, her explanation of her research and request to take notes produced an angry reaction from a non-White participant. This led to a barrage of criticism from many people, her eventual ejection from the meeting and the forced surrender of her notes. Later, another White participant in the meeting told her that if she had cried, those at the meeting would not have exiled her and labelled her as untrustworthy. Her ability to hide her suffering suggested to others that she did not sufficiently crave love from non-Whites, and thus she was not sufficiently aware of her stigmatised status (Slocum 2009: 19, 33).

At the institute, experiences of public betrayal did occur, although uncommonly. One colleague described how she was publicly insulted by a senior Indigenous man at a community meeting, and left undefended by any of her other Indigenous colleagues. 'I honestly nearly fell off the chair', she recalls. 'I'd worked with these people at the meeting for four years really, really closely, and not one of them spoke up for me ... I was devastated. I was betrayed, devastated, unloved, [and considered] untrustworthy'.[41] Elsewhere in the discussion she rationalises her treatment, recognising that she was a convenient scapegoat used to resolve a clan conflict without anyone from the community having to be 'shamed'. However, her acceptance of this behaviour on 'cultural' grounds does not overshadow her sense of betrayal and rejection.

The language she uses in recalling the episode suggests the importance of White stigma in experiences of betrayal. She laments that she is not only 'betrayed, devastated, unloved' but also considered to be 'untrustworthy' (this last accusation echoing Slocum's story recounted above). This is a desire not just to be loved, but to be worthy of being loved. A White anti-racist is marked by their privilege as untrustworthy and unworthy of Indigenous love. The importance of her efforts to overcome White stigma, through loving and being loved by her Indigenous colleagues, is revealed in the moment they are threatened. Rather than arguing that their treatment of her was unfair, she rationalises their behaviour and focuses on her feelings of betrayal. To her, the experience reveals not the potential cruelty of anti-racist practice, as highlighted in Slocum's account, but the pervasive nature of White stigma – she is unlovable, after all.

It is possible to interpret these experiences of suffering as extreme displays of tolerance. The toleration of frustration, discomfort and betrayal would then demonstrate the position of power from which White anti-racists can choose to suffer, or not to suffer. Hage argues that tolerance is 'a form of symbolic violence in which a mode of domination is presented as a form of egalitarianism' (Hage 1998: 87).[42]

When someone makes the observation 'He/She is tolerant', the extended phrase 'He/She is tolerant for someone who has the power not to be' is always implied. A powerless person is never thought of as 'tolerant': the title is reserved for those people who are in a position to tolerate, or not tolerate, others. The 'tolerant' person therefore benefits both from being judged as tolerant, and from the social power that makes this tolerance notable. Toleration involves setting the limit between the tolerable and the intolerable, or what he calls an 'empowered spatiality', a fantasy of ownership of the nation that decides where and when to tolerate outsiders. The futility of the symbolic denial of social distance is a convenient way to have one's cake and eat it too – to be considered a 'good' White person and retain the privileges of whiteness (Hage 1998: 87, 89).[43]

This analysis is congruent with the dominant thread of whiteness studies discussed previously in this chapter: the attempts of White people to be anti-racist are really conscious or subconscious efforts to reinstate or protect their privilege. The concept of White stigma sets this in a different light. For these Whites, the social power that makes tolerance noticeable is the very thing they wish to erase. They aim to deliberately privilege Indigenous desires and meanings over their own in an attempt at empowered disempowerment. However, like Hage, Bourdieu and others suggest, most find it impossible to transcend their privilege, no matter how vulnerable they make themselves or how much they suffer. In Chapter 2, I suggested that some White anti-racists respond to the unravelling of remediable difference by withdrawing from an anti-racist identity and retreating into other realms of intercultural conviviality (such as pleasure and friendship). In the light of this chapter, this withdrawal can be seen as a resignation to the stigma of whiteness, and an abandonment of attempts to be recognised as anti-racist (see Chapter 5). Such Whites no longer desire to disappear, but the cost of their continued presence is an incompatibility with the territory of anti-racism.

Notes

1. This is similar to the contemporaneous move against 'top-down' development and towards 'participatory development', whereby subaltern subjects are remade as the authors of their own improvement (Mosse 2005a, 2011; Li 2007). Other ethnographies of 'professional altruists' (as Arvidson calls them) reveal similar tendencies towards self-deprecation (Allahyari 2000; Riles 2004, 2006; Arvidson 2008).
2. Transcript: 15, 6.
3. Field Notes 12 Oct. 2004: 2, 8.
4. Parts of this chapter draw on material from Kowal 2011 and Kowal 2012a.
5. The Indigenous people that White anti-racists sympathise with are clearly stigmatised in Australian society. In relation to Indigenous stigma, White anti-racists play the role of sympathetic 'normal', what Goffman calls the 'wise'. Although beyond the scope of this chapter, the set of behaviours associated with being 'wise' to Indigenous stigma would intersect and interact with the behaviours that are explained by White stigma (Goffman 1963). Another related issue is the stigma of 'White trash', that is, poor White people (Wray 2006). However, there is likely to be little overlap between White anti-racist and 'White trash' segments of the White population.
6. Hughey argues that U.S. White anti-racists experienced 'stigma allure' whereby they actively 'embraced a stigmatized white racial identity as a lifelong burden' in order to demonstrate their commitment to anti-racism. Stigma acts as an 'integral marker of group identity' (Hughey 2012: 228, 237).
7. Progressive historians rebutted the charge of 'black armbands' by imputing that conservative historians wore 'white blindfolds' (Macintyre and Clark 2003).
8. See Chapter 4, note 23, for a discussion of the difference between settlers and migrants.
9. Although it is a voluntary stigma, I would argue that where it is passionately felt or fostered in childhood it could be experienced as involuntary. One way that white stigma can be fostered is through 'Sorry books', a community initiative popular in the late 1990s where ordinary Australian citizens assumed some responsibility for the cruelties of the colonial state by recording messages of sympathy for the Stolen Generations. A selection of publicly available messages are from children; for example, 'I've very sorry for taking your rights and liberties. Keiren Callahan, 9 years' (Australian Institute of Aboriginal and Torres Strait Islander Studies 2013).
10. Although it should be noted there are key differences between working overseas and working in a post-settler colonial context. Briefly, in general international development workers experience white privilege; those working in Indigenous affairs experience white stigma.
11. For another useful account, see Eriksson Baaz 2005; and for a recent review of the broader field, see Mosse 2013.

12. Hughey (2012) is similarly disapproving of White anti-racists complaining of bad treatment, and O'Brien (2003) assumes that willingness to suffer discomfort, pain and humiliation is the sign of a 'good' anti-racist.

13. On bad feelings and anti-racism, see Ahmed 2005; and Maddison 2011.

14. Transcript: 11, 16.

15. Transcript: 16, 7.

16. Transcript: 8, 2.

17. Transcript: 6, 16.

18. Transcript: 4, 5.

19. The empirical question of the impact of missions on Aboriginal lifeworlds requires a more complex consideration. See Swain and Bird Rose 1988 for Australian anthropological and historical material; and Swain 1993 for an influential argument about the impact of missionaries (and other external influences) on Aboriginal religions. See also Schwarz and Dussart 2010; and Laugrand 2012.

20. For an earlier exploration of this point, see Kowal and Paradies 2005.

21. Transcript: 15, 6.

22. Transcript: 15, 14.

23. Transcript: 13, 21.

24. Transcript: 5, 13.

25. Field Notes, 6 Apr. 2005.

26. Transcript: 15, 18. This discourse has been around for decades (Cowlishaw 1999; Tatz 1972). Batty describes yet another strategy for dealing with White stigma, where a senior Aboriginal person 'leases' their Aboriginality to a non-Indigenous person in order to give them authority to speak (Batty 2005).

27. Field Notes, 17 Mar. 2005.

28. Field Notes, 14 Apr. 2006.

29. Field Notes, 10 Sept. 2004.

30. The refusal of the label 'expert' is a recurring theme in White anti-racist discourse. For example, one non-Indigenous academic working in Indigenous studies tells how 'I daily resist other white academics desire to call me an "expert"' (Lampert 2003: 17), and berates some White academics who 'argu[e] with Indigenous academics that their opinions were misinformed, and quoting from "good" white sources as their proof' (Lampert 2003:19). At the same time, she draws on the discourse within whiteness studies discussed above, where the very rejection of privilege (in this case, rejection of the label 'expert') is actually a manifestation of privilege: 'It's very easy for me to smugly hide behind my role as an "expert" because even if I reject the label I acquire it from an academic institution that values and rewards "expertise". I can become this "expert" in Indigenous issues just by saying that's what I am, or allowing other white people to say it for me. My academic qualifications are written on my white body – plain in the colour of my skin, which grants me authority before I open my mouth' (Lampert 2003: 18).

31. Transcripts: 17, 20; and 15, 14. As I will explore in the conclusion, the Northern Territory Emergency Intervention that began in July 2007 signalled a paradigm shift away from self-determination and towards some new era that resolves the dilemmas of Indigenous improvement in another (equally contingent and provisional) way (Cowlishaw, Kowal and Lea 2006). Although there are important continuities between self-determination and the emerging era, the kind of White withdrawalism I have described here is now far less tenable.

32. Field Notes, 18 Apr. 2005. The follow sections appear in another form in Kowal 2012a.
33. Field Notes, 12 Aug. 2004.
34. Field Notes, 18 Apr. 2005: 4, 22–23.
35. As discussed in Chapter 5, many of these examples were discussed in a photocopied document called 'How to Stay Out of Trouble when Visiting Remote Aboriginal Communities' that was distributed to new employees at the institute.
36. Field Notes, 6 Dec. 2004.
37. Transcript: 9, 20.
38. Hughey also found that White anti-racist activists complained of hardships. In contrast to Thompson he did not find they were reluctant to talk about these difficulties, but rather they wore them as a 'white badge of pride' and used them to undermine the suffering of non-White Americans (Hughey 2012).
39. Field Notes, 18 Apr. 2005: 4, 23–24.
40. See Lea's discussion of 'Occupational Health & Safety' in the Northern Territory Health Department (Lea 2008).
41. Transcript: 17, 17–18.
42. Wendy Brown makes a related argument that tolerance is a practice of domination; see Brown 2006.
43. He sees this as an example of Bourdieu's 'strategies of condescension', whereby those in a superior social position symbolically deny the social distance between them and those below them by acting in a non-stereotypical fashion. The symbolic denial is simultaneously a recognition of the social distance, according the denier both 'the advantages of proximity and the advantages of distance' (Hage 1998: 78).

Conclusion

The White anti-racists depicted in this book find themselves trapped in the gaps they seek to close; the gap between remediable difference and radical difference, between sanitised difference and unsanitised difference, between improvement and assimilation, and between anti-racism and racism. In this conclusion, I consider the implications of my arguments for the current Australian political context, and for the broader project of multicultural recognition. What does my analysis mean for Australia, for Indigenous people, and for the capacity of liberal democracies to treat their subjects equitably and reckon with their colonial pasts? Is what I have described an aberration, a speed bump on the inevitable path towards statistical equality, with or without Indigenous self-determination? Or are the concerns of these White anti-racists a microcosm of the aporias of settler colonial Indigenous governance, or of national and international trends against the politics of recognition?

To address these questions, the dramatic change in Australian Indigenous affairs over the last decade must be taken into account. A paradigm shift away from self-determination is well underway. Although the logic of the self-determination era as I described it in Chapter 2 thrives in some pockets, in the main it is under attack. While the 'history wars' and the lack of a government apology to the Stolen Generations monopolised public debate in the 1990s (Macintyre and Clark 2003), after 2000 the issue of 'Aboriginal separatism' became a focus of conservative discourse (Johns 2001). Media stories increasingly proclaimed that 'Indigenous self-determination has failed' (Om 2006), and commentaries argued that land rights, access to welfare benefits, and culturally appropriate services have not improved the lives of Indigenous people (Neill 2002; Sandall 2001). Common to these varying accounts was the argument that the desire of a non-Indigenous progressive elite to assuage their 'White guilt' by preserving Indigenous culture has led to permissive practices (such as letting children abstain from school, and not pursuing violent offenders) that ironically have further damaged Indigenous societies.[1] Self-determination policies have been declared a humanitarian disaster, as remote communities wallow in 'welfare dependency' and widespread violence and sexual abuse is reported (Wild and Anderson 2007; Langton 2008; Sutton 2009).

In the last three years of the Howard conservative government's eleven year reign (1996–2007), it began pursuing policies that blatantly challenged the principles of the self-determination era, beginning with dismantling the Aboriginal and Torres Strait Islander Commission in 2004,[2] and culminating in the 2007 Northern Territory Emergency Response weeks before they lost office. 'The Intervention', as the Emergency Response is otherwise known, was an enormous and sudden increase in state investment in remote communities, which aimed, in the words of the then Indigenous Affairs Minister Mal Brough, to 'stabilize… normalize… and exit' remote communities (Altman and Hinkson 2007). The various measures taken in over 180 'prescribed' remote Northern Territory communities, community living areas and town camps included banning alcohol and pornography, abolishing the permit system that controlled movements into communities, and 'quarantining' 50 per cent of welfare payments of community residents into a separate account that could only be used at designated stores that supplied food, clothing and household items (and not alcohol). At the outset of this policy shift, the then federal health minister (and currently prime minister) outlined the principles underpinning his government's policies. They believed that self-determination had failed to improve Indigenous lives 'because of misplaced tact and fear of imposing what are now seen as outside standards, rather than universal ones. Australians' sense of guilt about the past and naive idealisation of communal life may now be the biggest obstacle to the betterment of Aborigines' (Abbott 2006).

Scepticism about self-determination has been a common theme on the conservative side of politics, but in the last few years this has spread across much of the political spectrum. Many Indigenous advocates have labelled the Intervention as a return to assimilation (Altman and Hinkson 2007). However, some progressive non-Indigenous commentators have aligned themselves with Indigenous leader Noel Pearson's arguments that self-determination has allowed the government to abdicate its responsibility to poorly functioning Indigenous organisations (Cowlishaw 2003). Accordingly, many White anti-racists feel ambivalent about the current Northern Territory Intervention, rather than rejecting it altogether as a rerun of the assimilation era, an issue I return to below. The historic and long-awaited apology to the Stolen Generations delivered in 2008 by the then newly elected progressive prime minister, Kevin Rudd, is another illustration of this vacillation. Alongside Rudd's moving words of apology, he stressed the need to uphold the previous government's Intervention in order to re-establish social norms in 'dysfunctional' remote communities enduring endemic levels of violence and substance abuse.[3]

Using the nomenclature of this book, these various developments indicate a movement away from Orientalism and radical difference, and towards unmitigated remedialism. 'Remediable difference' as I have described it has become unstuck, and the configuration of remedialism and Orientalism is in a state of flux. In the emerging paradigm, the 'fear of assimilation' is labelled as the problem, while the transformations in Indigenous communities that were once feared as assimilation are refashioned as 'inevitable cultural change'.[4] The concern that 'cultural change' will erode health-preserving aspects of Indigenous culture appears to have waned. In Robert Manne's terms, we have moved from the 'optimistic hope' of the self-determination era, when reviving Indigenous culture was broadly believed to offer the solution to Indigenous disadvantage, to a mode of 'pessimistic realism' where the autonomous liberal subject shaped by the right mix of incentives and sanctions is seen as the only rational goal of Indigenous policy (Manne 2007).

This emerging belief system supersedes remediable difference. If it continues to ascend, Indigenous difference will no longer be the quandary I have described in this book. Eventually, White anti-racists will cease to fear that essential indigeneity resides in the gaps they seek to close. Indigenous difference will not need to be parsed into sanitised and unsanitised portions to manage this fear. In effect, this move implicitly shifts all of Indigenous difference into the 'unsanitised' category. Indigenous difference can therefore be unproblematically erased as the statistical gaps close. If Indigenous people are no longer remediably *different*, but just remediable, this relieves much of the effort of charting a course between remedialism and Orientalism.

We can see this paradigm shift in the language of Indigenous policy. As noted, in 2007 the incoming progressive Labor government retained the Intervention with only minor modifications. As the Intervention's five-year expiration date of mid-2012 approached, the government considered its options. A discussion paper produced in 2011 (the basis of what became the 'Stronger Futures' legislation) outlines the possibilities for action, stating that the priorities would be 'making sure children get a good education, reducing alcohol abuse, and getting people into jobs' (Department of Families, Housing, Community Services and Indigenous Affairs 2011). The report includes no mention of self-determination, the keyword for Indigenous policy in the last three decades of the twentieth century. Even more instructive is the complete absence of the word 'culture'.[5] Words that are heavily used are 'training, building capacity, engagement', and most of all, 'responsibility' and 'partnership'. In this emerging paradigm, cultural difference is no longer relevant, and the task of Indigenous improvement is purely one of remediation.[6]

This reconfiguration of Indigenous affairs also reconfigures White anti-racist identities, initially heightening the fears and uncertainties that I have argued underlie attempts to 'do good' in Indigenous Australia.[7] The dilemmas I outlined in Chapter 2 are made more acute in the wake of the paradigm shift. The related fears of repeating the past (the dilemma of historical continuity) and the fear of making Indigenous people White (the dilemma of social improvement) were managed by remediable difference, for at least some White anti-racists. The normative anti-racist beliefs of the self-determination era promised that if Indigenous people had control of culturally appropriate services, and if Indigenous culture was restored, then Indigenous disadvantage would be addressed. This belief system maintained the moral integrity of White anti-racists who could help Indigenous people without the risk of inflicting further injuries on them.

For many White anti-racists, these normative beliefs have been badly shaken by the paradigm shift. The relative certainty of the self-determination era has been replaced with increasing uncertainty. There are two elements of this uncertainty. The first is uncertainty about which policy failure it is that we need to avoid repeating. For anti-racists who populate anti-intervention activist groups (such as 'Rollback the Intervention' and 'Concerned Australians'), assimilation still stands as the ultimate genocidal policy that is making a strong return. They equate the Intervention's welfare quarantining to rations, and employment programmes to forced assimilation, and they are unshaken in their conviction that genuine Indigenous control of policy is the answer (see, for example, Gibson 2009).[8] But for others, this certainty has been eroded by the revelations of widespread violence and abuse which many argue had worsened over the course of the self-determination era; by the work of Noel Pearson, Peter Sutton and Marcia Langton; and by shifting government policies. While White anti-racists once only had to avoid being assimilationist, now those who support distinctively 'Indigenous' lifeworlds must also ensure that they are not, as Pearson, Sutton and Langton argue, allowing romantic notions of the noble savage deny Indigenous people their citizenship rights to education and government services.

The self-determination era is becoming yet another chapter in the history of well-intentioned but ultimately misguided Indigenous policies, creating a quandary for many White anti-racists.[9] Where does the major source of human rights violations against Indigenous people lie: in the desire to make Indigenous people resemble other Australians, or in the abandonment of this aspiration in the 1970s? Some are sure of the answer to this question, one way or another. The Australian public sphere is full of people certain that the Intervention is only disempowering Indigenous people, and should immediately be stopped; and of people certain that the Intervention has been at least partially successful and that the conditions in remote communities warrant its continuation. Many more are uncertain.

The second source of uncertainly relates to the 'authentic Indigenous voice', a concept I outlined in Chapter 5. As we saw, this voice is the answer that some White anti-racists seek to any Indigenous policy problem – 'Just ask any Aboriginal person what should be done, and they will tell you! There's the answer!' (Troppo Armadillo 2004). In the self-determination era, concepts such as self-determination and community control depended on the idea that a community had a unified or at least consensual 'view' that could be determined through proper consultation.[10] This view was generally reinforced in the public sphere, where dissent amongst senior Indigenous leaders on ideological grounds was rare.[11] This end of this public Indigenous consensus has been marked by the increasing prominence of Indigenous intellectuals like Pearson and Langton. These figures have been divisive among the left. Whether one agrees with them or not, they have been instrumental in ending the fantasy that Indigenous people at a community, regional or national level present a unified view.

The recognition that Indigenous people have diverse views and interests allows a more accurate view of Indigenous political life. But it causes problems for White anti-racist subjectivities. The authentic Indigenous voice promised that if White anti-racists acted on the view of 'the community' they could avoid imposing their beliefs and desires on Indigenous people. One response to the uncertainty created by the breakdown of the authentic Indigenous voice is the introduction of another division into the space of Indigenous recognition (see Chapter 5): the division between the neoliberal, pro-Intervention and the progressive, anti-Intervention

Indigene. An example of this emergence is a 2005 piece by Eve Vincent and Clare Land in a left-wing online magazine (Land and Vincent 2005).[12] The article, 'Thinking for Ourselves', argued that it is acceptable to disagree with Noel Pearson. The fact that this argument must be made demonstrates the reluctance of White anti-racists to disagree with an Indigenous person and their corresponding need for Indigenous validation.

Is what I have described in this book a reflection of this paradigm shift? Are the White anti-racists who subscribe to the belief system I have set out simply suffering from 'misplaced tact' (as Abbott suggested), and will the crisis of remediable difference and the resulting fear and uncertainty be alleviated by the guilt-free universalism of the new era? Let us assume for a moment that the current critique of self-determination is, or will soon become, the dominant view among Whites who identify as anti-racist, and that the self-determination era is supplanted by another era, perhaps one of 'mutual responsibility' or 'partnerships'.[13] This may lessen White stigma and expand the space of recognition of anti-racism, diminishing the need for the convoluted performances I have described.

However, there are two related reasons why Orientalism will continue to exert its influence and require the persistence of some form of remediable difference. Tim Rowse has argued that the government's 'new arrangements' in Indigenous affairs cannot be a 'return to assimilation' because of two lasting legacies of the self-determination era: Aboriginal incorporated organisations, which number in the thousands and perform important state functions such as providing housing and health care; and the archive of Aboriginal statistics, including its many gaps (Rowse 2006). These phenomena will ensure that Indigenous difference continues to be visible and prominent.

At the interpersonal level, the experiences of White anti-racists in the contact zone will continue to unsettle the remedial project, even if the ascending policy paradigm downplays difference. Even the greatest confidence in universalism may be shaken in the midst of a ceremony, funeral, or hunting trip. Moments of radical difference are bound to generate suspicion that these aspects of Indigenous lifeworlds should not or cannot be packaged into the weekends of the otherwise Western lifestyle required if statistical gaps are to close.[14] Finally, if and when White anti-racists are able to overcome their fear of resembling the past, they may still be haunted by the future. They may still fear a future that might judge their universalism as false. The judgement of their predecessors as, at best, misguided, and at worst, racist (judgement that may soon include the practitioners of self-determination), makes their own future reckoning a persistent fear.

Dilemmas of Multiculturalism

The dilemmas I have described in this book illustrate the broader contradictions of liberal multiculturalism. At various points I have discussed the body of work that tries to reconcile the liberal state with a culturally diverse polity (Goldberg 1994; Taylor 1994; Kymlicka et al. 2000; Parekh 2000; Markell 2003; Kymlicka 2007, 2010; Winter 2011). At base, the contradictions this work grapples with reflect the crisis of universalism. Much has been written on the collapse of universal reason in the second half of the twentieth century. Theoretically, this has been encapsulated in the project of postmodernism (Lyotard 1984; Jameson 1991). Practically, it has played out in a variety of social movements, including Indigenous rights movements (Niezen 2003).[15]

Many scholars who write about the politics of recognition connect the collapse of universalism to the rise of 'culture'. The declining order is the classical liberal theory with its roots in the seventeenth century that sought to overcome the hold of religion and uncover the scientific principles of individual reason and individual need that could explain all aspects of social order. To European theorists it seemed 'natural' that pure reason resided in Europe. In the second half of the twentieth century, the social sciences rejected the idea of a universal human nature and contended that human nature could only be understood in its particular cultural context. Modernity itself was revealed as one of many contexts in which societies flourish. In the terms proposed by anthropologist James Boggs, 'liberal theory' that posits an essential human nature was replaced with 'culture theory' that recognises multiple ways of being human. Boggs argues that this shift is all but accomplished in social theory, with politics, law and economics lagging behind. This shift causes a collision between Western individualism – the 'essence of universal humanness' – and 'a new kind of human subject whose nature is inescapably cultural and therefore unavoidably situated' (Boggs 2002: 602).

Liberal multicultural theory and practice sits at the centre of this collision and the problems that erupt from it. As Gray puts it, the task of liberalism after universalism is 'to seek terms of coexistence among different cultural forms without the benefit – dubious as it proved to be – of the universalist perspective and the conception of rational choice' (Gray 1995: 96). Of all the variety of cultural forms that liberal multiculturalism attempts to accommodate, indigeneity generates some of the most complex problems.[16]

From the point of view of this shift from the universal to the particular, the unravelling of remediable difference could be considered the birth pangs of the new cultural paradigm, rather than the death knell of self-determination. Self-determination may not constitute a failure of cultural theory (as critics of self-determination might argue), but merely an early instantiation to be superseded with more nuanced models. Attempts by the current Australian government to resurrect universalism may be a temporary deviation as we slowly but inevitably move towards the formal recognition of Indigenous law and knowledge.[17]

How would the continuing rise of culturalism effect the beliefs of White anti-racists? It would have the opposite effect to the reinstatement of universalism typified by the Northern Territory Intervention. Rather than the triumph of remedialism over Orientalism, the universalism inherent in remedialism may eventually fade. The 'healthy' universal subject of the top line of the graph would cease to be the implicit reference point. It is difficult to imagine what this world without remedialism might be like. It could involve developing local, culturally specific ways to measure Indigenous well-being that replace the comparison of Indigenous and non-Indigenous statistics.[18] Indigenous development may seek out more imaginative culturalisms, and decouple from statistical equality and remedialism altogether, making the 'self-determination era' look like crude efforts too closely tied to Western aims.[19]

By taking a longer view, David Scott (2003) offers an alternative understanding of these shifts. He draws on Bernard McGrane's argument that Western societies have always ordered and explained difference, but that the taxonomy of difference has changed throughout history. In Renaissance Europe, the 'Other' were those who lacked Christianity. For Enlightenment scholars, the Other lacked reason. Nineteenth-century science created a gulf of evolutionary time between Europeans and non-Europeans in the form of advanced and primitive races. In the twentieth century, the dominant mode of explaining difference shifted again. The Other that once lacked Christianity, then lacked reason, and then belonged to a primitive race, became the Other which 'has culture' (McGrane 1989).

But this latest way to discern the Other has one distinctive feature. The negative valence of previous marks of otherness does not apply to the 'culturally diverse'. Many political theorists (among other social scientists) embrace the concept of culture because it is 'a cosmopolitan idiom in which the otherness of the West's Others, once a source of defensive anxiety and the object of truth-determining investigations, could now be understood … as *mere* difference' (Scott 2003: 111). Through culture, political philosophy can liberate itself from its oppressing and oppressive past. Culture performs the ironic task of meeting 'an ideological demand for a post ideological concept of difference' (ibid.: 109).[20] Like the White anti-racist belief system I have explored in this book, the project of lib-eral multiculturalism requires a conception of difference that contains the possibility of non-oppressive power relations.[21] Here we return to the central question of this book. When a group of relatively intelligent, well-meaning people, more or less supported by the state, attempt to enact a mode of difference that is non-oppressive, does this make any difference?

Political philosopher Wendy Brown is among those scholars who argue a politics of difference cannot transcend the conditions of oppression that produced those differences.[22] Through their emergence as a pro-test against marginalisation or subordination, politicised identities (like queer, refugee or Indigenous) become dependent on their own exclusion to remain salient. Acts of reparation can only potentiate suffering, in that they 'ceaselessly re-enact even as they redistribute the injuries of marginalization and subordination' within liberal society. Liberal multi-culturalism is severely constrained because the universalism of liberal-ism can only recognise difference through 'an economy of inclusion and exclusion' (Brown 1995: 70; see also Mehta 1999; Brown 2006; Ahmed 2012; Epstein 2007). Inevitably, 'the language of recognition becomes the language of unfreedom', even as it strives towards liberation (Brown 1995: 66). For Brown, an identity rooted in past and present oppressions can only reinforce its own marginalisation. Rather than sourcing identity from the wounds of the past and seeking justice through recognition, an emancipatory identity must be grounded in a vision of an alternative future that transcends liberal universalism.

This analysis suggests the ultimate problem with indigeneity, as it is recognised by progressive political forms, is that just Indigenous futures are bound to oppressive pasts. If this is the case, what are the alternatives? Scholars have proposed various post-racial possibilities. Paul Gilroy's vision of the future beyond difference has received perhaps the most attention. He argues that race-based affirmative action cannot deliver positive social change because of its reliance on racial categories. In a move similar to Brown's, Gilroy argues that 'raciology', defined as that which 'brings the virtual realities of "race" to dismal and destructive life', is too embedded in colonial oppression to offer any emancipatory potential (Gilroy 2000: 1). He envisages a Utopian 'planetary human-ism', where skin colour will be of no greater consequence than eye colour. He traces this project from Fanon, who argues in *Black Skin White Masks*: 'In no way should I dedicate myself to the revival of an unjustly recog-nized Negro civilization. I will not make myself the man of any past. I do not want to exalt the past at the expense of my present and of my future' (Fanon 1967: 226). For Gilroy, freedom from the encasement of colour is offered by a 'strategically universal' humanity.

This humanist vision relies on forgetting the past and abandoning the memories that produce wounded identities. Gilroy argues that this project of forgetting is in any case inevitable as the passage of time means the 'ebbing away of the brutal colonial relations that gave such a distinctive meaning to "race"' (Gilroy 2000: 335). Brown similarly prescribes a future-oriented politics as the antidote for wounded attachments, arguing that the ontological claims of identity politics of 'I am' should be replaced with the political claim, 'I want this for us' (Brown 1995: 75). The central question should not be 'what has happened to us', but 'what kind of a future do we want'?

By this logic, indigeneity is a troubled identity indeed, grounded as it is in past and ongoing injuries. One part is defined through ties to precolonial societies and in opposition to the European invaders, such that, as Muecke puts it, '"Indigenous modern" sounds like an oxymoron' (Muecke 2004: 138). The other part is defined through the collective wound of colonisation and continuing exclusion from the post-settler state. But while Gilroy sees the horizon of colonial brutality receding, Indigenous Australians continue to actively pursue compensation for the crimes of the past.[23] Brown concedes that although forgetting is a way forward, it aggravates the wounds of those for whom 'erased histories and historical invisibility are themselves such integral elements of the pain inscribed' (Brown 1995: 74). Leaving the past behind may make sense in theory, but as a political strategy it lacks politically viability and humanity.

Nonetheless, recent work by Indigenous scholars questions the utility of a concept of indigeneity anchored in the past. One target of this critical work is the concept of 'pan-indigeneity', a view that considers all Indigenous people as equally invested in an Indigenous identity, regardless of their social situation or diversity of ancestry. Pan-indigeneity has been the dominant construction of indigeneity in the self-determination era. It is an important strategy that served to counter historical invisibility and political marginalisation, but that ultimately illustrates the aporias of racialisation in post-settler nations. While acknowledging that pan-indigeneity has resulted in significant successes within the nation-state,[24] Indigenous scholar Yin Paradies argues this instrumental myth necessarily essentialises Indigenous people in multiple ways (Paradies 2006). He argues that these 'fantasies of Indigeneity' act to exclude most Indigenous people from authentic indigeneity and amount to 'internalised racism'. For example, people of Indigenous descent who choose to identify as 'part-Indigenous' are seen as misguided and politically treacherous, playing into the hands of conservative groups who seek to deny their authenticity.[25] To escape essentialised indigeneity, both Indigenous and non-Indigenous people 'must decouple Indigeneity from disadvantage and marginality, from cultural and physical alterity and from callow moral dichotomies' (Paradies 2006: 363). By loosening the definition of indigeneity to include middle-class Indigenous people, and even non-Indigenous people adopted by Indigenous people, indigeneity could be radically redefined in a way that may free it from its opposition to whiteness and from its anchor in the past.[26]

Lynette Russell presents a similar political project in her rejection of the dichotomy of Indigenous and non-Indigenous. In her historical scholarship and in personal accounts of her Indigenous identity, she rejects the imperative to state something is *either* Aboriginal *or* non-Aboriginal, instead choosing 'an identity that states emphatically I am neither one thing nor another. For me, the binaries of Indigenous/non-Indigenous, native/newcomer are meaningless. Instead, I found myself reaching for the possibility of another space or, perhaps, two (or more) spaces, each mutually occupying the same locale' (Russell 2006: 13).[27] According to Brown and others, such redefined notions of indigeneity may better facilitate future-orientated political projects.

This book has extended the politics of recognition to understand how dominant subjectivities are formed through mutual recognition with subalterns. In that light, Brown's observation that 'the language of recognition becomes the language of unfreedom' has implications for White anti-racists who recognise and are recognised by Indigenous people (Brown 1995: 66). Just as Indigenous subjectivities that are founded in opposition paradoxically limit the possibilities for emancipation, White identities founded in opposition to Indigenous people may be impotent at driving change, even where the White identity in question is the shamed, stigmatised and sorry settler.

An alternative politics would explore non-stigmatised, non-settler identities.[28] The aim of this exercise is not to let White people 'off the hook' or to ignore White privilege, but to create a society that did not curtail its own emancipatory possibility. Following Russell, descendants of non-Indigenous settlers may reject a settler identity, perhaps pointing to their deeply felt connections to the Australian landscape (see Trigger 2008; and Chapter 4).[29] The dissolution of the settler–native boundary may resolve the challenges and aporias of White anti-racist subjectivities I have outlined, but at enormous political cost. Without recognisable settlers and recognisable Indigenous people, one cannot have compensation or reparation for the wrongs of colonialism. Dismantling the 'fantasies of Indigeneity' could also dismantle the hard-won successes of Indigenous political movements. A more reasonable goal may be a plurality of identity – 'settler-and' rather than 'settler-or' – which would reject the idea of mutually exclusive categories without abandoning categories altogether.

It is hard to imagine what viable, non-oppositional identities might look like. The political utility of such identities might seem slim to some and morally bereft to others. But given the limitations inherent in current modes of recognition, they are worth exploring.

Notes

1. Noel Pearson has been a prominent Indigenous proponent of this argument; see Pearson 2000; 2007.
2. ATSIC was the national representative body for Indigenous Australians that offered policy advice and delivered Indigenous programmes. ATSIC leaders were the subject of various scandals (including rape and corruption charges) which preceded the organisation's demise, although many Indigenous advocates maintain these were convenient excuses for the government to do what it wanted. A memorable policy experiment of that time that foretold the Intervention was the introduction of Shared Responsibility Agreements (SRAs) under a policy of Mutual Obligation from late 2004. The first SRA was established in the remote WA community of Mulan. Residents agreed to wash their children's faces every day to prevent the eye disease trachoma in return for increased services and a petrol bowser (Kowal 2006b).
3. This decision to continue nearly every aspect of the Intervention was supported by the progressive Northern Territory government (which included a number of Indigenous ministers) and was fuelled by continuing revelations in 2007 and 2008 of child sexual abuse in remote communities in the Northern Territory, Far North Queensland and remote Western Australia.
4. See, for example, Nicolas Peterson's chapter on 'secular assimilation' in Altman and Hinkson 2010.
5. However the document does use the adjective 'cultural' twice: once when it reinforces that culture cannot be used as a mitigating factor in sentencing, and the other in the reference list, listing a government report completed by consultants Cultural and Indigenous Research Australia.
6. An argument that deserves further research is whether and how a muted form of difference persists in the concept of 'partnership'.
7. This shift, which is also occurring within Indigenous populations beyond Australia, reconfigures Indigenous identities along with White identities. Emerging Indigenous identities are outside the scope of my research, but see, for example, de la Cadena and Starn 2007; Rowse 2008; Merlan 2009; Fortun, Fortun and Rubenstein 2010; Trigger and Dalley 2010; Scott 2011; and Gagné and Salaün 2012.
8. Also see http://rollbacktheintervention.wordpress.com/ and http://www.concerned australians.com.au/.
9. For anthropological scholarship on this paradigm shift, see Sanders 2009; Sutton 2009; Altman and Hinkson 2010; Austin-Broos 2011; Sullivan 2011; Lea 2012; Morphy and Morphy 2013; and Merlan and Peterson 2013.
10. The assumptions of unity and homogeneity underlying community consultation have been noted in relation to Australia, and internationally. See, for example, Peters-Little 1999; and Cooke and Kothari 2001.

11. An exception to this was the negotiations over the Native Title Act in 1993 when Pearson and Langton formed part of the 'A team' that negotiated a deal with the then Prime Minister Paul Keating that was unsuccessfully fought by a 'B team' of opposing Aboriginal leaders. Such a significant moment of public intra-racial dissent was not repeated until the mid-2000s.

12. The website of the activist group 'Rollback the Intervention' contains another illustration of this argument. It links to a comprehensive critique of Noel Pearson (by prominent journalist Chris Graham) arguing he is not recognised as either a leader or an elder by Aboriginal people, and should be disregarded.

13. Already at the time of my fieldwork, elements of the critique of self-determination were popular among some White anti-racists, seen for instance in the support for Noel Pearson and in the concern about the 'enslaving' [Transcript: 16, 12] effect of 'welfare passivity': 'We've been *so irresponsible* with how we've put these people on welfare, with no obligations to work with them and support them like [teaching them] this is how you manage money' [Transcript 17, 6–7].

14. Noel Pearson's concept of 'orbiting', whereby Indigenous people move away from their communities for work and study and then return, is designed to address these suspicions by proposing that Indigenous people can maintain cultural and family connections at the weekends and during holidays, while still pursuing Western success.

15. This collapse of universalism is also related to the 'crisis of whiteness' discussed in Chapter 6 (Winant 2004: 4).

16. An important case in point is native title, which gives Indigenous people with traditional links to land the right to undertake traditional activities and to be consulted about proposed land developments. The state's recognition of native title must be buttressed with a non-recognition of Indigenous customary law, as such a recognition of an alterior system of law would 'shatter the skeletal structure' of the common law (Patton 2001; Povinelli 2002: 176; Langton and Palmer 2004).

17. This hypothesis may be supported by the current campaign to change the Australian constitution to formally recognise Indigenous Australians.

18. See Burgess et al. 2005 for one example focusing on Indigenous people's relationship to their land. Another example is the attempts to use individualised quality of life measures to obtain culturally relevant measures of programme effects (Chenhall et al. 2009).

19. Jon Altman's 'hybrid economy' could perhaps be seen as an example of a culturally based model of development, although it is firmly tied to the dominant Australian economy (Altman 2009).

20. A similar argument is made by Patchen Markell (2003).

21. Culture thus performs the task of enacting historical discontinuity (see Chapter 2).

22. Other work relevant to this question considers the inherent violence of all affective relations – see, for example, Hardt 2011; and Berlant 2011.

23. The most prominent campaigns were seeking compensation for the Stolen Generations and for 'stolen wages' (wages withheld and underpaid to Indigenous people who worked on Queensland reserves for much of the twentieth century); see Human Rights and Equal Opportunity Commission 1997; and Kidd 2006. Although the historic apology offered by Prime Minister Rudd to the Stolen Generations in 2007 was highly moving for Indigenous people and White anti-racists alike, compensation for the members of the Stolen Generations remains unresolved, and the ongoing Northern Territory Intervention has produced another wave of injury claims.

24. In Australia, the definition of an Indigenous person is someone who has Indigenous ancestry, who identifies as Indigenous and is identified as Indigenous by an Indigenous community. This definition is far more flexible than comparable definitions in the U.S. and Canada. Self-declaration is sufficient to access many Indigenous-specific services (for example, extra health checks), although accessing some benefits (such as scholarships) usually requires certification from an Indigenous organisation.

25. An example of this is seen in Aboriginal filmmaker Leah Purcell's *Black Chicks Talking* (2001) where she interviews Kathryn Hay, a former beauty queen and, later, member of parliament. Kathryn says she thinks of herself as 'part-Aboriginal' because she looks White and does not know anything about Indigenous culture. Leah replies 'Which part?', and proceeds to tell her that she should not think that way, as she is entirely Aboriginal. These issues came to the fore in the 2011 case of racial discrimination brought against conservative commentator Andrew Bolt (discussed in Chapter 4) for claiming in his articles that 'light-skinned' Aboriginal people were only identifying as Aboriginal to gain benefits.

26. Pearson (2006) similarly argues against the view that Indigenous educational and economic success 'automatically pose challenges for the preservation of identity. … Indigenous Australian identity … is often said to be so intimately connected with the organisation of our traditional society that it will cease to exist if we embrace modernity'. Nyamnjoh's concept of 'flexible indigeneity' is another related project that seeks to loosen the 'ever-diminishing circles' of 'authentic' indigeneity (Nyamnjoh 2007).

27. See, also, Russell 2001a, 2001b, 2005. Her position draws on Homi Bhabha (1994).

28. See Hage's discussion of the complex relationship between the migrant and the Australian national dyad of settler/Aborigine (Hage 2003: 79–107).

29. For a discussion of this issue in a New Zealand context, see Dominy 1995.

REFERENCES

Abbott, T. 2006. 'Misplaced Tact Stands in the Way of Help', *Sydney Morning Herald* (21 June).

ABC Online Indigenous News. 2011. 'Ex-Victorian Premiers Back Aboriginal Welcome' (19 May). Retrieved 6 Dec. 2012 from http://www.abc.net.au/news/stories/2011/05/19/3221321.htm?site=indigenous&topic=latest.

ACT Government: Community Services. 2013. *Welcome to Country*, Retrieved 20 March 2013 from http://www.dhcs.act.gov.au/atsia/welcome_to_country.

Adams, C. 2002. 'Ethics, Power and Politics in Aboriginal Health Research', *The Asia Pacific Journal of Anthropology* 3(2): 44–64.

Adams, V. 1996. *Tigers of the Snow and Other Virtual Sherpas: An Ethnography of Himalayan Encounters*. Princeton, NJ: Princeton University Press.

Agamben, G. 1998. *Homo Sacer: Sovereign Power and Bare Life*. Stanford, CA: Stanford University Press.

Agrawal, A. 2005. *Environmentality: Technologies of Government and the Making of Subjects*. Durham, NC: Duke University Press.

Ahmed, S. 2004. 'Declarations of Whiteness: The Non-Performativity of Anti-Racism', *Borderlands* 3(2).

———. 2005. 'The Politics of Bad Feeling', *Australian Critical Race and Whiteness Studies Association Journal* 1(1): 72–85.

———. 2012. *On Being Included: Racism and Diversity in Institutional Life*. Durham, NC: Duke University Press.

Allahyari, R. 2000. *Visions of Charity: Volunteer Workers and Moral Community*. Berkeley: University of California Press.

Alphen, E. van. 1991. 'The Other Within', in *Alterity, Identity, Image: Selves and Others in Society and Scholarship*, edited by R. Corbey and J. Leerssen. Amsterdam: Rodopi.

Althusser, L. 1971. *Lenin and Philosophy and Other Essays*. New York: Monthly Review Press.

Altman, J. 2009. *Beyond Closing the Gap: Valuing Diversity in Indigenous Australia*. Canberra: Centre for Aboriginal Economic and Policy Research.

Altman, J., and M. Hinkson (eds). 2007. *Coercive Reconciliation: Stabilise, Normalise, Exit Aboriginal Australia*. Melbourne: Arena Publications.

Altman, J., and M. Hinkson (eds). 2010. *Culture Crisis: Anthropology and Politics in Aboriginal Australia*. Sydney: UNSW Press.

Anderson, I. 1988. *Koorie Health in Koorie Hands: An Orientation Manual in Aboriginal Health for Health-Care Providers*. Melbourne: Koorie Health Unit, Health Department, Victoria.

———. 2003. 'Black Bit, White Bit', in *Blacklines: Contemporary Critical Writing by Indigenous Australians*, edited by M. Grossman. Melbourne: Melbourne University Press.

Anderson, W. 2002. *The Cultivation of Whiteness: Science, Health and Racial Destiny in Australia*. Melbourne: Melbourne University Press.

Anonymous. 2005. 'Our Third World Shame', *The Age* (15 May).

Arvidson, Malin. 2008. 'Contradictions and Confusions of Development Work: Exploring the Realities of Bangladeshi NGOs', *Journal of South Asian Development* 3(1): 109–34.

Atkinson, Judy. 2002. *Trauma Trails, Recreating Song Lines: The Transgenerational Effects of Trauma in Indigenous Australia*. Melbourne: Spinifex Press.

Attwood, B., and J. Arnolds. 1992. 'Power, Knowledge and Aborigines: Special Edition', *Journal of Australian Studies* 35.

Attwood, B., and A. Markus. 1999. *The Struggle for Rights for Aborigines: A Documentary Collection*. Sydney: Allen & Unwin.

Austin, J.L. 1962. *How To Do Things With Words: The William James Lectures delivered at Harvard University in 1955*. London: Oxford University Press.

Austin, T. 1993. *I Can Picture the Old Home So Clearly: The Commonwealth and 'Half-Caste' Youth in the Northern Territory, 1911–39*. Canberra: Aboriginal Studies Press.

Austin-Broos, Diane. 2011. *A Different Inequality: The Politics of Debate about Remote Aboriginal Australia*. Sydney: Allen & Unwin.

Australian Broadcasting Corporation. 2006. *Lateline TV Program Transcript*. Retrieved 15th June 2006 from http://www.abc.net.au/lateline/content/2006/s1639127.htm.

Australian Bureau of Statistics. 1973. 'Year Book Australia 1973'. Canberra.

———. 2001. 'National Health Survey: Summary of Results, 2001'. Canberra: Australian Government Publishing Service.

———. 2003. 'General Social Survey: Summary Results, Australia, 2002'. Canberra: Australian Government Publishing Service.

———. 2004a. 'Deaths, Australia 2003'. Canberra: Australian Government Publishing Service.

———. 2004b. 'National Aboriginal and Torres Strait Islander Social Survey, 2002'. Canberra: Australian Government Publishing Service.

———. 2006. 'National Aboriginal and Torres Strait Islander Health Survey, 2004–05'. Canberra: Australian Government Publishing Service.

———. 2009. 'Experimental Life Tables for Aboriginal and Torres Strait Islander Australians, 2005–2007'. Canberra.

———. 2010. 'Population Characteristics, Aboriginal and Torres Strait Islander Australians, 2006'. Canberra.

Australian Institute of Aboriginal and Torres Strait Islander Studies. 2013. *The Sorry Books*, retrieved 13 September 2013.

Australian Institute of Health and Welfare. 2009. 'Expenditure on Health for Aboriginal and Torres Strait Islander people 2006–07', in *Health and Welfare Expenditure Series No. 39*. Canberra.

———. 2013. 'Expenditure on Health for Aboriginal and Torres Strait Islander People 2010–11'. Canberra.

Australian Institute of Health and Welfare, and Australian Bureau of Statistics. 2008. *The Health and Welfare of Australia's Aboriginal and Torres Strait Islander Peoples, 2008*. Canberra.

Australian Museum. 2006. *Dreaming Online: Spirituality*. Retrieved 16 Oct. 2006 from http://www.dreamtime.net.au/indigenous/spirituality.cfm.

Aveling, N. 2004a. 'Critical Whiteness Studies and the Challenges of Learning to be a "White Ally"', *Borderlands* 3(2).

———. 2004b. 'Being the Descendants of Colonialists: White Identity in Context', *Race, Ethnicity and Education* 7(1): 57–71.

———. 2012. '"Don't talk about what you don't know": On (not) Conducting Research with/in Indigenous Contexts', *Critical Studies in Education* 54(2): 203–14.

Barker, Joanne. 2011. *Native Acts: Law, Recognition, and Cultural Authenticity*. Durham, NC: Duke University Press.

Barry, A., T. Osborne and N. Rose. 1996. *Foucault and Political Reason: Liberalism, Neo-Liberalism and Rationalities of Government*. Chicago: University of Chicago Press.

Batty, P. 2005. 'Private Politics, Public Strategies: White Advisers and their Aboriginal Subjects', *Oceania* 75(3): 209–21.

Beck, U. 1992. *Risk Society: Towards a New Modernity*. London: Sage.

Beckett, J. 1988. 'Aboriginality, Citizenship and Nation State', *Social Analysis* 24: 3–18.

——— (ed.). 1994. *Past and Present: The Construction of Aboriginality*. Canberra: Aboriginal Studies Press.

Benedict, R. 1934. 'Anthropology and the Abnormal', *Journal of General Psychology* 10: 59–82.

Biehl, J., B. Good, and A. Kleinman (eds) 2007. *Subjectivity: Ethnographic Investigations*. Berkeley: University of California Press.

Berlant, Lauren. 2011. 'A Properly Political Concept of Love: Three Approaches in Ten Pages', *Cultural Anthropology* 26(4): 683–91.

Bhabha, Homi K. 1994. *The Location of Culture*. London: Routledge.

———. 2011. *Our Neighbours, Ourselves: Contemporary Reflections on Survival*. Berlin and New York: Walter de Gruyter.

Bird Rose, D., and R. Davis. 2005. *Dislocating the Frontier: Essaying the Mystique of the Outback*. Canberra: ANU E Press.

Blainey, G. 1993. 'Drawing up a Balance Sheet of Our History', *Quadrant* 37(7–8): 10–15.

Boggs, J. 2002. 'Anthropological Knowledge and Native American Cultural Practice in the Liberal Polity', *American Anthropologist* 104(2): 599–610.

Bolt, Andrew. 2010. 'Don't Welcome Me to My Own Country'. *Herald Sun* (15 March).

———. 2011. 'Baillieu Made the Right Call on Welcome Ceremonies'. *Herald Sun* (21 May). Retrieved 6 December 2012 from http://www.heraldsun.com.au/opinion/baillieu-made-the-right-call-on-welcome-ceremonies/story-e6frfifx-1226059908884.

Bonnett, A. 2000a. *Anti-racism*. London: Routledge.

———. 2000b. *White Identities: Historical and International Perspectives*. Harlow: Prentice Hall.

———. 2006. 'The Americanisation of Anti-racism? Global Power and Hegemony in Ethnic Equity', *Journal of Ethnic and Migration Studies* 32(7): 1083–1103.

Bourdieu, P. 1977. *Outline of a Theory of Practice*. Cambridge: Cambridge University Press.

———. 1990. *The Logic of Practice*. Stanford, CA: Stanford University Press.

———. 1993. *Sociology in Question*. London: Sage.

Brady, M. 1993. 'Giving Away the Grog: An Ethnography of Aboriginal Drinkers who Quit without Help', *Drug and Alcohol Review* 12: 401–11.

———. 2004. *Indigenous Australia and Alcohol Policy: Meeting Difference with Indifference*. Sydney: University of New South Wales Press.

Briggs, C.L., and C. Mantini-Briggs. 2003. *Stories in the Time of Cholera: Racial Profiling during a Medical Nightmare*. Berkeley: University of California Press.

Brodkin, K. 1998. *How Jews Became White Folks and What That Says About Race in America*. Chapel Hill, NC: Rutgers University Press.

Brown, W. 1995. *States of Injury: Power and Freedom in Late Modernity*. Princeton, NJ: Princeton University Press.

————. 2006. *Regulating Aversion: Tolerance in the Age of Identity and Empire*. Princeton, NJ and Oxford: Princeton University Press.

Buchanan, Nicholas, and Eve Darian-Smith. 2011. 'Introduction: Law and the Problematics of Indigenous Authenticities', *Law & Social Inquiry* 36(1): 115–24.

Burchell, G. 1993. 'Liberal Government and Techniques of the Self', *Economy and Society* 22(3): 267–82.

Burchell, G., C. Gordon and P. Miller (eds). 1991. *The Foucault Effect: Studies in Governmentality*. Chicago: The University of Chicago Press.

Burgess, C., F. Johnston, D. Bowman and P. Whitehead. 2005. 'Healthy Country: Healthy People? Exploring the Health Benefits of Indigenous Natural Resource Management', *Australian and New Zealand Journal of Public Health* 29(2): 117–22.

Butler, J. 1997. *The Psychic Life of Power: Theories in Subjection*. Stanford, CA: Stanford University Press.

Cadena, M. de la, and O. Starn (eds). 2007. *Indigenous Experience Today*. New York: Berg.

Carrier, J. 1995. *Occidentalism: Images of the West*. Oxford: Clarendon Press.

Carter, J. 1988. 'Am I Too Black To Go With You?', in *Being Black: Aboriginal Culture in 'Settled' Australia*, edited by I. Keen. Canberra: Aboriginal Studies Press.

Castles, I. 1986. *Year Book Australia*. Vol. 70. Canberra: Australian Bureau of Statistics.

Cattelino, Jessica R. 2010. 'The Double Bind of American Indian Need-based Sovereignty', *Cultural Anthropology* 25(2): 235–62.

Chenhall, Richard, Kate Senior, David Cole, Teresa Cunningham and Ciaran O'Boyle. 2009. 'Individual Quality of Life among At Risk Indigenous Youth in Australia', *Applied Research in Quality of Life* 5(3): 171–83.

Chesterman, J., and B. Galligan. 1997. *Citizens Without Rights: Aborigines and Australian Citizenship*. Cambridge: Cambridge University Press.

Clouston Associates. 2005. 'Report of Tiwi Shopping Centre Development Public Consultation Meeting'. Darwin.

Commonwealth of Australia. 1937. 'Aboriginal Welfare: Initial Conference of Commonwealth and State Aboriginal Authorities, held at Canberra, 21st to 23rd April, 1937'. Canberra: Commonwealth Governent Printer.

Condon, J., A. Barnes, J. Cunningham and L. Smith. 2004. 'Improvements in Indigenous Mortality in the Northern Territory over Four Decades', *Aust NZ J Public Health* 28: 445–51.

Conklin, B. 1997. 'Body Paint, Feathers and VCRs: Aesthetics and Authenticity in Amazonian Activism', *American Ethnologist* 24(4): 711–37.

Conroy, John. 2009. 'Aborigines Interrupt "Welcome"' (*The Border Mail*, 15 October). Retrieved 6 December 2012 from http://www.bordermail.com.au/news/local/news/general/aborigines-interrupt-welcome/1651152.aspx.

Convery, Stephanie. 2010. 'Lip Service', *Overland*. Retrieved 6 December 2012 from http://overland.org.au/2010/03/lip-service/.

Cooke, B., and U. Kothari. 2001. *Participation: The New Tyranny?* London and New York: Zed Books.

Coombs, H.C., and D. Smith. 1994. *Aboriginal Autonomy: Issues and Strategies*. Melbourne: Cambridge University Press.

Cooper, F., and A.L. Stoler. 1997. *Tensions of Empire: Colonial Cultures in a Bourgeois World*. Berkeley: University of California Press.

Cornwall, Andrea, and Karen Brock. 2005. 'What do Buzzwords Do for Development Policy? A Critical Look at "Participation", "Empowerment" and "poverty reduction"', *Third World Quarterly* 26(7): 1043–60.

Cowlishaw, G. 1999. *Rednecks, Eggheads and Blackfellas: A Study of Racial Power and Intimacy in Australia*. St Leonards, NSW: Allen & Unwin.

———. 2003. 'Euphemism, Banality, Propaganda: Anthropology, Public Debate and Indigenous Communities', *Australian Aboriginal Studies* 1: 2–18.

———. 2011. 'Mythologising Culture', *The Australian Journal of Anthropology* 22(2): 170–88.

Cowlishaw, G., E. Kowal and T. Lea. 2006. 'Double Binds', in *Moving Anthropology: Critical Indigenous Studies*, edited by T. Lea, E. Kowal and G. Cowlishaw. Darwin: Charles Darwin University Press.

Crewe, E., and E. Harrison. 1998. *Whose Development? An Ethnography of Aid*. London: Zed Books.

Cummings, B. 1990. *Take this Child: From Kahlin Compound to the Retta Dixon Home*. Canberra: Aboriginal Studies Press.

Dauth, Tim. 2011. 'Group Names and Native Title in South-East Australia', in *Unsettling Anthropology: The Demands of Native Title on Worn Concepts and Changing Lives*, edited by T. Bauman and G. Macdonald. Canberra: Australian Institute of Aboriginal and Torres Strait Islander Studies.

Day, B. 1994. *Bunji: A Story of the Gwalwa Daraniki Movement*. Canberra: Aboriginal Studies Press.

———. 2001. 'Aboriginal Fringe Dwellers in Darwin: Cultural Persistence or Culture of Resistance?' Ph.D. dissertation. University of Western Australia.

———. 2005a. 'The Death of a Long Grass Man', *National Indigenous Times* 5.

———. 2005b. 'A View from the Long Grass', *Parity* 12(3): 21.

Dempster, Elizabeth. 2007. 'Welcome to Country: Performing Rights and the Pedagogy of Place', *About Performance* 7.

Department of Families, Housing, Community Services and Indigenous Affairs. 2011. *Stronger Futures in the Northern Territory Discussion Paper*. Retrieved 15 May 2012 from http://www.fahcsia.gov.au/our-responsibilities/indigenous-australians/publications-articles/closing-the-gap-in-the-northern-territory/stronger-futures-in-the-northern-territory-discussion-paper.

Dominy, M. 1995. 'White Settler Assertions of Native Status', *American Ethnologist* 22(2): 358–74.

Douglas, Heather. 2006. 'Customary Law, Sentencing and the Limits of the State', *Canadian Journal of Law and Society* 20(1): 141–56.

Dussart, F. 2009. 'Diet, Diabetes and Relatedness in a Central Australian Aboriginal Settlement: Some Qualitative Recommendations to Facilitate the Creation of Culturally Sensitive Health Promotion Initiatives', *Health Promotion Journal of Australia* 20(3): 202–7.

Dyck, Noel. 1985. *Indigenous Peoples and the Nation-State: 'Fourth World' Politics in Canada, Australia, and Norway*. St Johns, Newfoundland: Institute of Social and Economic Research.

Dyer, R. 1997. *White*. London and New York: Routledge.

Elder, Catriona. 2007. *Being Australian: Narratives of National Identity*. Crows Nest, NSW: Allen & Unwin Academic.

Elias, Norbert. 1978. *The Civilizing Process: The History of Manners*. New York: Urizen.

Epstein, S. 2007. *Inclusion: The Politics of Difference in Medical Research*. Chicago: University of Chicago Press.

Eriksson Baaz, M. 2005. *The Paternalism of Partnership: A Postcolonial Reading of Identity in Development Aid*. London: Zed Books.

Escobar, A. 1995. *Encountering Development: The Making and Unmaking of the Third World*. Princeton, NJ: Princeton University Press.

Everett, K. 2009. 'Welcome to Country... Not', *Oceania* 79(1): 53–64.

Fabian, J. 1999. 'Remembering the Other: Knowledge and Recognition in the Exploration of Central Africa', *Critical Inquiry* 26(1): 49–69.

Fairclough, N. 2003. '"Political Correctness": The Politics of Culture and Language', *Discourse and Society* 14(1): 17–28.

Fanon, F. 1967. *Black Skin, White Masks*. New York: Grove Press.

Fassin, Didier. 2011. *Humanitarian Reason: A Moral History of the Present*. Berkeley: University of California Press.

Ferguson, J. 1990. *The Anti-Politics Machine: Development, Depolitization, and Bureaucratic Power in Lesotho*. New York: Cambridge University Press.

Fine, Michelle, Lois Weis, Linda Powell and L. Mun Wong. 1997. *Off White: Readings on Race, Power and Society*. New York: Routledge.

Fisher, Daniel. 2012. 'Running Amok or Just Sleeping Rough? Long-Grass Camping and the Politics of Care in Northern Australia', *American Ethnologist* 39(1): 171–86.

Fortun, K.I.M., Mike Fortun and Steven Rubenstein. 2010. 'Editor's Introduction to "Emergent Indigeneities"', *Cultural Anthropology* 25(2): 222–34.

Foucault, M. 1983. 'The Subject and Power', in *Michel Foucault: Beyond Structuralism and Hermeneutics*, edited by H. Dreyfus and P. Rabinow. Chicago: University of Chicago Press.

———. 1988. 'Practicing Criticism, or, Is It Really Important to Think?', in *Politics, Philosophy, Culture*, edited by L. Kritzman. New York and London: Routledge.

Frankenberg, R. 1993. *White Women, Race Matters: The Social Construction of Whiteness*. Minneapolis: University of Minnesotta Press.

Fraser, N. 2000. 'Rethinking Recognition', *New Left Review* 3: 107–20.

Friedman, J. 1999. 'Rhinoceros 2', *Current Anthropology* 40(5): 679–88.

Gagné, Natacha, and Marie Salaün. 2012. 'Appeals to Indigeneity: Insights from Oceania', *Social Identities* 18(4): 381–98.

Gallagher, C. 1997. 'White Racial Formation: Into the Twenty-First Century', in *Critical White Studies: Looking behind the Mirror*, edited by R. Delgado and J. Stefancic. Philadelphia: Temple University Press.

Gelder, K., and J. Jacobs. 1998. *Uncanny Australia: Sacredness and Identity in a Postcolonial Nation*. Carlton, VIC: Melbourne University Press.

Gibson, Paddy. 2009. 'The NT Intervention: Grass-roots Experience and Resistance'. Discussion Paper. Sydney: Jumbunna Indigenous House of Learning, University of Technology Sydney.

Giddens, A. 1990. *The Consequences of Modernity*. Palo Alto, CA: Stanford University Press.

Gilroy, P. 2000. *Against Race: Imagining Political Culture Beyond the Color Line*. Cambridge: Harvard University Press.

Goffman, E. 1959. *The Presentation of Self in Everyday Life*. New York: Anchor Books.

———. 1963. *Stigma: Notes on the Management of Spoiled Identity*. Englewood Cliffs, NJ: Prentice-Hall.

Goldberg, D.T. 1994. 'Introduction: Multicultural Conditions', in *Multiculturalism: A Critical Reader*, edited by D.T. Goldberg. Oxford: Blackwell.

Goudge, P. 2003. *The Whiteness of Power: Racism in 'Third World' Development and Aid*. London: Lawrence & Wishart.

Gray, D., S. Saggers, T. Stockwell, P. Gruenewald, J. Toumbourou and W. Loxley. 2005. 'The Evidence Base for Responding to Substance Misuse in Indigenous Minority Populations', in *Preventing Harmful Substance Use: The Evidence Base for Policy and Practice*. London: John Wiley & Sons.

Gray, J. 1995. *Liberalism*. Minneapolis: University of Minnesota Press.

Gray, J., M. Bagramanian and A. Ingram. 2000. 'Where Pluralists and Liberals Part Company', in *Pluralism: The Philosophy and Politics of Diversity*. London: Routledge.

Greco, M. 2004. 'The Politics of Indeterminacy and the Right to Health', *Theory, Culture and Society* 21: 1–22.

Griffiths, Michael R. 2012. 'The White Gaze and its Artifacts: Governmental Belonging and Non-Indigenous Evaluation in a (Post)-settler Colony', *Postcolonial Studies* 15(4): 415–35.

Haebich, A. 2000. *Broken Circles Fragmenting Indigenous Families 1800–2000*. Freemantle: Freemantle Arts Centre Press.

Hage, G. 1995. 'The Limits of Anti-Racist Sociology', *UTS Review* 1(1): 59–82.

———. 1998. *White Nation: Fantasies of White Supremacy in a Multicultural Society*. Annandale, NSW: Pluto Press.

———. 2003. *Against Paranoid Nationalism: Searching for Hope in a Shrinking Society*. Annandale: Pluto Press.

Hale, C. 2006. 'Activist Research v. Cultural Critique: Indigenous Land Rights and the Contradictions of Politically Engaged Anthropology', *Cultural Anthropology* 21(1): 96–120.

Hall, S. 1994. 'Cultural Identity and Diaspora', in *Colonial Discourse and Postcolonial Theory*, edited by P. Williams and L. Chrisman. New York: Columbia University Press.

———. 1996. 'When was "the Post-Colonial"? Thinking at the Limit', in *The Post-Colonial Question: Common Skies, Divided Horizons*, edited by I. Chambers and L. Curti. London: Routledge.

———. 2002. 'Race, Articulation, and Societies Structured in Dominance', in *Race Critical Theories: Text and Context*, edited by P. Essed and D.T. Goldberg. Malden, MA: Blackwell.

Hall, T. 1996. *Mercenaries, Missionaries and Misfits: Adventures of an Under-Age Journalist*. London: The Muncaster Press.

Hamilton, A. 1981. *Nature and Nurture: Aboriginal Child-Rearing in North-Central Arnhem Land*. Canberra: Australian Institute of Aboriginal Studies.

Haraway, D. 1997. *Modest_Witness@second_Millennium. FemaleMan_Meets_OncoMouse*. New York: Routledge.

Hardt, Michael. 2011. 'For Love or Money', *Cultural Anthropology* 26(4): 676–82.

Hartigan, J. 1999. *Racial Situations: Class Predicaments of Whiteness in Detroit*. Princeton, NJ: Princeton University Press.

———. 2005. *Odd Tribes: Toward a Cultural Analysis of White People*. Durham, NC: Duke University Press.

Hayes, Bronwyn, and Ann Bonner. 2010. 'Job Satisfaction, Stress and Burnout Associated with Haemodialysis Nursing: A Review of Literature', *Journal of Renal Care* 36(4): 174–79.

Hays, S. 1994. 'Structure and Agency and the Sticky Problem of Culture', *Sociological Theory* 12(1): 57–72.

Healy, C. 2008. *Forgetting Aborigines*. Sydney: University of New South Wales Press.

Heatley, A. 1986. *A City Grows: A History of the Darwin City Council 1957–1984*. Darwin: North Australia Research Unit, Australian National University.

Henkel, H., and R. Stirrat. 2001. 'Participation as Spiritual Duty: Empowerment as Secular Subjection', in *Participation: The New Tyranny?*, edited by B. Cooke and U. Kothari. London: Zed Books.

Henry, J., T. Dunbar, A. Arnott, M. Scrimgeour, S. Matthews, L. Murakami-Gold and Allison Chamberlain. 2002a. *Indigenous Research Reform Agenda: Changing Institutions*. Darwin: Cooperative Research Centre for Aboriginal and Tropical Health.

———. 2002b. *Indigenous Research Reform Agenda: Rethinking Research Methodologies*. Darwin: Cooperative Research Centre for Aboriginal and Tropical Health.

Heppell, M., and J. Wigley. 1981. *Black Out in Alice Springs: A History of the Establishment and Development of Town Camps in Alice Springs*. Canberra: Australian National University.

Heron, B. 2007. *Desire for Development: Whiteness, Gender and the Helping Imperative*. Waterloo, Ontario: Wilfrid Laurier University Press.

Hinkson, M. 2003. 'Encounters with Aboriginal Sites in Metropolitan Sydney: A Broadening Horizon for Cultural Tourism?', *Journal of Sustainable Tourism* 11(4): 295–306.

Holmes, C., and E. McRae-Williams. 2009. 'An Investigation into the Influx of Indigenous "Visitors" to Darwin's Long Grass from Remote NT Communities – Phase 2', in *Monograph Series* 33. Hobart: National Drug Law Enforcement Research Fund, Commonwealth of Australia.

Holmes, Douglas, and George Marcus. 2005. 'Cultures of Expertise and the Management of Globalization: Toward the Re-Functioning of Ethnography', in *Global Assemblages: Technology, Politics, and Ethics as Anthropological Problems*, edited by A. Ong and S. Collier. Oxford: Blackwell, pp. 235–52.

Huggins, J. 1998. *Sister Girl: The Writings of Aboriginal Activist and Historian Jackie Huggins*. St Lucia: University of Queensland Press.

Hughey, Matthew. 2012. 'Stigma Allure and White Antiracist Identity Management', *Social Psychology Quarterly* 75(3): 219–41.

Human Rights and Equal Opportunity Commission. 1997. 'Bringing Them Home: Report of the National Inquiry into the Separation of Aboriginal and Torres Strait Islander Children from Their Families'. Canberra.

Humphery, K. 2000. 'Indigenous Health and "Western Research"'. Discussion Paper. Melbourne: VicHealth Koori Health Research and Community Development Unit.

———. 2001. 'Dirty Questions: Indigenous Health and "Western Research"'. *Aust NZ J Public Health* 25(3): 197–202.

Ignatiev, N. 1995. *How the Irish Became White*. London: Routledge.

Ivers, R., A. Castro, D. Parfitt, R. Bailie, P.H. D'Abbs and R. Richmond. 2006. 'Evaluation of a Multi-component Community Tobacco Intervention in Three Remote Australian Aboriginal Communities', *Aust J Public Health* 30(2): 132–36.

Jacobs, M. 2009. *White Mother to a Dark Race: Settler Colonialism, Maternalism, and the Removal of Indigenous Children in the American West and Australia*. Lincoln: University of Nebraska Press.

Jameson, F. 1991. *Postmodernism, or, the Cultural Logic of Late Capitalism*. Durham, NC: Duke University Press.

Jensen, R. 2006. *The Heart of Whiteness: Confronting Race, Racism and White Privilege*. San Francisco: City Lights Publishers.

John, B. 2005. 'Tiwi Camper Health Risks', *Northern Territory News* 13.

Johns, G. 2001. 'The Failure of Aboriginal Separatism', *Quadrant* 45(5): 9–18.

Johnson, M. 2011. 'Reconciliation, Indigeneity, and Postcolonial Nationhood in Settler States', *Postcolonial Studies* 14(2): 187–201.

Johnston, V. 2008. 'Smoking Behaviours in a Remote Australian Indigenous Community: The Influence of Family and Other Factors', *Social Science and Medicine* 67(11): 1708–16.

Jordan, M.E. 2005. *Balanda: My Year in Arnhem Land*. Crows Nest, NSW: Allen & Unwin.

Kauanui, J. Kehaulani. 2008. *Hawaiian Blood: Colonialism and the Politics of Sovereignty and Indigeneity*. Durham, NC: Duke University Press.

Kaufmann, E. 2005. *The Rise and Fall of Anglo-America: The Decline of Dominant Ethnicity in the United States*. Cambridge, MA: Harvard University Press.

Kaufmann, G. 1997. 'Watching the Developers: A Partial Ethnography', in *Discourses of Development: Anthropological Perspectives*, edited by R. Grillo and R. Stirrat. Oxford: Berg, pp. 107–31.

Keen, I. 1988. *Being Black: Aboriginal Cultures in 'Settled' Australia*. Canberra: Aboriginal Studies Press.

Kerr, B. 2005. 'Itinerants from Hell', *Northern Territory News* 13.

Khoo, S.-E., B. Birrell and G. Heard. 2009. Intermarriage by Birthplace and Ancestry in Australia. *People & Place* 17(1): 15–28.

Kidd, R. 2006. *Trustees on Trial: Recovering the Stolen Wages*. Canberra: Aboriginal Studies Press.

Kirton, Jean F., and Nero Timothy. 1977. 'Yanyuwa Concepts Relating to "Skin"', *Oceania* 47(4): 320–22.

Kowal, E. 2006a. 'Moving Towards the Mean: Dilemmas of Assimilation and Improvement', in *Moving Anthropology: Critical Indigenous Studies*, edited by T. Lea, E. Kowal and G. Cowlishaw. Darwin: Charles Darwin University Press.

———. 2006b. 'Mutual Obligation and Indigenous Health: Thinking through Incentives and Obligations', *Medical Journal of Australia* 184(6): 292–93.

———. 2010. 'Welcome to Country?', *Meanjin* 69(2).

———. 2011. 'The Stigma of White Privilege: Australian Anti-racists and Indigenous Improvement', *Cultural Studies* 25(3): 313–33.

———. 2012a. 'Stigma and Suffering: White Anti-racist Identities in Northern Australia', *Postcolonial Studies* 15(1): 5–21.

———. 2012b. 'Responsibility, Noel Pearson and Indigenous Affairs in Australia', in *Responsibility*, edited by G. Hage and R. Eckersley. Melbourne: Melbourne University Press, pp. 43–56.

Kowal, E., I. Anderson and R. Bailie. 2005. 'Moving Beyond Good Intentions: Indigenous Participation in Aboriginal and Torres Strait Islander Health Resarch', *Aust J Public Health* 29(5): 468–70.

Kowal, E., H. Franklin and Y. Paradies. 2013. 'Reflexive Antiracism: A Novel Approach to Diversity Training', *Ethnicities* 13(3): 316–37.

Kowal, E., and Y. Paradies. 2005. 'Ambivalent Helpers and Unhealthy Choices: Public Health Practitioners' Narratives of Indigenous Ill-health', *Social Science and Medicine* 60(6): 1347–57.

Kroll-Smith, J.S., and S. Couch. 1990. 'Sociological Knowledge and the Public at Risk: A "Self-Study" of Sociology, Technological Hazards and Moral Dilemmas', *Sociological Practice Review* 1(2): 120–27.

Kulick, D. 2006. Theory in Furs : Masochist Anthropology. *Current Anthropology* 47(6): 933–52.

Kunz, C., and L. Costello. 2003. '2001 Census: Ancestry – Detailed Paper'. Canberra: Australian Bureau of Statistics.

Kymlicka, W. 1995. *Multicultural Citizenship: A Liberal Theory of Minority Rights*. Oxford: Clarendon University Press.

———. 2007. *Multicultural Odysseys: Navigating the New International Politics of Diversity*. Oxford: Oxford University Press.

———. 2010. 'The Rise and Fall of Multiculturalism? New Debates on Inclusion and Accommodation in Diverse Societies', *International Social Science Journal* 61(199): 97–112.

Kymlicka, W., R. Cohen-Almagor, M. Bagramanian and A. Ingram. 2000. 'Ethnocultural Minorities in Liberal Democracies', in *Pluralism: The Philosophy and Politics of Diversity*. London: Routledge.

Laclau, E., and C. Mouffe. 1985. *Hegemony and Socialist Strategy: Towards a Radical Democratic Politics*. London: Verso.

Lambert-Pennington, K. 2007. 'What Remains? Reconciling Repatriation, Aboriginal Culture, Representation and the Past', *Oceania* 77(3): 313–36.

Lampert, J. 2003. 'The Alabaster Academy: Being a Non-Indigenous Academic in Indigenous Studies', *Social Alternatives* 22(3): 17–23.

Land, C., and E. Vincent. 2005. 'Thinking for Ourselves', *New Matilda Magazine*.

Langford, J. 2002. *Fluent Bodies: Ayurvedic Remedies for Postcolonial Imbalance*. Durham, NC: Duke University Press.

Langton, M. 2008. 'Trapped in the Aboriginal Reality Show', *Griffith Review* 19: 1–17.

Langton, M., L. Morris and L. Palmer. 1998. 'The Long Grass People of Darwin', *Parity* 11(4): 24.

Langton, M., and L. Palmer. 2004. 'Treaties, Agreement Making and the Recognition of Indigenous Customary Polities', in *Honour Among Nations? Treaties and Agreements with Indigeous Peoples*, edited by M. Langton, L. Palmer, M. Tehan and K. Shain. Melbourne: Melbourne University Press.

Latour, B. 2003. 'The Promises of Constructivism', in *Chasing Technoscience: Matrix for Matereality*, edited by D. Ihde and E. Selinger. Bloomington, IN: University of Indiana Press.

———. 2004a. 'How to Talk About the Body? The Normative Dimension of Science Studies', *Body & Society* 10(2–3): 205–29.

———. 2004b. Why has Critique Run Out of Steam? From Matters of Fact to Matters of Concern. *Critical Inquiry* 30(2): 224–48.

Latour, B., and S. Woolgar. 1979. *Laboratory Life: The Social Construction of Scientific Facts*. Beverly Hills, CA: Sage Publications.

Lattas, A. 1993. 'Essentialism, Memory and Resistance: Aboriginality and the Politics of Authenticity', *Oceania* 63(3): 240–68.

Laugrand, Frédéric. 2012. 'The Transition to Christianity and Modernity among Indigenous Peoples', *Reviews in Anthropology* 41(1): 1–22.

Lea, T. 2002. 'Between the Pen and the Paperwork: A Native Ethography of Learning to Govern Indigenous Health in the Northern Territory'. Ph.D., University of Sydney.

———. 2008. *Bureaucrats and Bleeding Hearts: Indigenous Health in Northern Australia*. Sydney: University of New South Wales Press.

———. 2012. 'Contemporary Anthropologies of Indigenous Australia', *Annual Review of Anthropology* 41(1): 187–202.

———. 2014. *Darwin*. Sydney: NewSouth.

Levine, Hal. 2011. 'Visiting Tieke K ainga: The Authenticity of a Maori Welcome', *Oceania* 81(2): 137–47.

Li, T.M. 2000. 'Articulating Indigenous Identity in Indonesia: Resource Politics and the Tribal Slot', *Comparative Studies in Society and History* 42(1): 149–79.

———. 2003. 'Masyarakat Adat, Difference and the Limits of Recognition in Indonesia's Forest Zone', in *Race, Nature and the Politics of Difference*, edited by D.S. Moore, J. Kosek and A. Pandian. Durham, NC: Duke University Press.

———. 2007. *The Will to Improve: Governmentality, Development and the Practice of Politics*. Durham, NC: Duke University Press.

Link, B.G., and J.C. Phelan. 2001. 'Conceptualizing Stigma', *Annual Review of Sociology* 27(1): 363–85.

Loney, M. 2001. *Missionaries, Mercenaries and Misfits*. Manchester: Clinamen Press.

Luhmann, N. 1993. *Risk: A Sociological Theory*. New York: Aldine de Gruyter.

Luhrmann, T.M. 2000. 'The Traumatized Social Self: The Parsi Predicament in Modern Bombay', in *Cultures under Siege: Collective Violence and Trauma*, edited by M.M. Suarez-Orozco and A.C. Robben. Cambridge: Cambridge University Press.

Lupton, D. 1995. *The Imperative of Health: Public Health and the Regulated Body*. London: Sage.

Lutschini, M. 2005. 'Engaging with Holism in Australian Aboriginal Health Policy – A Review', *Australia and New Zealand Health Policy* 2(15).

Lyotard, J.F. 1984. *The Postmodern Condition: A Report on Knowledge*. Minneapolis: University of Minnesota Press.

Macdonald, G. 1988. 'A Wiradjuri Fight Story', in *Being Black: Aboriginal Cultures in 'Settled' Australia*, edited by I. Keen. Canberra: Aboriginal Studies Press.

Macintyre, S., and A. Clark. 2003. *The History Wars*. Carlton, VIC: Melbourne University Press.

Maddison, S. 2011. *Beyond White Guilt: The Real Challenge for Black–White Relations in Australia*. Sydney: Allen & Unwin.

Manne, R. 2007. 'Pearson's Gamble, Stanner's Dream', *The Monthly* (August): 30–40.

Marcus, G. 1983. 'Elite as a Concept, Theory and Research Tradition', in *Elites: Ethnographic Issues*. Alberquerque: University of New Mexico Press.

———. 1998. *Ethnography through Thick and Thin*. Princeton, NJ: Princeton University Press.

Marcus, G., and M. Fischer. 1986. *Anthropology as Cultural Critique: An Experimental Moment in the Human Sciences*. Chicago: University of Chicago Press.

Markell, Patchen. 2003. *Bound by Recognition*. Princeton, NJ: Princeton University Press.

Martin, D.F. 2001. 'Is Welfare Dependency "Welfare Poison"? An Assessment of Noel Pearson's Proposals for Aboriginal Welfare Reform'. Canberra: Centre for Aboriginal Economic Policy Research.

Masanauskas, John. 2012. 'Ratepayers Shell Out for Welcome to Country Ceremonies'. *Herald Sun* (30 July).

Masanauskas, John, and Chris Gillet. 2012. 'Kennett Hails Baillieu's Move Away from Indigenous Acknowledgements' (19 May). Retrieved 6 Dec. 2012 from http://www.heraldsun.com.au/news/premier-ted-baillieu-drops-compulsory-aboriginal-welcome/story-e6frf7jo-1226058528404.

Maypilama, L., J. Garnggulkpuy, M. Christie, J. Greatorex and J. Grace. 2004. *Yolngu Long Grassers on Larrakia Land*. Darwin: Charles Darwin University.

McAuley, Gay. 2009. 'Unsettled Country: Coming to Terms with the Past', *About Performance* 9.

McClintock, A. 1995. *Imperial Leather: Race, Gender and Sexuality in the Colonial Contest.* New York: Routledge.

McDermott, M. 2006. *Working Class White: The Making and Unmaking of Race Relations.* Berkeley: University of California Press.

McDonald, H. 2003. 'East Kimberley Concepts of Health and Illness: Cross-Cultural Issues in the Provision and Reception of Medical Services, 2003'. Presentation given 27 October at Australian Institute for Aboriginal and Torres Strait Islander Studies, Canberra. Retrieved 6 March 2006 from http://www.aiatsis.gov.au/_files/research/pdfs2003/McDonald.pdf

McGrane, B. 1989. *Beyond Anthropology: Society and the Other.* New York: Columbia University Press.

McGregor, R. 1997. *Imagined Destinies: Aboriginal Australians and the Doomed Race Theory, 1880–1939.* Melbourne: Melbourne University Press.

———. 2011. *Indifferent Inclusion: Aboriginal People and the Australian Nation.* Canberra: Aboriginal Studies Press.

McIntosh, P. 1990. 'White Privilege: Unpacking the Invisible Knapsack', *Independent School* (Winter): 31–36.

McKinney, K.D. 2003. '"I Feel 'Whiteness' When I Hear People Blaming Whites": Whiteness as Cultural Victimization', *Race and Society* 6(1): 39–55.

McNay, Lois. 2008. *Against Recognition.* Cambridge: Polity.

Mehta, U.S. 1999. *Liberalism and Empire: A Study in Nineteenth-Century British Liberal Thought.* Chicago and London: The University of Chicago Press.

Mellor, D. 2004. 'Responses to Racism: A Taxonomy of Coping Styles Used by Aboriginal Australians', *American Journal of Orthopsychiatry* 74(1): 56–71.

Memmott, P. 2000. 'Report on the Social Conditions of Aboriginal Campers in the Todd River and Other Public Places in Alice Springs'. Alice Springs: Tangentyere Council Inc.

Memmott, P., and S. Fantin. 2001. '"The Long Grassers": A Strategic Report on Indigenous "Itinerants" in the Darwin and Palmerston Area'. Brisbane: University of Queensland.

Merlan, F. 2006. 'Explorations toward Intercultural Accounts of Socio-Cultural Reproduction and Change', *Oceania* 75(3): 167–82.

———. 2009. 'Indigeneity: Global and Local', *Current Anthropology* 50(3): 303–33.

———. 2014. 'Recent Rituals of Indigenous Recognition in Australia: Welcome to Country', *American Anthropologist* 116(2): 1–14.

Merlan, Francesca, and Nicolas Peterson. 2013. 'Anthropology, Public Policy and Social Process in Indigenous Australia', *The Asia Pacific Journal of Anthropology* 14(4): 297–303.

Michaels, E. 1988. 'Bad Aboriginal Art', *Art & Text* 28.

Minde, R., and K. Minde. 1995. 'Socio-cultural Determinants of Psychiatric Symptomatology in James Bay Cree Children and Adolescents', *Canadian Journal of Psychiatry* 40: 304–12.

Mookherjee, Nayanika, Nigel Rapport, Lisette Josephides, Ghassan Hage, Lindi Renier Todd and Gillian Cowlishaw. 2009. 'The Ethics of Apology: A Set of Commentaries', *Critique of Anthropology* 29(3): 345–66.

Moon, D., and L. Flores. 2000. 'Antiracism and the Abolition of Whiteness: Rhetorical Strategies of Domination among "Race Traitors"', *Communication Studies* 51(2): 97–115.

Mooney, G., V. Wiseman and S. Jan. 1998. 'How Much should we be Spending on Health Services for Aboriginal and Torres Strait Islander People?', *Medical Journal of Australia* 169: 508–9.

Moran, A. 2005a. *Australia: Nation, Belonging and Globalization*. New York: Routledge.

———. 2005b. 'Trust and Uncertainty in a Settler Society: Relations between Settlers and Aborigines in Australia', in *Trust, Risk and Uncertainty*, edited by S. Watson and A. Moran. New York: Palgrave Macmillan.

———. 2009. 'What Settler Australians Talk About when They Talk About Aborigines: Reflections on an In-depth Interview Study', *Ethnic and Racial Studies* 32(5): 781–801.

Moreton-Robinson, A. 2000. *Talkin' Up to the White Woman: Indigenous Women and Feminism*. St Lucia: University of Queensland Press.

———. 2003. 'I Still Call Australia Home: Indigenous Belonging and Place in a White Postcolonizing Society', in *Uprootings/Regroundings: Questions of Home and Migration*, edited by S. Ahmed, C. Castaneda, A. Fortier and M. Sheller. Oxford: Berg.

———. 2005. 'The House that Jack Built: Britishness and White Possession', *Australian Critical Race and Whiteness Studies Association Journal* 1(2): 21–29.

Morphy, Frances, and Howard Morphy. 2013. 'Anthropological Theory and Government Policy in Australia's Northern Territory: The Hegemony of the "Mainstream"', *American Anthropologist* 115(2): 174–87.

Moses, A.D. 2011. 'Official Apologies, Reconciliation, and Settler Colonialism: Australian Indigenous Alterity and Political Agency', *Citizenship Studies* 15(2): 145.

Moses, D. 2007a. 'The Non-German German and the German German: Dilemmas of Identity after the Holocaust', *New German Critique* 101: 45–94.

———. 2007b. 'Stigma and Sacrifice in the Federal Republic of Germany', *History and Memory* 19(2): 139–80.

Mosse, D. 2001. 'People's Knowledge, Participation and Patronage: Operations and Representations in Rural Development', in *Participation: The New Tyranny?*, edited by B. Cooke and U. Kothari. London and New York: Zed Books.

———. 2005a. *Cultivating Development: An Ethnography of Aid Policy and Practice*. London: Pluto Press.

———. 2005b. 'Global Governance and the Ethnography of International Aid', in *The Aid Effect: Giving and Governing in International Development*, edited by D. Mosse and D. Lewis. London: Pluto.

———. 2004. 'Is Good Policy Unimplementable? Reflections on the Ethnography of Aid Policy and Practice', *Development and Change* 35(4): 639–71.

———. 2011. *Adventures in Aidland: The Anthropology of Professionals in International Development*. New York: Berghahn Books.

———. 2013. 'The Anthropology of International Development', *Annual Review of Anthropology* 42(1): 227–46.

Muecke, S. 2004. *Ancient and Modern: Time, Culture and Indigenous Philosophy*. Sydney: UNSW Press.

———. 2005. *Textual Spaces*. Perth: API Network.

Muehlebach, A. 2001. '"Making Place" at the United Nations: Indigenous Cultural Politics at the U.N. Working Group on Indigenous Populations', *Cultural Anthropology* 16(3): 415–48.

Nader, L. 1972. 'Up the Anthropologist: Perspectives Gained from Studying Up', in *Reinventing Anthropology*, edited by D. Hymes. New York: Pantheon Books.

Narayan, K. 1993. 'How Native is a "Native" Anthropologist?', *American Anthropologist* 95(3): 671–82.

National Aboriginal Health Strategy Working Party. 1989. 'A National Aboriginal Health Strategy'. Canberra: Australian Government Publishing Service.

National Health and Medical Research Council (NHMRC). 2003a. 'Values and Ethics: Guidelines for Conduct of Aboriginal and Torres Strait Islander Health Research'. Canberra.

———. 2003b. 'NHMRC Strategic Plan 2003–6'. Available from http://www.nhmrc.gov.au/publications/_files/nh46.pdf.

———. 2006. 'Keeping Research on Track: A Guide for Aboriginal and Torres Strait Islander Peoples about Health Research Ethics'. Canberra.

Neill, R. 2002. *White Out: How Politics is Killing Black Australia*. Crows Nest, NSW: Allen & Unwin.

Nguyen, V.K. 2005. 'Uses and Pleasures: Sexual Modernity, HIV/AIDS and Confessional Technologies in a West African Metropolis', in *Sex in Development: Science, Sexuality and Morality in Global Perspective*, edited by V. Adams and S.L. Pigg. Durham, NC: Duke University Press.

Niemonen, Jack. 2007. 'Antiracist Education in Theory and Practice: A Critical Assessment', *The American Sociologist* 38: 159–77.

Niezen, R. 2003. *The Origins of Indigenism*. Berkeley: University of California Press.

NSW Health. 2005. *Welcome to Country Protocols Policy*. Sydney: Department of Health, New South Wales.

NT Licensing Commission. 2003a. 'Reasons for Decision: Alawa Shops'. Darwin: Northern Territory Licensing Commission.

NT Licensing Commission. 2003b. 'Reasons for Decision: Tiwi Supermarket'. Darwin: Northern Territory Licensing Commission.

Nyamnjoh, Francis B. 2007. '"Ever-Diminishing Circles": The Paradoxes of Belonging in Botswana', in *Indigenous Experience Today*, edited by M. de la Cadena and O. Starn. Oxford: Berg.

O'Brien, Amanda, and Lex Hall. 2010. 'Ernie Dingo Claims First Welcome', *The Australian* (17 March).

O'Brien, Eileen. 2003. 'The Political is Personal: The Influence of White Supremacy in White Antiracists' Personal Relationships', in *White Out: The Continuing Significance of Racism*, edited by A. Doane and E. Bonilla-Silva. New York: Routledge.

———. 2009. 'From Antiracism to Antiracisms', *Sociology Compass* 3(3): 510–12.

Om, J. 2006. 'Indigenous Self-Determination Has Failed', ABC Transcripts (Australia), Retrieved 28 Oct. 2006.

Omi, M. 1996. 'Racialization in the Post-Civil Rights Era', in *Mapping Multiculturalism*, edited by A. Gordon and C. Newfield. Minneapolis: University of Minnesotta Press.

Paradies, Y. 2006. 'Beyond Black and White: Essentialism, Hybridity and Indigeneity', *Journal of Sociology* 42(4): 355–67.

Parekh, B. 2000. *Rethinking Multiculturalism: Cultural Diversity and Political Theory*. London: Macmillan.

Patterson, R. 2006. *From Vietnam to Timor: Misfit, Missionary or Mercenary*. Loftus, NSW: Australian Military History Publications.

Patton, P. 2001. 'Reconciliation, Aboriginal Rights and Constitutional Paradox in Australia', *Australian Feminist Law Journal* 15(1): 25–40.

Pearson, L. 2010. *Ted Bailieu, That is Just UnAustralian*. ABC Unleashed Website. Retrieved 4 May 2010 from http://www.abc.net.au/unleashed/2722866.html.

Pearson, N. 2000. *Our Right to Take Responsibility*. Cairns: Noel Pearson & Associates.

———. 2006. *Layered Identities and Peace*. Retrieved 1 October 2006 from http://www.cyi.org.au/viewfile.aspx?article=IJL3E9TM2Z1D4SQSU59L&file=LAYERED%20IDENTITIES%20AND%20PEAC1.pdf.

———. 2007. 'White Guilt, Victimhood and the Quest for a Radical Centre', *Griffith Review* 16: 1–39.

Peters-Little, F. 1999. 'The Community Game: Aboriginal Self-Definition at the Local Level'. Canberra: Australian Institute of Aboriginal and Torres Strait Islander Studies.

———. 2006. *Return of the Noble Savage: Aboriginal Representation in the Australian Film and Television Industry*. Canberra: Aboriginal Studies Press.

Peterson, N. 1993. 'Demand Sharing: Reciprocity and the Pressure for Generosity among Foragers', *American Anthropologist* 95(4): 860–74.

Pholi, K., D. Black and C. Richards. 2009. 'Is "Close the Gap" a Useful Approach to Improving the Health and Wellbeing of Indigenous Australians?', *Australian Review of Public Affairs* 9(2): 1–13.

Pilkington, D., and N. Garimara. 1996. *Follow the Rabbit-Proof Fence*. Brisbane: University of Queensland Press.

Povinelli, E. 2001. 'Radical Worlds: The Anthropology of Incommensurability and Inconceivability', *Annual Review of Anthropology* 30: 319–34.

———. 2002a. 'Notes on Gridlock: Genealogy, Intimacy, Sexuality', *Public Culture* 14(1): 215–38.

———. 2002b. *The Cunning of Recognition: Indigenous Alterities and the Making of Australian Multiculturalism*. Durham, NC and London: Duke University Press.

———. 2010. 'Indigenous Politics in Late Liberalism', in *Culture Crisis: Anthropology and Politics in Aboriginal Australia*, edited by J. Altman and M. Hinkson. Sydney: UNSW Press.

Pratt, Mary Louise. 1992. *Imperial Eyes: Travel Writing and Transculturation*. London and New York: Routledge.

Price, B., and D. Price. 1998. 'Unheard Voices', *Journal of Australian Indigenous Issues* 1(2): 15–23.

Probyn, F. 2004. 'Playing Chicken at the Intersection: The White Critic of Whiteness', *Borderlands* 3(2): 14–29.

Pyett, P. 2002. 'Working Together to Reduce Health Inequalities: Reflection on a Collaborative Participatory Approach to Health Research', *Aust J Public Health* 26(4): 332–36.

Reconciliation Australia. 2010. 'Welcome to and Acknowledgement of Country'. Available from http://www.reconciliation.org.au/home/resources/factsheets/q-a-factsheets/welcome-to-and-acknowledgement-of-country.

Reconciliation Australia, and Auspoll. 2012. 'Australian Reconciliation Barometer 2012'. Canberra.

Redfield, Peter. 2013. *Life in Crisis: The Ethical Journey of Doctors Without Borders*. Berkeley: University of California Press.

Reid, J., and M. Trompf (eds). 1991. *The Health of Aboriginal Australia*. Sydney: Harcourt Brace Jovanovich.

Reynolds, H. 1987. *Frontier: Aborigines, Settlers and Land*. St Leonards: Allen & Unwin.

Rigney, L.I. 1999. 'Internationalization of an Indigenous Anticolonial Cultural Critique of Research Methodologies: A Guide to Indigenist Research Methodology and its Principles', *Wicazo SA Review* (Fall): 109–21.

Riles, Annaleise. 2004. 'Real Time: Unwinding Technocratic and Anthropological Knowledge', *American Ethnologist* 31(1): 1–14.

————. 2006. 'Anthropology, Human Rights, and Legal Knowledge: Culture in the Iron Cage', *American Anthropologist* 108(1): 52–65.

Roche, Ann M., Vinita Duraisingam, Allan Trifonoff and Amanda Tovell. 2013. The Health and Well-being of Indigenous Drug and Alcohol Workers: Results from a National Australian Survey, *Journal of Substance Abuse Treatment* 44(1): 17–26.

Roediger, D. 1991. *The Wages of Whiteness: Race and the Making of the American Working Class*. London: Verso.

————. 1994. *Towards the Abolition of Whiteness: Essays on Race, Politics, and Working Class History*. New York: Verso.

Rose, N. 1999. *Powers of Freedom: Reframing Political Thought*. Cambridge: Cambridge University Press.

Rowley, C.D. 1972a. *Outcasts in White Australia*. Ringwood: Penguin.

————. 1972b. *The Remote Aborigines*. Ringwood: Penguin.

Rowse, T. 1990. 'Are We All Blow-ins?', *Oceania* 61(2): 185–91.

————. 1992. *Remote Possibilities: The Aboriginal Domain and the Administrative Imagination*. Darwin: North Australia Research Unit, Australian National University.

————. 2000. *Obliged to be Difficult: Nugget Coombs' Legacy in Indigenous Affairs*. Melbourne: Cambridge University Press.

————. 2002. *Indigenous Futures: Choice and Development for Aboriginal and Islander Australia*. Sydney: University of New South Wales Press.

————. 2005. 'Introduction: Contesting Assimilation', in *Contesting Assimilation*. Perth: API Network.

————. 2006. 'The Politics of Being "Practical": Howard's Fourth Term Challenge', in *Moving Anthropology: Critical Indigenous Studies*, edited by T. Lea, E. Kowal and G. Cowlishaw. Darwin: Charles Darwin University Press.

————. 2008. 'Indigenous Culture: The Politics of Vulnerability and Survival', in *The Sage Handbook of Cultural Analysis*, edited by T. Bennett and J. Frow. Los Angeles: Sage.

————. 2012. *Rethinking Social Justice: From 'Peoples' to 'Populations'*. Canberra: Aboriginal Studies Press.

Rudd, K. 2008. 'Address to the Indigenous Welcome to Country, Opening of the 42nd Federal Parliament, Member's Hall, Parliament House, Canberra'. Available from http://www.pm.gov.au/media/speech/2008/speech_0071.cfm.

Russell, L. 2001a. *Savage Imaginings: Historical and Contemporary Constructions of Australian Aboriginalities*. Melbourne: Australian Scholarly Publishing.

———— (ed.). 2001b. *Colonial Frontiers: Indigenous–European Encounters in Settler Societies*. Manchester: Manchester University Press.

————. 2005. '"Either, or, Neither Nor": Resisting the Production of Gender, Race and Class Dichotomies in the Pre-Colonial Period', in *The Archaeology of Plural and Changing Identities*, edited by E.C. Casella and C. Fowler. New York: Springer Verlag.

————. 2006. 'Introduction', in *Boundary Writing: An Exploration of Race, Culture, and Gender Binaries in Contemporary Australia*, edited by L. Russell. Honolulu: University of Hawaii Press.

Saggers, S., and D. Gray. 1991. *Aboriginal Health and Society: The Traditional and Contemporary Aboriginal Struggle for Better Health*. Sydney: Allen & Unwin.

Said, E. 1978. *Orientalism*. New York: Pantheon.

Sandall, R. 2001. *The Culture Cult: Designer Tribalism and Other Essays*. Boulder, CO: Westview.

Sanders, W. 2004. 'Thinking About Indigenous Community Governance'. Canberra: Centre for Aboriginal Economic Policy Research.

Sansom, B. 1980. *The Camp at Wallaby Cross: Aboriginal Fringe Dwellers in Darwin.* Canberra: Australian Institute of Aboriginal Studies.

Schwab, J. 1995. *The Calculus of Reciprocity: Principles and Implications of Aboriginal Sharing.* Canberra: Centre for Aboriginal Economic and Policy Research.

Schwarz, Carolyn, and Françoise Dussart. 2010. 'Christianity in Aboriginal Australia Revisited', *The Australian Journal of Anthropology* 21(1): 1–13.

Scott, Colin. 2011. *Aboriginal Autonomy and Development in Northern Quebec and Labrador.* Vancouver: UBC Press.

Scott, D. 2003. 'Culture in Political Theory', *Political Theory* 31(1): 92–115.

Scott, J.C. 1990. *Domination and the Arts of Resistance: Hidden Transcripts.* New Haven, CT: Yale University Press.

Shepherd, Tory. 2011. 'Welcome to Country Unwelcome in Some Quarters'. *Daily Telegraph* (21 May). Retrieved 6 December 2012 from http://www.dailytelegraph.com.au/news/opinion/welcome-to-country-unwelcome-in-some-quarters/story-e6frezz0-122 6059864190.

Shore, Cris. 2002. 'Introduction: Towards an Anthropology of Elites', in *Elite Cultures: Anthropological Perspectives*, edited by C. Shore and S. Nugent. London: Routledge.

Shore, C., and S. Wright. 1997. *Anthropology of Policy: Critical Perspectives on Governance and Power.* London and New York: Routledge.

Short, Damien. 2012. 'When Sorry Isn't Good Enough: Official Remembrance and Reconciliation in Australia', *Memory Studies* 5(3): 293–304.

Sillitoe, P. 1998. 'The Development of Indigenous Knowledge: A New Applied Anthropology', *Current Anthropology* 39(2): 223–53.

Silverman, C. 2005. 'Misfits, Mercenaries and Missionaries', *The New Canadian Magazine* (Spring): 11–13.

Slocum, R. 2009. 'The Embodied Politics of Pain in US Anti-racism', *ACME: An E Journal for Critical Geographies* 8(1): 18–45.

Slotkin, R. 1992. *Gunfighter Nation: The Myth of the Frontier in Twentieth Century America.* New York: Atheneum.

Smart, Ninian. 1973. *The Science of Religion and the Sociology of Knowledge: Some Methodological Questions.* Princeton, NJ: Princeton University Press.

Smith, L.T. 2012. *Decolonizing Methodologies, Research and Indigenous Peoples.* 2nd edn. London and New York: Zed Books.

Spark, R., R. Donovan and P. Howat. 1991. 'Promoting Health and Preventing Injury in Remote Aboriginal Communities: A Case Study', *Health Promotion Journal of Australia* 1(2): 9–16.

Stepan, N.L. 1982. *The Idea of Race in Science: Great Britain 1800–1960.* London: Macmillan.

Stirrat, R. 2008. 'Missionaries, Mercenaries and Misfits: Representations of Development Personnel', *Critique of Anthropology* 28(4): 406–25.

Stocking, G.W. 1968. *Race, Culture and Evolution: Essays in the History of Anthropology.* New York: The Free Press.

———. 1982. *Race, Culture and Evolution.* Chicago: University of Chicago Press.

Stoczkowski, W. 2009. 'UNESCO's Doctrine of Human Diversity: A Secular Soteriology?', *Anthropology Today* 25(3): 7–11.

Stokes, G. 1997. 'Citizenship and Aboriginality: Two Conceptions of Identity in Aboriginal Political Thought', in *The Politics of Identity in Australia.* Cambridge: Cambridge University Press.

Sullivan, P. 1996. *All Free Man Now: Culture, Community and Politics in the Kimberley Region, North-Western Australia*. Canberra: Aboriginal Studies Press.

———. 2011. *Belonging Together: Dealing with the Politics of Disenchantment in Australian Indigenous Policy*. Canberra: Aboriginal Studies Press.

Sutton, P. 2001. 'The Politics of Suffering: Indigenous Policy in Australia since the 1970s', *Anthropological Forum* 11(2): 125–73.

———. 2003. *Native Title in Australia: An Ethnographic Perspective*. Cambridge University Press.

———. 2009. *The Politics of Suffering: Indigenous Australians and the End of the Liberal Consensus*. Melbourne: Melbourne University Press.

Swain, T. 1993. *A Place for Strangers: Towards a History of Australian Aboriginal Being*. Cambridge: Cambridge University Press.

Swain, T., and D. Bird Rose. 1988. *Aboriginal Australians and Christian Missions: Ethnographic and Historical Studies*. Bedford Park: Australian Association for the Study of Religions.

Taffe, S. 2005. *Black and White Together: FCAATSI, the Federal Council for the Advancement of Aboriginal and Torres Strait Islanders, 1958–1972*. Brisbane: University of Queensland Press.

Tatz, C. 1972. 'The Politics of Aboriginal Health', *Australian Journal of Political Science* 7(S1): 3–23.

———. 2001a. 'Confronting Australian Genocide', *Aboriginal History* 25: 16–36.

———. 2001b. 'Use of the term "Indigenous"', *Med J Aust* 174: 256–57.

Taussig, M. 1987. *Shamanism, Colonialism and the Wild Man: A Study in Terror and Healing*. Chicago: Chicago University Press.

———. 1993. *Mimesis and Alterity: A Particular History of the Senses*. New York: Routledge.

Taylor, C. 1994. 'The Politics of Recognition', in *Multiculturalism: Examining the Politics of Recognition*, edited by A. Gutmann. Princeton, NJ: Princeton University Press.

Taylor, P., S.J. Walker and B. Marawili. 2011. *Message in the Bottle: A Survey of Drinking Patterns and Attitudes about Alcohol Policy amongst Darwin's Homeless*. Darwin: Larrakia Nation Aboriginal Corporation Research Division.

Thiele, Steven. 1991. 'Reconsidering Aboriginality: Special Issue', *Australian Journal of Anthropology* 2(2).

Thomas, D.P. 2004. *Reading Doctors' Writing: Race, Politics and Power in Indigenous Health Research, 1870–1969*. Canberra: Aboriginal Studies Press.

Thompson, B. 2001. *A Promise and a Way of Life: White Antiracist Activism*. Minneapolis: University of Minnesota Press.

Tonkinson, R. 2007. 'Aboriginal "Difference" and "Autonomy" Then and Now: Four Decades of Change in a Western Desert Society', *Anthropological Forum* 17(1): 41–60.

Trewin, D., and R. Madden. 2003. *The Health and Welfare of Australia's Aboriginal and Torres Strait Islander Peoples*. Canberra: Australian Bureau of Statistics; Australian Institute of Health and Welfare.

Trigger, D. 2008. 'Place, Belonging and Nativeness in Australia', in *Making Sense of Place*, edited by F. Vanclay, M. Higgins and A. Blackshaw. Canberra: National Museum of Australia.

———. 2009. 'Indigenous Knowledge: Notes for Conversation with Michael Williams, Brisbane Festival of Ideas' (29 March).

Trigger, D., and C. Dalley. 2010. 'Negotiating Indigeneity: Culture, Identity, and Politics', *Reviews in Anthropology* 39: 46–65.

Trigger, D., and J. Mulcock. 2005. 'Forests as Spiritually Significant Places: Nature, Culture and "Belonging" in Australia', *The Australian Journal of Anthropology* 15(3): 306–20.

Troppo Armadillo. 2004. *Troppo Armadillo Blog*. Retrieved 5 Jan. 2005 from http://troppoarmadillo.ubersportingpundit.com/archives/001041.html#024099.

Trotter, L. 1997. 'Key Findings of 1996 and 1997 Household Surveys', in *Quit Evaluation Studies: Volume 9*, edited by R. Mullins, J. Boulter and R. Borland. Melbourne: Victorian Smoking and Health Program.

Trouillot, M.R. 1991. 'Anthropology and the Savage Slot: The Poetics and Politics of Otherness', in *Recapturing Anthropology: Working in the Present*, edited by R. Fox. Santa Fe, NM: School of American Research Press.

Trudgen, R. 2000. *Djambatj Mala: Why Warriors Lie Down and Die*. Darwin: Aboriginal Resource and Development Services.

Tsing, A.L. 1999. 'Becoming a Tribal Elder, and Other Green Development Fantasies', in *Transformation of the Indonesian Uplands*, edited by T.M. Li. London: Harwood.

———. 2005. *Friction: An Ethnography of Global Connection*. Princeton, NJ: Princeton University Press.

Turrell, G., G. Stanley, M. de Looper and B. Oldenburg. 2006. *Health Inequalities in Australia: Morbidity, Health Behaviours, Risk Factors and Health Service Use*. Canberra: Queensland University of Technology and the Australian Institute of Health and Welfare.

UNESCO. 2003. 'Convention for the Safeguarding of the Intangible Cultural Heritage'. Paris.

Veracini, Lorenzo. 2011. 'Introducing Settler Colonial Studies', *Settler Colonial Studies* 1(1): 1–12.

Warah, Rasna (ed.). 2008. *Missionaries, Mercenaries and Misfits: An Anthology*. Milton Keynes, UK: AuthorHouse.

Watt, B. 2002. 'Youths Jailed over Bashing of Blacks', *Northern Territory News* 4.

Wells, J., and T. Rowse. 2005. 'The Arafura Pearl: Assimilating Darwin', in *Contesting Assimilation*. Perth: API Network.

Whitlam, G. 1973. 'Aboriginals and Society', Press Statement No. 74. Sydney: Whitlam Institute, University of Western Sydney.

Wild, R., and P. Anderson. 2007. 'Ampe Akelyernemane Meke Mekarle "Little Children Are Sacred": Report of the Northern Territory Board of Inquiry into the Protection of Aboriginal Children from Sexual Abuse'. Darwin: Northern Territory Government.

Wilson, T., J. Condon and A. Barnes. 2007. 'Northern Territory Indigenous Life Expectancy Improvements, 1967–2004', *Australian and New Zealand Journal of Public Health* 31(2): 184–88.

Winant, H. 2004. 'From behind Blue Eyes: Whiteness and Contemporary U.S. Racial Politics', in *Off White: Readings on Race, Power and Society*, edited by M. Fine, L. Weis, C. Powell and L. Mun Wong. New York: Routledge.

Windschuttle, K. 2002. *The Fabrication of Aboriginal History*. Sydney: Macleay Press.

———. 2012. 'Sacred Traditions Invented Yesterday', *Quadrant* 56(12): 15–16.

Winter, E. 2011. *Us, Them, and Others: Pluralism and National Identities in Diverse Societies*. Toronto: University of Toronto Press.

Wray, M. 2006. *Not Quite White: White Trash and the Boundaries of Whiteness*. Durham, NC: Duke University Press.

Wu, F.H. 2002. 'The Model Minority: Asian American "Success" as a Race Relations Failure', in *Yellow: Race in America Beyond Black and White*. New York: Basic Books.

Young, I.M. 1990. *Justice and the Politics of Difference*. Princeton, NJ: Princeton University Press.

Zajicek, Anna M. 2002. 'Race Discourses and Antiracist Practices in a Local Women's Movement', *Gender and Society* 16(2): 155–74.

Zhou, M. 2004. 'Are Asian Americans Becoming White?', *Context* 3(1): 29–37.

Zizek, S. 1993. *Tarrying with the Negative: Kant, Hegel, and the Critique of Ideology*. Durham, NC: Duke University Press.

INDEX